NOTRE DAME COLLEGE OF EDUCATION
MOUNT PLEASANT
LIVERPOOL L3 5SP

GEOGRAPHY.

Sig. Head of Dept. ....

4' 74

THEORY OF THE LOCATION
OF INDUSTRIES

ALFRED WEBER

Theory of the Location
of Industries

Translated with an Introduction and Notes by

CARL J. FRIEDRICH

THE UNIVERSITY OF CHICAGO PRESS

CHICAGO & LONDON

Standard Book Number: 226-26469-6
THE UNIVERSITY OF CHICAGO PRESS, CHICAGO 60637
The University of Chicago Press, Ltd., London

PREFACE

In presenting this book to the public I am spared an embarrassment that many writers encounter; I do not need to give an apology for the topic with which it deals. Alfred Weber's treatise is a pioneering venture. He attempts to master by theoretical analysis a complete wilderness of facts which has grown up around us during the last two centuries concerning the location of our modern manufacturing industries. To be sure, others have ventured upon the task of describing and classifying the phenomena of geographical distribution; but, as Weber points· out, previous writers did not get beyond a mere enumeration of various factors which played a part in determining the location of industries.

While I am quite impressed with the importance of Weber's work itself, if clearly understood, it is precisely this task of making it understood about which I feel very apologetic. In spite of the help and advice which Professors Leon C. Marshall and Frank W. Taussig, as well as Drs. E. H. Chamberlin, William Y. Elliot, Edward Mason, Talcott Parsons, and Andreas Predöhl have so generously afforded me, I do not feel confident that I have succeeded in conquering the difficulties which confront the translator of such a highly abstract treatise. Had not Professor Marshall and Dr. Mason read the entire manuscript through and made numerous suggestions for its improvement, I fear I should not have found the courage to let it see the light of day.

It will be conceded by those who have embarked on the hazardous adventure of translating abstract thought from one language into another that nothing is more perplexing. It is in such thought that the *Sprachgeist* develops its subtlest distinctions, successfully defying either translating, transcribing, or paraphrasing. For this reason the paging of the German edition of Weber's book has been inserted as marginal notes throughout. These notes are usually inserted at the end of a sentence, even though that sentence overlaps the page in the original. The interested reader will consult the German text wherever the English translation becomes too obscure. Had space permitted, I should have included the German text itself. But, after all, the greatest usefulness of such a translation is the assistance it may give to the student who knows the original language, but does not know it sufficiently well to enable him to make the entire translation himself.

Comparison with the German text will show that Weber's preface to the first and second (unaltered) edition, as well as his two notes *(Exkurse)* have been omitted. We should have been glad to include Weber's contribution to the *Grundriss der Sozialökonomik*[1] could it have been arranged. I can only refer to this treatise all readers who are particularly interested in those aspects of location which Weber touches upon in his introduction and in his last chapter as well as in the paragraphs throughout the book on tendencies of development. It seemed important to include the mathematical appendix by Georg Pick. I sincerely hope that the indulgent reader will not feel as did that student who wrote on top of Alfred Marshall's mathematical appendix to his *Principles:* "A bad case of appendicitis—cut it out." In translating this mathematical appendix I have had the valuable advice of Mr. Paul S. Bauer.

This study would probably not have been possible without the constant encouragement of Professor Leon C. Marshall. I wish to thank him and all others who have helped me.

C. J. F.

---

[1] "Industrielle Standortslehre (Reine und kapitalistische Theorie des Standorts)," in *Grundriss,* Abteilung VI, B, particularly the second part dealing with capitalistic theory.

TABLE OF CONTENTS

EDITOR'S INTRODUCTION

THE THEORY OF LOCATION IN RELATION TO THE THEORY OF LAND RENT

"Knowledge insufficient for prediction may be most valuable for guidance," wrote John Stuart Mill, in discussing economic theory in general.[2] This statement might very properly have been made the motto of Weber's attempt to analyze a much-neglected problem by what Mill would have called a strictly deductive method. This problem is: what causes an industry[3] to change its location?

The change of industrial location is among the most generally discussed economic problems of today. In the nation-wide agitation for power development in the United States, for example, the argument is quite generally used that it will "decentralize" industries.[4] English economic theory, however, has neglected a strictly theoretical analysis of the problem. From Adam Smith to Pigou no adequate deductive treatment of the causes determining economic location has been attempted, in spite of the fact that such an analysis may be capable of aiding in further refining the theories of monopoly, transportation rates, and international trade.

John Stuart Mill[5] touches upon the problem when consid-

[2] *Logic,* Book 6, chap. ix, §2.

[3] "Industry" is used here and throughout in the sense of manufacturing industry, unless stated otherwise.

[4] So Secretary Hoover. Compare his address at the First International Power Conference, London, 1927, *Prosperity Through Power Development.* Compare also the many generalizations which are made in order to explain the movement of industries to the South.

[5] It is, of course, arbitrary to begin with Mill, but it may be justified on grounds of expediency, since he more or less systematized and correlated the thought of those before him. I, for one, should like to include at least Adam

ering value. In enumerating the various channels through which labor cost influences the cost of production he, like previous writers, includes the cost of transporting materials to the place of production and the cost of "conveyance of products to the market."[6] But he does not consider the variability of this factor as affecting the place of production, although some of the direct effects of purely locational factors did attract his attention. "Almost all kinds of raw material extracted from the interior of the earth—metals, coals, precious stones, etc., are obtained from mines differing considerably in fertility, that is, yielding very different quantities of the product to the same quantity of labor and capital." But he apparently despaired of explaining this phenomenon, since he goes on: "Whatever the causes, it is a fact that mines of different degrees of richness are in operation, and since the value of the produce (the costs) must be proportional to the cost of production at the worst mine (fertility and *situation* taken together), it is more than proportional to that of the best."[7] Here "situation" (which corresponds to our term "location") emerges for a moment as a factor, but immediately disappears again behind the more usual consideration of "fertility." But this factor of "location," whose determining causes seem so elusive to Mill, may be capable of rational explanation if only we carry our inquiry one step farther and analyze the factors which determine what is and what is not a "favorable" location. We shall return to this point presently. It remains to call attention here to the fact that the passages just discussed appear in

---

Smith and Ricardo, because of their relation with the system of Von Thünen. But the peculiarities of their theories of rent would require too much time to review for the particular problem in hand (cf. Schumpeter, *Epochen der Dogmen-und Methodengeschichte,* pp. 87 ff.). It is not very difficult, moreover, to apply what is here said about John Stuart Mill to the earlier thinkers.

[6] *Principles* (New York, 1874, from the 5th London edition), Book III, chap. iv, §1. In succeeding notations Roman numerals refer to book, Arabic to section, unless otherwise indicated.

[7] *Principles,* III, chap. v, 3. The italics are mine.

connection with Mill's analysis of rent in its relation to value. It may not be amiss to quote another passage which may shed more light upon this aspect of the matter: "Land is used for other purposes than agriculture, ... and when so used yields a rent. . . . . The ground rent of a house in a small village is but little higher than the rent of a similar patch of ground in the open fields, but that of a shop in Cheapside[8] will exceed these, by the whole amount at which people estimate the superior facilities of money-making in the more crowded place."[9] But all this hardly explains why Cheapside came to be Cheapside! Why did Cheapside happen to become a "favorable" location? A theory of location will consider the situation or location rent a problem rather than merely a fact, and therefore the theory of location may serve as a fruitful avenue of approach to certain obscure aspects of the theory of rent, value, and distribution. We shall have occasion later to indicate briefly how it becomes important for the theory of monopoly, for the theory of international trade, and for the theory of railway rates. While it would be interesting to consider here Mill's analysis of the influence of the progress of industry upon rents,[10] we shall have to content ourselves with a mere mention of the problem and proceed to a few observations upon the position of Alfred Marshall.

The strong interest of Marshall in production naturally led him to touch upon the question of what causes the location (or, as he called it, "localisation") of industries to change. From the point of view of anyone interested in the history of economic ideas in general and in the history of the theory of location in particular it is quite interesting that Alfred Marshall (in the introduction to the first edition of his *Principles of Economics*) acknowledges his great indebtedness to Thünen. It will be remembered that it was Thünen who advanced a theory of the lo-

[8] An expensive trading section in London.

[9] *Principles,* III, chap. v, 3; cf. also III, chap. v, 4.

[10] *Principles,* IV, chap. iii.

cation of agricultural production.[11] But while Thünen related his theory very definitely to his theory of rent, modifying the position of Adam Smith,[12] Marshall did not approach this problem of location from a theoretical point of view, and consequently attempted no answer to that aspect of the theory of rent which we have just pointed out. There is a twofold explanation for this. For one thing, Marshall's main effort was directed toward working into the theory of rent the supposedly new equilibrium theory of demand and supply,[13] contenting himself with carefully restating the theory that "rent does not enter the cost of production,"[14] Marshall does not inquire into the problem which he, like Mill before him, encounters. In discussing the argument which arose between Ricardo and Smith regarding the "price at which coals can be sold for any considerable time,"[15] he is inclined to agree with Ricardo that "it is the least fertile mine which regulates the price." Omitting the matter of a royalty which enters on account of the exhaustibility of a mine, Marshall, like Mill, does not explain why a less fertile mine should be in use at all. Like Mill,

[11] *Der Isolierte Staat,* particularly Part I. For a recent interpretation of the significance of this treatise in the history of economic thought, cf. Edgar Salin, "Der Isolierte Staat 1826–1926," in *Zeitschrift für die gesamte Staatswissenschaft,* 1926.

[12] He made the distinction between rent of land and profit on capital invested on the land, like Ricardo.

[13] While this name was not used by Mill, the essential aspects of the concept of "equilibrium," as far as they matter for the problem here in hand, were treated by Mill as indicated above.

[14] It is stated as follows: "When land capable of being used for producing one commodity is used for producing another, the price of the first is raised by the consequent limitation of its field of production. The price of the second will be the expense of production (wages and profits) of that part of it which only just pays its way. . . . . And if for the purposes of any particular argument we take together the whole expenses of the production on that land, and divide these among the whole commodity produced, then the rent, which ought to count in, is not that which the land would pay if used for producing the first commodity, but that which it does pay when used for producing the second" (*Principles,* 4th ed., p. 483).

[15] Cf. *loc. cit.,* p. 484.

he speaks of the fact that a rise in rent may cause a manufacturer to move into another town or into the country, but he does not say why the rent *does rise* in the first instance. Similarly, he explains that the demand for exceptionally valuable urban land comes from traders of various kinds, wholesale and retail, more than from manufacturers. But why such increase in the demand should come, he does not explain at all. Still, the most striking instance where Marshall encounters the problem of location (or situation) without undertaking to solve it is in his discussion of what he calls situation rent.[16]

If in any industry, whether agricultural or not, two producers have equal facilities in all respects, except that one has a more convenient situation than the other, *and can buy or sell in the same markets with less cost of carriage,* the differential advantage which his situation gives him, is the aggregate of the excess charges for cost of carriage to which his rival is put. And, we may suppose, that *other advantages of situation,* such, for instance, as the *near access to a labour market especially adapted to his trade,* can be translated in like manner into money values. When this is done for, say, a year, and all are added together we have the annual money value of the advantages of situation which the first business has over the second; and the corresponding difference in the incomes derived from the two businesses is commonly regarded as a difference of *situation rent.*[17]

But why does not the second manufacturer move to the more favorable location? This fact certainly needs an explanation! In a footnote Marshall refers to two examples, in both of which the competitive position of two productive units is the same because the additional cost of production due to capital and labor of one are compensated for by the more favorable location of the other in relation to the market. "Favorable location" in both cases refers to advantages in transportation costs. But these, obviously, are not examples of production which have any bearing upon the problem of location, because when

[16] *Principles,* V, chap. x.

[17] The italics in this quotation are mine.

locational advantages of one kind (labor, etc.) are balanced by locational advantages of another, *no change of location will take place*. On the other hand, it is not clear how the advantage due to reduced transportation costs can be called a "rent," since it is not explained why the other productive unit is not quite free to go to a place with the same balance of advantage.[18] Feeling perhaps the inconclusiveness of his reasoning, Marshall proceeds to treat of "exceptional cases in which the income derived from advantageous situation is earned by individual effort and outlay." Much of this uncertain generalizing could have been subjected to rational explanation by an adequate understanding of the underlying locational problem. It remains to say a word regarding certain forms of quasi-rent (as Marshall called it) which are due to the fact that a certain location is made more favorable by environmental factors. The true nature of rents of this kind, which are due to a disturbed equilibrium of locations, becomes recognizable only if the locational network of the underlying regular stratum of locations is distinguished quite clearly.

Marshall's reluctance to undertake their analysis in connection with these rent problems does not, however, prevent him from treating "the concentration of specialized industries in particular localities."[19] But what he gives is, as Alfred Weber pointed out later, a more or less systematic survey of various

---

[18] The actual examples refer to extractive industries. These involve the question of increased output, as did the example of Mill we have cited. It is curious that Marshall should at this point quote Thünen's *Der Isolierte Staat* with outspoken approval, while failing to make use of Thünen's theory of location contained therein.

[19] *Principles,* IV, chap. x. Cf. also his interesting discussion in *Industry and Trade* (1923), chap. ii, and elsewhere, where he quotes Alfred Weber (p. 27). But it seems rather doubtful whether he appreciated the full significance of Weber's theory, since he says of it that it is a development of Lardner's Law of Squares in transport and trade (as set forth in *Railway Economy* [1850], p. 14). The connection is rather far fetched, to say the least.

locational factors; but—much like Roscher[20]—he does not in any way develop or even employ the theoretical concepts which Thünen had first worked out. This is rather interesting (or shall I say astonishing?) in view of the close relation between him and Thünen. But, as has been noted before, Marshall seems mainly concerned with working into the classical system the new equilibrium theory which is also to be found in Thünen. Marshall was probably too deeply concerned by the "psychological" foundation which he and others had given to that theory to be willing to bother with Thünen's concept of an isolated economic system.[21] It may be helpful, therefore, to sketch in a few sentences the main outline of Thünen's theory of location,[22] although it involves in some respects repeating what is known to economists in connection with his theory of rent.

Thünen, like Ricardo, studied an imagined state of facts in

[20] W. Roscher, *Studien ueber die Naturgesetze, welche den natürlichen Standort der Industriezweige bestimmen.* Similar catalogues of possible factors have been published by others, compare, for example, F. S. Hall, "The Localization of Industries," Twelfth Census, *Manufacturers,* Part I; and Edward A. Ross, "The Location of Industries," *Quarterly Journal of Economics,* X (1896), 247 ff. For a discussion of these and many other minor contributions cf. Witold Krzyzanowski, "Literature of Location of Industries," in *Journal of Political Economy,* XXXV (1927), 278 ff.

[21] It is rather hard to withstand the temptation to take up this aspect in the history of economic thought in greater detail; but such an undertaking could not be given justice within the scope of this brief essay. Similar considerations compel me to pass over without more than a casual reference the difficult problems which arise from the twelfth chapter of the sixth book of Marshall's *Principles* where he deals with the influence of progress on value. Such further discussion would have afforded an opportunity to consider the work of some of the writers of the next generation, particularly A. C. Pigou and J. M. Clark *(Principles of Overhead Costs).*

[22] His theory is to be found in *Der Isolierte Staat,* 2d ed., 1842, and later. Edgar Salin, writing upon the history of economic theory, expressed the belief that Thünen was the most important German theorist of the nineteenth century. However, the part of his system in which he expounds his theory of location has least been heard of and is seldom referred to in any theoretical treatises written in English. Not even special studies such as that of Ross mentioned in footnote 20 above, seem to have been aware of it.

which all nonessential aspects of the real case have been eliminated. In his totally isolated economic system[23] he finds that the
location of different kinds of agricultural production is determined by the relation between the price of the products in the
market place and the distance from the market place. The most
significant result of this approach to the problem is that the cost
of transporting the products to the market place is isolated as the
basic element and made the starting-point of the analysis of location. It is possible to do this because it is supposed anyway
for the purpose of this analysis that labor cost (wages) are equal
throughout the plain.[24] Besides, equal fertility is assumed
throughout. It is worth noting that Thünen does not consider
the effect of the cost of transporting appliances (such as plows,
etc.) to the place of production. This omission unduly simpli-
fies his analysis as compared with that of Alfred Weber. But it
should not be forgotten, anyhow, that the theory of location of
Thünen was the by-product of quite a different problem, namely, "how will the kind of agricultural production of a certain
farm be affected by a gradual decline of the prices of its produce
in its [fixed] market"?[25] It is well known that Thünen finds
rent to be due primarily to the advantage which is caused by a
smaller distance from the consuming center, i.e., smaller costs
of transportation.[26] This finding is based upon the law: "The
value of produce at the place of production decreases with the
distance of the place of production from the market place."[27]

[23] The picture of this system is well-known. He supposes a town (market
place) within a fertile plain, without navigable rivers or canals, and of given fertility throughout, which ends somewhere far away from the town in the wilderness. Thünen himself calls this ". . . . eine bildliche Darstellung, eine Form, die
den Ueberblick erleichtert und erweitert; die wir aber nicht aufgeben dürfen,
weil sie, wie die Folge ergeben wird, so reich an Resultaten ist."

[24] This supposition, while not expressly made in the first part, is noted by
Thünen in the third part, p. 73.

[25] *Der Isolierte Staat*, I, p. 21.

[26] *Op. cit.*, p. 227.   [27] *Op. cit.*, p. 37.

But Thünen was, of course, well aware of the fact that this is not a complete explanation of rent. In the third part of his work he finds rent based upon differences in the wage level. This second explanation seems to contain a contradiction to the first. Such seeming contradiction is due to different premises; in the one case it is assumed that the wage level is constant; in the other, that the value of the produce is constant, i.e., that cost of transportation is constant (according to the rule just cited). It is possible to assume this theoretically in spite of the fact that the wage level is changing—indeed, this possibility is of central importance for all that follows. This second assumption that the value of the produce is constant further involves the assumption that no more uncultivated soil is available. In the first case, then, the value of the produce is the variable, dependent upon the larger or smaller costs of transportation to the market place. In the second case, the wage level is the variable. What is common to both cases is that the cost of production does not rise in proportion to the value of the produce, so that if the value of the produce rises above a certain point there remains a surplus which is the basis of a rent.[28] Expressing this finding in relation to the main problem before referred to, Thünen formulates (stated with slight alterations for the present purpose) that the price of the produce must be so high that the rent of that farm for which it is most expensive to transport the produce to the market place does not become less than zero. Unfortunately, Thünen did not work out the significance of this second aspect for his implied theory of location. It would have been necessary to analyze the variations produced by the introduction of this second factor: labor cost. Had he done so, his theory would be more clearly related to that of Alfred Weber. It will be observed that Thünen, considering agricultural production only (an extractive industry), assumes here a definite and constant limit of production at any given place (so and so many bushels

[28] *Der Isolierte Staat*, I, p. 73.

of wheat per acre, for example). The validity of this assumption is, even in agriculture, subject to the further assumption that the most intensive methods are already in use equally throughout. Such an assumption would not be in accord with the generally accepted modern doctrine of the variability of productive forces. Be this as it may, such supposition has obviously no significant application to manufacturing industries. It is, on the contrary, possible to assume that a practically unlimited amount of one kind of production may be carried on at one place rather than another. More of this later.

I have said before that Thünen's theory of agricultural location was a by-product of his effort to determine which kind of production would best be carried on at a given place. Alfred Weber, on the other hand, undertakes the analysis of industrial location for its own sake.[29] It is useful to bear this difference in mind. Observing the gigantic movements of manufacturing industries, Weber asks: What causes a given industry to move from one location to another? What are the general economic laws determining these movements? Theoretically, Weber, like Thünen, might have asked: Which industry should be carried on at any given place? But, as a matter of fact, such an approach to the problem appears mistaken at first sight because the possibilities of manufacture are legion. This point reveals a third limitation of Thünen's analysis: he assumes a very limited group of products, namely, the agricultural produce of German farms in the beginning of the nineteenth century. This made it possible for him to find a reasonably satisfactory answer to his question, what kind of production would best be carried on at a

---

[29] Alfred Weber, *Ueber den Standort der Industrien,* I. Teil, *Reine Theorie des Standorts,* and Alfred Weber, "Industrielle Standortslehre (Allgemeine und kapitalistiche Theorie des Standorts)," in *Grundriss der Sozialökonomik,* Abteilung VI, B. The few points which are emphasized here are chosen with reference to the focusing point of this essay, rent. They do not propose to describe the theory itself. That will best be understood from Weber's own work.

given place. But this answer is satisfactory only within the limits just indicated.

Weber, who concentrates upon the problem of location as such, is not hampered by this limitation. He, of course, is interested only in discovering the operation of such general factors as influence manufacturing industries. But before going into the questions connected with that issue, it may be useful to compare the theoretical picture from which he starts with that of Thünen. Like Thünen, he assumes an absolutely even plain and equal transportation rates throughout. But he does not assume one consuming center; he assumes many of them scattered over the plain. Instead of equal fertility throughout, which would correspond to equal amounts of fuel and raw materials at equal cost throughout, Weber assumes only equal cost of fuel and raw materials at all deposits,[30] but retains the uneven distribution of such deposits. These, and these only, are Weber's assumptions.

The variable general factors are of two kinds: those which are primary causes of the regional distribution of industry (regional factors), and those which are secondary causes of a redistribution of industry (agglomerating and deglomerating factors), being themselves effects of those regional factors. By analyzing one given industrial process Weber deductively finds two general regional factors of cost: transportation costs and labor costs. It might be objected here that transportation costs are themselves partly determined by labor costs. This is true; but it is essential for the analysis of location to isolate costs of transportation as a separate element, since the problem of location is one of spatial distribution. The term "labor costs" is therefore used here and elsewhere in the sense of *labor costs as applied to*

[30] When Weber wishes to express possible differences in the price of fuel and raw materials at different deposits by additions to the distance between them and the place of production, this amounts theoretically to assuming equal cost of fuel and raw material throughout at their deposits, since the theoretical premises contain no assumption regarding the "real" distance of any point.

a given industry. This simplification is justified by the fact that
Weber's problem is: What causes a given industry to move
from one location to another? It is even possible to assume variations in the wage level (labor costs) of such a given industry
without necessarily implying a change in the labor costs of any
other industry, like the transporting agency. Apparently these
are exactly the same factors which Thünen had found. But, un-
like Thünen, Weber analyzes the effects of a change in both
variables. After having ascertained the laws determining the location when labor costs are constant, he proceeds to ascertain
the alterations resulting from varying costs of labor. He is able
to formulate his result in definite rules. Firstly, he finds that *the
location of manufacturing industries is determined* (transportation costs being variable, labor costs constant) *by the ratio between the weight of localized*[31] *material and the weight of the
product.*[32] This ratio Weber calls the material index. The explanatory value of this general rule need not be discussed here
in detail.[33] This result was reached upon the assumption of
equal labor costs throughout. What variations will be caused
by varying costs of labor? Weber finds: The extent of the
variation caused by varying labor costs is determined by the
ratio between cost of labor per ton of product (labor index) and
the total weight of all goods (product, materials, fuel, etc.)

[31] Localized are such materials as are not to be had everywhere; the latter
are called ubiquities. Cf. *infra*, p. 51. An interesting discussion of these concepts
will be found in Oskar Engländer, *Theorie des Güterverkehrs und der Frachtsätze*, p. 121 ff. It is convincingly urged there that the decisive point is whether
a material is to be had everywhere *at equal prices*.

[32] It is fairly simple to relate this rule to the theory of land rent as it becomes a function of location. A fuller discussion will be undertaken below in
connection with the indirect general agglomerating and deglomerating factors
determining the location of manufacturing industries.

[33] By way of illustration, this may be said: Certain materials enter with
their entire weight into the product (silver, etc.); others not at all (coal, etc.).
This distinction is of considerable significance. Weber is able to make the formula that the production of all industries whose material index is not greater
than 1 is located at the place of consumption (cf. *infra*, p. 61).

transported. This total weight is called locational weight, and the ratio just described is called labor coefficient. Now Weber can deduce the second general rule: *When labor costs are varied, an industry deviates from its transport locations in proportion to the size of its labor coefficient.*

The writer wishes Alfred Weber had analyzed the locations which result when transportation costs are eliminated, before studying the variations due to varying labor costs, while cost of transportation remained variable.[34] The results of such an analysis would enable us to check upon the results of the previous analysis by introducing transportation costs into a network of locations first solely determined by cost of labor.[35] It would have served also as an excellent basis of defense against the criticism of Werner Sombart,[36] which does not really touch the foundation of Weber's theory at all because Sombart does not take up the problem from the point of view of economic theory. It is not possible to go into details, but the final result of such an analysis seems quite obvious. If transportation costs were constant, all production would go to the locations with lowest labor costs. To illustrate this "rule" let us assume that the labor costs are equal at A, B, and C, and a given distribution of a given industry between A, B, and C exists. If, then, the labor costs at A fall, all production will move at once from B and C to A.[37] It

[34] It is necessary for a clear understanding of this discussion to bear in mind that an elimination of transportation costs would only result if it were assumed that it costs the same to ship goods of any kind and any weight any distance.

[35] It will be remembered that Thünen made this first step, although incompletely, due probably to his preoccupation with the problem of rent (cf. above, p. xviii). But he failed to carry his analysis beyond this elemental stage and did not study either the variations caused by introducing labor costs into a system of locations determined by transportation costs or the variations caused by introducing transportation costs into a system determined by labor costs.

[36] Cf. his review in the *Archiv für Sozialwissenschaft und Sozialpolitik*, XXX (1910), 748, and *Der Moderne Kapitalismus*, 3d ed., Vol. II, 2, p. 800, 901 ff.

[37] It must not be objected here that this is inconceivable, because the "demand" for labor in A would at once raise the cost of labor in A, since it is an

would be easy to show that an introduction of transportation costs into these simple equations would give results identical with those obtained by Weber. Obviously the rule just stated, if we should be willing to call it such, has no explanatory value, because its application to different industries shows no "typical" alterations for each industry,[38] but affects all industries alike; whether they had high labor costs per ton of product, or low, they would obviously go to the location which rendered this part of their cost lowest.

The main reason for entering upon the discussion contained in the foregoing paragraph is to show that Weber was methodologically fully justified in starting his analysis with variable transportation costs and constant labor costs, because the locational significance of variations in labor costs becomes capable of analysis only in its relation to the total weight of all goods to be transported during the particular process of production. It seems to the writer that it is of the greatest importance that Alfred Weber has thus succeeded in laying bare the fact that transportation costs are theoretically the most fundamental element determining location, because it is only in relation to these two fundamental figures, the material index and the locational weight, that general rules can be stated whose application to particular industries shows significant alterations for each industry.[39] The only question which arises regarding Weber's deductions is whether it would not have been better to stick to transportation costs as the only "general" factor of location, and to treat labor as an indirect factor. Andreas Predöhl seems to be inclined to take this view, although his claim that "there is

_____

implication of our hypothesis that there is an abundant supply of labor at every location at the prevailing wage level.

[38] This may be the reason why Thünen refrained from stating it in relation to the problem of location.

[39] This entire reasoning is based upon a theory of theory which chooses among different possible theories upon the basis of their explanatory value.

no logical difference between the labor factor and any other local factor" goes too far.[40]

What has been said thus far may suffice to explain the location of industries as affected by factors which are both common to all industries (general factors) and direct in their operation. But, as was noted before, certain further variations are caused by factors which are themselves partly caused by those direct or primary (Weber calls them regional) factors just discussed. These indirect factors (agglomerating and deglomerating) are not capable of the same deductive analysis as the direct factors discussed before, because they follow from the social nature of production. Quite generally speaking, such an indirect factor is an advantage which follows from the fact that not less than a certain quantum of production is agglomerated at *one* place (agglomerating factor), or from the fact that not more than a certain quantum of production is agglomerated at *one* place (deglomerating factor). The agglomerating factors (advantages from large-scale production through technical apparatus, labor organization, etc.) are related to the nature of the particular industry, while the deglomerating factors are all traceable to the inevitable increases in the rent of land which accompany the agglomeration of industry.

How far, then, will agglomeration go? The significance of an answer to this question for an understanding of rent is obvious. Let us follow Weber's analysis. He returns to the assumption of constant labor costs in order to study the deviations caused by these agglomerating and deglomerating factors within the network of locations as determined by costs of transportation alone. He eliminates the deglomerating factors by treating them as lessening the force of agglomerating factors. But,

[40] Cf. his "The Theory of Location in Its Relation to General Economics," *Journal of Political Economy,* Vol. XXXVI (1928), where he bases his arguments to some extent upon Alfred Marshal; and "Das Standortsproblem in der Wirtschaftstheorie," *Weltwirtschaftliches Archiv* (1925), XXI, where he bases his arguments upon Gustav Cassel.

according to Weber, this can only be assumed as long as isolated industries are considered; otherwise there exists the possibility of "accidental" agglomeration of several different industries, which would create deglomerating tendencies quite apart from an agglomeration of any particular industry.[41] This leads Weber to consider the effect of the agglomerating factors upon an isolated industry, whose locations have been determined by the costs of transportation. The economies per ton of product for each quantum of agglomeration constitute a function of the agglomerating factors, the "function of economy." The increases of the economies from quantum to quantum constitute another function of the agglomerating factors, the "function of agglomeration." This latter function is the real measure for the extent of agglomeration. The extent of agglomeration is determined by the ratio between this function of agglomeration and the locational weight, the latter multiplied by the (uniform!) rate of transportation. Weber finds that a formula exists which shows which quantum of agglomeration will be realized.[42]

The reintroduction of variable labor costs shows the two "deviating" tendencies, labor and agglomeration, competing with each other, with the result that the tendency of industry to concentrate at a few locations will be further increased. This finding would support our earlier suggestion regarding the position of labor costs within a theoretical treatment of location.

The foregoing may suffice to show that Alfred Weber and Thünen both point out the fundamental importance of transportation costs for any theoretical understanding of location. Hence, upon the basis of the assumptions made in the beginning,

[41] The writer is wondering whether it can even then be assumed. Labor costs, we saw, may concentrate a given industry in one or two places which would create these deglomerating tendencies. As a matter of fact, even when only transportation costs are variable, a concentration of industries in one location may cause a sufficient rise in rent to "deglomerate" them. This was pointed out partly and from another point of view by Predöhl, *loc. cit.*

[42] Cf. *infra*, p. 153 ff.

rent is capable of analysis as a function of location.[43] It is at this point, the writer believes, that the importance of the theory of location for general economic theory becomes apparent, for it was in connection with this problem that Thünen developed whatever theory of location he did develop.

Among the problems which have presented major difficulties to economic theory, the effect of forces operating to restrain trade has occupied a very important place. Monopolies, transportation rates, and international tariffs stand out among such forces. Their separate theories must necessarily be interrelated. The connecting link between them is an adequate theory of rent.

As to the theory of monopoly, I shall venture no more than a hint. A more elaborate discussion would necessitate an analysis of the work of at least A. C. Pigou and J. M. Clark.[44] But one thought suggests itself at once: if all deglomerating tendencies are related to the rise of land value, i.e., rents, then, where no rise in land values becomes apparent (let us say in a socialist system), the result would seem to be a considerable acceleration of agglomeration.[45] But most economists today would hold that

[43] Predöhl, *loc. cit.*, suggests a threefold basis of location for the purpose of a general theory of location: rent, other local cost as a whole, and transportation cost. But if rent is, as I think was shown sufficiently, a function of location, it is theoretically quite unsatisfactory to assume it as a general or direct "factor" of location. This aspect of Predöhl's arguments was also questioned by O. Engländer (although from another viewpoint), "Kritisches und Positives zu einer allgemeinen reinen Lehre vom Standort," *Zeitschrift für Volkswirtschaft und Sozialpolitik*, Vol. V, Nos. 7–9 (1926), and Predöhl's reply, "Zur Frage einer allgemeinen Standortstheorie," *Zeitschrift für Volkswirtschaft und Sozialpolitik*, Vol. V, Nos. 10–12 (1927).

[44] Cf., for example, J. M. Clark, *Economics of Overhead Costs*, particularly pp. 82–83.

[45] I do not know how much weight can be attached to Russian statistics in matters of this kind, but if the recent census is fairly correct, the development in Soviet Russia seems to be at least in accordance with this statement. Cf. *Foreign Affairs*, VI, 333. In this connection it is amusing to note that Weber's theory of location has been translated into Russian in recent years and acquired a great vogue in that country, I am told. The independence of its conclusions from the price mechanism lends it significance there, perhaps.

since rent would be an element of the cost of production in a socialist state, such an acceleration would be impossible in the long
run, and that the final equilibrium would be identical. However,
what has been said about the locational foundation of rent, suggests a more complex situation, as we are apparently dealing
with interdependent variables.

In applying the theory of location to the theory of transport
rates, a suggestive start has been made by Oskar Engländer. A
good deal of light is shed also upon this aspect by Stuart R. Dag-
gett.[46]

Finally international trade was taken up by Alfred Weber
himself.[47] In his general work he attacked the theory of the "international division of labor," thus taking a stand opposed to
that of many other economists.[48] The forces which seem to determine the location of industries would obviously permeate the
international field, and this led Weber to apply the rules which he
had found to the problems of international trade. One might
start from the assumption of an even distribution of the different
kinds of production over the entire earth rather than from the
assumption of the "international division of labor." The classical
doctrine of free trade, says Weber, takes only capital and labor

[46] Cf. his *The Principles of Inland Transportation* and Oskar Engländer,
Theorie des Güterverkehrs und der Frachtsätze.

[47] "Die Standortslehre und die Handelspolitik," *Archiv fuer Sozialwissenschaft und Sozialpolitik,* XXXII (1911), 667 ff. There is some hope that this
whole aspect of the theory of location will be further developed soon. Bertil Ohlin has recently ventured upon the bold assertion that "the theory of international trade is nothing but an international theory of location" ("Ist eine Mod-
ernisierung der Aussenhandelstheorie erforderlich?" *Weltwirtschaftliches Archiv,*
XXVI, 97 ff.). It does not become very clear from this article, unfortunately,
how Ohlin expects to elaborate upon his theme.

[48] Cf., for example, A. B. Clark (in Palgrave's *Dictionary,* 1923): "By localization of industry is meant the concentration of different industries in different
localities, a phenomenon in its international aspects aptly described by Torren's
phrase 'territorial division of labor.'" This in 1923; the article [on localization]
does not even mention the *Standort der Industrien.*"

into consideration when discussing costs of production, while the "natural" factors are supposedly eliminated by the Ricardian theory of rent. This approach makes it impossible to appreciate the independent significance of the costs of transportation. The picture of the "natural" tendencies of the distribution of economic forces shows really four stages (or layers):

1. The farming population will be distributed rather evenly around the historical centers of culture and population (Thünen's belts).

2. All industries which remain so oriented under the influence of costs of transportation (i.e., industries which use more "pure" materials or ubiquities than weight-losing materials) will be evenly distributed upon this foundation.

3. Industries which show considerable weight losses during the process of production will be attracted to the deposits of raw materials and fuels.

4. Industries with high labor costs per ton of products will be concentrated at the favorable international labor markets.

From this it will appear that the classical doctrine (probably upon the basis of actual events in England at the time) concentrated its attention upon the fourth stage and attributed to it a good deal of what was probably due to the third. However, there is a certain recognition of Weber's point of view (although, as we have shown, without the theoretical foundation) in Marshall.[49] Friedrich List, in a sense, represents a reaction

[49] *Principles,* 4 ed., p. 761. "It is no slight gain that she [England] can make cheaply clothes and furniture and other commodities for her own use; but those improvements in the arts of manufacture which she has shared with other nations have not directly increased the amount of raw produce which she can obtain from other countries with the product of a given quantity of her own capital and labor. Probably more than three-fourths of the whole benefit she has derived from the progress of manufactures during the present century has been through its indirect influence on *lowering the transport of men and goods, of water and light, of electricity and news; for the dominant economic fact of our own age is the development, not of the manufacturing, but of the transport*

against the classical overemphasis upon labor costs when he says that wherever there is agriculture there must also be industry. But he does not undertake to construct a theoretical foundation for this aspect of his protest. Only upon the basis of an adequate theory of location is it possible to fit the two points of view into a satisfactory theoretical harmony.

It seemed primarily desirable to point out the significance of isolating costs of transportation for any theory of location. In spite of the apparent distortions which the network of locations as determined by transportation costs alone is subject to in the international field, a clear analysis of the working of this factor has much to contribute toward a deeper understanding of the forces underlying the international distribution of industries.[50] Weber's new approach enables him to restate the doctrine of free trade. If the natural evolution tends to develop new industrial centers, such tendencies may be retarded or accelerated, but they cannot be eliminated.

To summarize, land rents, i.e., advantages due to favorable

---

industries. It is these that are growing most rapidly in aggregate volume and individual power, ... they also which have done by far the most toward increasing England's wealth." (Italics mine.) But why? If the costs of transportation are so important, their operation ought to be given the appropriate attention. That this whole matter is in some way related to the question of land value and rent is also asserted by Marshall: "The influence on values which has been exerted in the modern age by the means of transport is nowhere so conspicuous as in the history of land; its value rises with every improvement in its communications with markets in which its produce can be sold, and its value falls with every new access to its own markets. . . . ."

[50] Says Weber (*Archiv, loc. cit.,* p. 668): "Jede äussere Handelspolitik bedeutet, wenn sie einen bewussten, willkürlichen Eingriff in das natural Gegebene darstellt, den Versuch, Produktionszweige in einen Wirtschaftskörper hinein und aus anderen herauszuziehen, sie in ihrer geographischen Lagerung zu beeinflussen, zu verschieben." This aspect has recently been expanded upon and has been made the basis of historical systematization of the problem of the interrelation between locational development and the growth of the modern state by Hans Ritschl, "Reine und historische Dynamik des Standorts der Erzeugungszweige" in *Schmollers Jahrbuch,* Vol. 51, pp. 813 ff.

locations of industry in relation to raw material deposits and market areas, appear to be variable functions of the locations of industry which are in turn variable functions of dynamic (or creative) factors, such as the development of new material resources, transportation facilities, or increases in population which determine economic development in the long run. An adequate theory of location seems bound to enrich the theory of land rent and thereby perhaps carry repercussions into other aspects of the theory of value.

CARL JOACHIM FRIEDRICH

Theory of the Location of Industries

INTRODUCTION

The question of the location of industries[1] is a part of the general problem of the local distribution of economic activities. In each economic organization and in each stage of technical and economic evolution there must be a "somewhere" as well as a "somehow" of production, distribution, and consumption. It may be supposed that rules exist for the one as well as for the other. Still, political economy, in so far as it goes beyond the analysis of elemental facts and beyond pure theory, is of necessity primarily description and theory of the nature of economic organization *(Wirtschaftsart)*. The presentation and theoretical analysis of the nature, the sequence, and the juxtaposition of the different kinds of economic organization is its natural content as soon as it attacks concrete reality. This is such an enormous content that it should not occasion wonder if a young science, limiting itself in its initial tasks, treats the "somewhere" of economic processes simply as a function of the nature of that process, although the location of an economic process is only partly a function of its nature. In other words, political economists have dismissed this problem of location with some general references to rules of local and international division of labor, etc., or political economy has left to economic geography the theoretical consideration of the distribution of economic processes over a given area. Naturally, the latter is able to approach the problem only in so far as it can be explained by purely physical facts. The result is as unsatisfactory as if we had left the analysis of the nature of economic processes, i.e., political economy, to the technical sciences.

But while problems of location have been treated by geogra-

[1] Industries is here and throughout the text used in the sense of manufacturing industries.—EDITOR.

phers primarily, Thünen is a notable exception. There are, too, several later attempts in this field. But they are insignificant when compared with the magnitude of the problem. We witness today enormous displacements of economic forces, migrations of capital and human labor such as no other age has ever seen. We see "empires rise, empires fall," apparently as the consequence of such locational changes. We follow these developments with a strong feeling of their significance; we predict the tendencies of future accumulation and distribution, the development of industrial states and their collapse. We even interfere with these matters by our trade and tariff policies *(Handelspolitik)*, and try to master them. In short, we do repeatedly a thousand things which we should really attempt only after we have secured a clear understanding of the laws which operate within this sphere. But can we say that we possess such a knowledge? Can we say that in our discussions we make use of much more than some vague notions about the division of labor, etc., while assuming location to be determined by the nature of the particular process? We work, in spite of Thünen and his successors, almost entirely with such tools, I believe.

We also notice enormous displacements taking place within national boundaries. We observe that certain regions rapidly grow poor in human beings and capital, while others become saturated. We see in metropolitan centers great masses conglomerate, seemingly without end. We philosophize about these matters, talk about the advantages and disadvantages which result, about *Asphaltkultur*, or "decline of morals." Of course we have long since become partisan in these matters. To some of us it seems that the populace "runs" to the big cities only for "pleasure's" sake—to the ultimate ruin of itself and its posterity; to others it appears that these people follow inevitable laws, as for
3 example the flow toward the place of lowest pressure socially, etc. Much thought has been spent upon the "rush to the city" (not only upon its consequences, but also upon its causes), but

is it possible for us to arrive at any conclusion about its causes
when we do not possess as yet any real knowledge of the general
rules determining the location of economic processes—when the
purely economic laws which without any doubt somehow influence location are not discovered?

Everybody who moves into a large city goes there, among
other purposes, in order to follow some economic pursuit. Is it
sensible for us to argue about cultural and social motives when
perchance we are simply fettered by the iron chains of hard economic forces? It may be that the enormous agglomerations of
today are nothing but inevitable results of a certain stage of economic and technical development; or perhaps they are the consequence of the social organization of our economic system.
Concerning this we really ought to have some exact knowledge.
At any rate we cannot very well go ahead assuming that there are
no rules of economic location at all, or that people are guided by
"pleasure" and other irrational motives when choosing the location of their economic pursuits, although we know them to be
controlled by hard-and-fast rules in every other economic situation.

Ambition might tempt us to formulate a general theory of location. For it seems possible only on the basis of general rules
of locational distribution of economic forces to disclose the causal relation between them and those large displacing processes
which we observe. With such general rules known, it would be
possible to show how and to what extent the aggregation of population is determined by economic forces. Having acquired this
knowledge, we might become able to say how far forces of a 4
general cultural nature determine the location of economic processes.

But certain reasons make it advisable to limit our inquiry to
a theory of *industrial* location, reasons quite apart from such entirely personal facts as the time and strength of an individual.

For one thing, the theory dealing with the nature of economic processes has, with much profit, separated the spheres of production, distribution, and consumption. We gradually gain the basis for a general understanding of the economic system by learning how the phenomena of different spheres are interrelated.

Still, as a matter of fact, the locational forces operating *between* the different spheres are quite peculiar. We may separate production, distribution, and consumption as far as we please, but, analyzing the locational character of an economic system *(Wirtschaft)*, we need to explain a large part of each of these at the same time. For example, the locational distribution of consumption appears to be, with slight exceptions, nothing but locational distribution within the other two spheres, seen from a different point of view. Only the relatively inconsiderable number of people who are, economically speaking, merely consumers, such as officials, soldiers, and persons of private means, move about independently of the other two spheres. For the rest, each producer, laborer, merchant, or the like, wherever he may be, affects to some extent the location of consumption. In turn, each consumer, wherever he may be, affects to some extent 5 the locational distribution within the other two spheres.

The limitation assigned to our study is, therefore, in fact, to a large extent a matter of appearance only. That part of distribution which represents the actual movement of goods is geographically imbedded either between the different parts of production (productive process of distribution) or between production and consumption (consumptive process of distribution). It is impossible to explain the sphere of production locationally without including in this explanation the distribution of material goods in all its aspects. In the theory dealing with the nature of economic processes it may be possible to have production end at the point where the product is sold to a merchant, at least abstractly; but for the purpose of explaining the economic location of production this procedure is impossible. Each part of production orients itself geographically with consumption in mind. The explanation of this orientation—locational theory—cannot neglect consideration of the place of consumption. Thus in fact we include the distribution of goods in our theory.

Because of this inevitable interaction our theory does not, however, become a complete theory of the location of distribution. We in no way explain thereby the location of the seats of the wholesale merchants, of the agents who direct the actual movement of goods, i.e., the location of the trading centers. The headquarters directing the circulation of the goods and this circulating process itself must be disconnected geographically.

Moreover, we say nothing definite regarding obligations and money, that is, we say nothing definite concerning the location of the centers of capital and credit. This being true, some aspects of the collateral spheres of the economic system remain unexplained. These collateral spheres must be treated separately when one method is that of isolating[2] the various factors. And, for that matter, these collateral spheres have a geographical movement of their own, and their location should accordingly be explained separately.

As has been indicated, if we take the sphere of production and explain its location completely, we shall of necessity explain 6 also the larger part of all other locational problems within the economic organism. Practically speaking, we approach the total problem of economic location from one particular point; the first steps will be a theory of the location of production, but the last ones will be essentially a general theory of location—or at least it will not be very difficult to arrive at such a theory.

Limiting ourselves thus to the sphere of production, it is of prime importance to seek an explanation of the location of industrial production. There are good reasons why we should content ourselves with this analysis. We have a theory of the location of agricultural production by Thünen, although it needs, I

---

[2] This isolating process, it is true, is largely formal and abstract.

believe, some reshaping, and particularly some developing. But
we do not as yet have any theory of the location of industries—
we may say that without doing injustice to the work of Roscher
and Schaeffle—although it is obvious that industrial location is
far more important for explaining the large modern displacing
processes. To be sure, very nice and interesting facts determine
the locational displacements of the different methods of agricultural production. But they are upon the whole simple, extensively analyzed, well-known matters, at least to the extent to which
they go beyond technical details and influence international economic displacements and the modern aggregations of population.
Moreover, they have in a certain sense created only the basis of
the general locational revolution of recent times; they have provided merely the groundwork upon which other forces have
arisen to displace economic processes and to determine the agglomerations of population. This we sense quite distinctly as
the modern "enigma" which is to be solved. Mysteries are not
contained in the agricultural sphere. If they can be found anywhere in economic matters, and especially if they can be found
in the sphere of production, they will have to be discovered in
the industrial sphere and in the locational rules which control it.
The locations of the industries form the "substance" (I do not
7 say the cause) of the large agglomerations of people today. We
view their movements quite superficially, and with perhaps too
few misgivings as to the international implications of the shifting of forces. We argue seriously about tendencies in this sphere.
It is highly important, therefore, to begin by clarifying these
tendencies, not only because they are greatly neglected, but also
because they are most far reaching in fact.

How shall that be done?

It is well worth noticing that we know the simple *facts* about
the distribution of agriculture better than those about the distribution of industry. This situation is quite easily explained by
the greater complexity of the industrial sphere. We have well-

developed statistics which cover fairly well the areas of cultivation of the different agricultural products, the size of the crops, and their international as well as their local distribution, the latter at least in many countries. We have data, and we can even say that on the whole the data are scientifically analyzed. The essential aspects of agricultural locational distribution and development are known to us; if not, it is our own fault.

With regard to industries, however, we are confronted at the very outset with gigantic difficulties in getting the mere material.[3] We do not even know the raw figures of international distribution of production of more than a few trades, such as mines, salt works, sugar, tobacco, and perhaps the mechanical part of the textile industry—in other words, trades whose production is analyzed statistically for fiscal or other special purposes. For all other industries we use, for want of better data, the import and export figures in a manner scientifically quite inadmissible. When we talk of international distribution of industrial resources we use figures which we should not use at all except in terms of their relation to the size of the original production. The trade censuses which, by giving the number of persons employed, give us suggestions regarding size, are very difficult to compare, and for that reason are not thus used. This is the situation regarding the distribution of industries internationally.

8

What is to be said concerning the distribution within the national boundaries? Material exists regarding this, although partly hidden so far. Here the trade censuses, or at least their preliminary and intermediary materials, can give us information about local displacements of a very exact kind and free from all objection. We do not do injustice to anyone by saying that this really extensive material has so far not been analyzed for these purposes. The geographical conditions of distribution and local

[3] This was written in 1909. But even today many of the essential facts are not available.—EDITOR.

accumulation have nowhere as yet been analyzed in a careful quantitative way for even one industry. Of what use for our purposes are beautiful maps showing us the regions within which one industry is practiced "primarily" if we learn that this same industry is also practiced "outside" of these regions within the same country?[4] We ought to know, for purposes of any exact locational study, to what extent they are practiced "inside" and "outside," i.e., the relation, quantitatively speaking, between the two. Similarly useless for our purpose are otherwise quite estimable maps which show us the "relative geographical importance" of various industries in relation to the population;[5] they give us information concerning the different composition of the population here and there, but not concerning the geographical distribution of the industry itself. If we search for quantitatively well defined information regarding the local distribution of industries, we soon find that we grope in the dark concerning all industries in all countries, with perhaps the single exception of mining and smelting production. We grope in the dark concerning every single period of the development of a given industry —and how much more so concerning its entire development! My respects, therefore, to economic treatises including any discussion of local distribution of industry at present! Nothing is to be said against them as things stand. We ought to realize, however, that they are in fact little more than rather sketchy silhouettes.

Obviously a change should be brought about in this situation. It is necessary to canvass systematically the existing ma-

₄ Compare the maps of numerous writings on the English industries; similarly, the maps of distribution of industries which are added to the reports of factory inspection.

₅ Compare the maps of the official German reports on the Trade Census. They are used and even elaborated for the purpose of illustrating the location of industry in Teubner's *Handbuch der Wirtschaftskunde Deutschlands,* I suppose *faute de mieux.* For evidence that they are not only useless in principle, but that one gets quite a distorted idea about the whole matter, compare Part II.

terial available upon one period, and we shall choose the German development since 1860 for that purpose. It is further necessary to get a reliable picture by making an exact quantitative analysis of the interrelated forces which affect the distribution and agglomeration of the individual industries. This is the first and unavoidable part of our investigation, to get exact data regarding the actual locational relations and displacements in any one tolerably isolatable district for some period of time, even if quite limited. We need to have before us the object with which we are dealing, clear and discernible, and particularly *measurable,* in all its parts.

But we want still more, and we must attempt more, as has been indicated earlier. We want to discover "laws" for the movements within this (industrial) body—laws sufficiently exact to enable us to measure, with their help, the displacement of economic forces in such a way that we can state to what extent these displacements, and to what extent other factors cause the vast geographical revolutions of our time.

The empiricist will at best look askance at this larger and more essential enterprise. He will in his well-known fashion tell us that we should have to be able to subject the social life and its forces to experiments if we wish to find exact, i.e., scientific, laws;[6] that inasmuch as we cannot do that, we ought to content ourselves with stating "probabilities" and more or less certain "relationships," "regularities," "phenomena of evolution." Anything else is useless from his point of view, and we cannot, therefore, expect sympathy from that side. But we may hope for sympathy among those who believe with us that it is possible without experiments to analyze further by purely theoretical, intensive labor empirical evolutionary phenomena, in spite of their complexity. By making use of the method of isolating analysis,

[6] Scientific stands here for the German term *naturwissenschaftlich,* as opposed to *geisteswissenschaftlich.* The distinction roughly corresponds to "scientific" and "philosophic." Cf. Rickert, *Kulturwissenschaft und Naturwissenschaft,* 4th ed., 1921.—EDITOR.

we may ascertain, if not all, at least some, causal relationships, and prepare for a perfect causal understanding, and even for measurement. By the adherents of the method of isolation, then, this essay, whether successful or not, will probably be approved, 10 at least in principle. We hope that the writer, and not the essay, will be blamed for its possible failure.

This will make clear how we must proceed with this essay. Obviously, two different purposes should be achieved. First, we shall have to develop the pure laws of industrial location, laws in the strictest sense of the term pure, i.e., independent of any particular kind of economic system *(Wirtschaftsart)*.[7] Secondly, we shall have to show what *particular form* these laws receive in the modern economic order, and what *additional* rules, or perhaps only regularities, enter. The second phase of the work will of course contain an explanation of the interesting relationship[8] between these two kinds of laws and the large social revolutions referred to.

Methodologically we shall always proceed by isolation, not

[7] The concept of a system of "pure" economics as indicated here occurs in German theoretical literature. It is the outcome of an attempt to regain for economic theory a position which it seemed to have lost completely under the impact of the historical school. Books like Karl Bücher's *Introduction to Political Economy* treated economics in terms of economic development. Usually several stages were being distinguished, of which the last is the capitalistic stage, or lately the high capitalistic *(hochkapitalistische Stufe)*. In order to get a foothold outside this evolutionary view and to return to theory, the expedient of such an abstract "pure" system was used. It seemed sensible to say that if all these systems were designated as economic systems, it was justifiable to search for the characteristics which they had in common, although some will hold that the thought of the earlier thinkers like Smith and those following him is "capitalistic" and representative of the stage of development with which they were concerned. The assumption of such a "pure" system of economics simply marks the return to what would be styled "economic theory" in England and America. Cf. also *infra*, p. 226, footnote.—EDITOR.

[8] Relationship is here used for *Dynamik*, a German word which is not always suited for translation into the English "dynamics," and which therefore has occasionally been rendered by "forces" and "relationship," respectively, depending upon the particular meaning it has in the respective connections.—EDITOR.

only in the first part dealing with the pure theory, but in the second part[9] as well. There is one difference, however. For the task of stating the pure rules of location it will be possible to use deduction exclusively. We shall be able to start from certain very simple premises and to deduce therefrom the entire system *(Mechanik)* of "pure" rules of location. Naturally, this system will apply only in terms of these premises and no further. It will become apparent that it is possible to develop these pure rules of location fully in so far as they are of a general nature, and apply therefore more or less to all industries. For the details compare chapter i.

The further task of formulating the laws of location under modern capitalism cannot be achieved by simple deduction. The premises which determine the particular application of the pure rules as well as the additional rules governing reality are not known without further investigation. In order to formulate them we must first secure the actual picture of industrial orientation (location), as it is moulded by the modern economic life. Once we have this actual picture we shall have to show to what extent this orientation is affected by unexplained special[10] causes which the general theory has ignored and may properly ignore.[11] Finally, we shall have to show the effects of unexplained causes of a general kind. For these latter we shall have to find the premises which must somehow be due to the particular nature of modern economic or social life. Only from these premises may we deduce the rules of location "governing reality," which can give us a complete picture of the distribution of locations and at the same time can perhaps give us the means of understanding the general aggregations of population in modern times—that is,

[9] An outline of this second part is contained in Alfred Weber, "Industrielle Standortslehre (Allgemeine und kapitalistische Theorie des Standorts)" in *Grundriss der Sozialökonomik* (1914), Abteilung VI, 1, 70–82.—EDITOR.

[10] Due to circumstances in particular industries.—EDITOR.

[11] Details in chap. i.

so far as such a thing can be done by an abstract theory, which never explains entirely a concrete reality.

Obviously then, the preliminary canvass of facts which I mentioned earlier is a necessary introduction to the later task of a "realistic" theory. I had, in fact, undertaken this preliminary work of ascertaining precisely the evolution of German industrial location since 1860 before I had acquired any theoretical conception. I believe, however, that it will be better to present this factual material where it belongs, both as a matter of logic and as a matter of practical presentation: after the pure theory and before the realistic theory. It is impossible to analyze or arrange this material at all without an abstract theory of location. I have indeed gained it myself from this analysis; only out of an abstract theory and a clear survey of the facts can the realistic theory be compounded.[12]

We shall organize this work, then, as follows: The first part will contain the pure theory. This is divided into two parts: (a) the abstract disclosure of the economic forces which control the orientation of industries, i.e., the analysis of the constituent elements (locational factors) determining the location of industries, and (b) the formulation of the laws according to which these factors work.

The second part will contain the "realistic" theory and will be based upon:

a) An analysis of the locational distribution (*Lagerung*) of German industries since 1860.

b) An analysis of some other data which are available concerning the aggregation of population in modern capitalistic countries.

We shall see that the kind of industrial location which we have today is not entirely explained by the "pure" rules of loca-

---

[12] It has to be kept in mind that Professor Weber does not work out his so-called "realistic" theory in this volume. An approach to it is made in his contribution to the Grundriss der Sozialökonomik.—EDITOR.

tion, and therefore is not purely "economic." It results to a large extent rather from very definite central aspects of modern capitalism and is a function of modern capitalism which might disappear with it. It results, we may say in hinting at the main point, from degrading labor to a commodity bought today and sold tomorrow, and from the ensuing laws determining the labor market (*Gesetze der "Arbeitsmarktgestaltung"*) and from the local "agglomeration of workers" created thereby. This agglomeration of workers produces by necessity the particular kind of industrial aggregations which we find today and which I shall call "progressive agglomeration of industry" (*Stufenagglomeration der Industrie*). Therefrom results, as we shall have to show, the phenomenon of modern aggregations of population and, of course, many other things.

I say this only to indicate that the "realistic" theory will enable us to arrive at certain fairly general conclusions which explain at least a part of the dynamics of the large modern geographical revolution. But only a *part;* the limit of the conclusions of the second section of our study will be found in the limits of its material. This material deals mainly with the movements of industry within only a part of the international economic organism—within a territory which represents a politically, and, generally speaking, a nationally uniform organization. This limitation in the material has the advantage that the movements of industry thus studied present themselves to the observer as, in a sense, "pure." They take place without regard, on the one hand, to any differences of political organization and to the influence of trade and tariff policies; and without regard, on the other hand, to differences of race, climate, and environment. Our studies thus provide without doubt an analysis for *one* country, and apparently they provide the first necessary step toward a similar theory for the *Weltwirtschaft* (economic system of the world); for a general theory would, at the outset, also disregard the constituent differential elements just mentioned and would introduce them afterward.[13] The limitation in the material has, however, a disadvantage in that it does not help us to ascertain precisely the significance of each of the differentiating factors mentioned above. In this respect the limitations of the material set a limit to everything attempted in this essay, a fact which cannot be emphasized strongly enough.

This is, of course, the point at which further study is desirable. It should be said, however, that further research becomes rather difficult. We need, in order to get ahead, rather diversified new data. We need primarily clarity as to ideas and facts concerning the general significance of such fundamental factors as national disposition (*Volksanlage*) and environment—both their general significance and their relationship to what we call labor supply *(Arbeiterstamm)*. We need to ascertain precisely how far the quality in its different parts of industrial output depends upon the "stock of industrial workers" in different climates *(Zonen)* and among different nations, and how far this dependence changes within the framework of the modern technical and economic development, etc.[14] For an understanding of the international problem we need, moreover, investigations into the actual effects of political interferences (such as trade policies and labor policies) upon the local grouping of economic forces— studies which we do not possess at present in spite of all our theorizing regarding international trade and tariff policies. We

[13] There is no question that the importance of some of these differentiating factors (particularly the trade and tariff policy) is generally very much overestimated today. But there is no question, either, that others, like climate and cultural environment, perhaps even "race," have considerable importance—so considerable, in fact, that they will be felt even in analyzing the seemingly uniform German body, and that some "dark spots" which remain can hardly be explained except by them. The available statistical material unfortunately does not allow to solve these problems.

[14] Cf. in this connection the researches of American sociologists, i.e., Clark Wissler, *Man and Culture,* F. Stuart Chapin, *Cultural Changes,* and P. Sorokin, *Social Mobility.*—EDITOR.

should also secure an enormous mass of material concerning the international distribution of industrial location (*internationale Industrielagerung*), etc. These are many and difficult matters.

But irrespective of this, we shall of course find that much of what is presented within the narrow frame of this essay must be corrected, and the reader will observe that there remain unsolved problems, a fact which will not be concealed.

This book is expected to be a beginning, not an end. 15

CHAPTER I

LOCATIONAL FACTORS AND LOCATIONAL DYNAMICS

The economic causes determining the location of an industry seem to be a network of complex, diverse elements, often in individual instances so arbitrarily, or at least incidentally, composed that there appears to be no place for more than an analysis of the individual case.[1] It seems impossible to make any general statement for most industries concerning the places to which their factories must go or concerning the causes upon which their locations depend. If we approach the individual manufacturer with a question concerning the choice of his location, he will at most give us a quaint concoction of general and particular reasons, unless he points to the past and says: "I am here because this industry grew up here." This concoction will be different for each factory and will present whatever general causes it contains in a particular individual setting. Thus one might well despair, as I have said, of discovering general formulas for the solution of the different elements, or even of ascertaining precisely their limits. Still, an attempt to do so is quite necessary from a theoretical point of view. However difficult it seems, we must try to disentangle the knot of causes which confronts us everywhere in reality, and to isolate and group the elements composing it.

I. TERMS

In order to do this we need a clear understanding of two terms: first, the forces which operate as economic causes of lo-

---

[1] Cf. R. M. Haig, "Some Aspects of the Regional Plan of New York and Its Environs," and "Toward an Understanding of the Metropolis," *Quarterly Journal of Economics,* Vol. XL.—EDITOR.

16 cation, the "locational factors"; and second, the objects which we believe those causes to act upon, the "locational units."

By "locational factor" we mean an advantage which is gained when an economic activity takes place at a particular point or at several such points rather than elsewhere. An advantage is a saving of cost, i.e., a possibility for the industry to produce at this point a certain product at less cost than elsewhere, to accomplish the entire productive and distributive process of a certain industrial product cheaper at one place than at another.

We say the productive and distributive process of a certain product. We shall always compare for one and the same product the advantages of production as represented by locational factors; since only the production of one and the same product constitutes a unit with regard to the spatial distribution of which we may speak with sufficient accuracy.

It is necessary to be exact in this respect: a given commodity of better quality is not the same product as the same commodity of inferior quality, at least not in principle. The production of each is, from a theoretical point of view, a "unit" in itself which is distributed over an area according to its peculiarities. These units can and do compete with each other; the better commodity may supplant the less good, or vice versa, and this may also affect their locations eventually. But this competition or displacement is not essentially a locational struggle; it is based upon competitive causes of a different kind. It does not concern us for the moment. It represents the displacement of one industry by another, in the same way in which wood and clay products are superseded by iron goods. It is, however, an object of our study to learn whither the victorious or the defeated industry and the production of the different qualities move. We have to solve that problem by analyzing the local distribution of the productive advantages which are decisive for this particular

17 quality, this "locational unit."

It is obvious that, practically speaking, it may and frequently will be the case that the extent and the importance of a given productive advantage is negligible as between different qualities of the same product. It may happen that for different qualities of a product the locational factors are so similar that they are, practically speaking, equal. But even so, these different qualities represent independent units for the purpose of locational analysis. It must be kept in mind that each of the qualities has its particular sphere of consumption, competing, perhaps, but separate. It is consequently not possible to treat the productions of these different qualities as one locational unit, even though they are in close proximity (have deposits of raw materials and other real locational elements in common). We have to deal with two different productions which happen to find their locations according to similar causes.

The foregoing, however, is the abstract position of pure theory. As a matter of fact, there is in reality an enormously wide field in which the competition of quality changes to that of price, and in which products of a different but closely approximate quality are in fact treated as one and the same product at different prices. Viewing the matter closely, one is compelled to admit that each "competition of price" rests partly upon such a difference in quality; because the quality of no product is truly equal to that of any other. Competition of price is possible only by disregarding differences of quality.

Still, whenever in reality no difference of quality is recognized, we do not need to recognize it when applying theory to reality. In such a case we have before us, for this one application at least, "units" of location of production. The different qualities of product have been welded together into a unit by life through 18 being treated as one by consumption. Accordingly, we shall treat as locational units varied products whose distribution of production over an area is properly to be analyzed as a unit.

This much regarding the nature of the terms, locational factors and locational units.

How shall we group these locational factors? We seek a general theory of location; that is to say, we wish to resolve the seeming chaos of the local distribution of production into theoretically general rules. Such general rules would result only from the operation of locational factors of a *general* nature, if at all. Such general locational factors must be considered for every industry, asking in the case of each industry in what way they exercise their general influence and to what extent. Thus the first question is: Are there such general causes of location which concern every industry? And the next question is: Are there any special causes of orientation which concern only this or that industry, or this or that group of industries? Such special causes obviously are the result of the peculiar technical or other nature of an industry or group of industries. How far can the location of industries be explained by general causes, and how far only by introducing special causes? It is obviously helpful to classify locational factors as general and special. It may elucidate the difference to state at this point that the cost of transportation, of labor, and rent are general factors, since they should be considered in the case of every industry, influencing it "more or less in one way or in another." On the other hand, the perishability of raw materials, the influence of the degree of humidity of the air upon the manufacturing process, the dependence upon fresh water, etc., are special locational factors, because they concern particular industries only.

All locational factors, whether general or special, are to be further classified according to the influence which they exercise (1) into such as distribute the industries regionally and (2) into such as "agglomerate" or "deglomerate" industries within the regional distribution. To "distribute regionally" means to direct industry toward places on the surface of the earth which are geographically determined and given, to draw industry to definite regions and thus to create a fundamental framework of industrial locations. To "agglomerate" and to "deglomerate" means to contract industry at certain points within such a framework (irrespective of where the framework may be situated geographically), and thus to determine the agglomerations which industry shows within the framework—something quite distinct from the process of regional distribution.

If industry is influenced by the cost of transportation or by geographical differences in the cost of labor, industry is drawn to. points geographically quite definite, though changing their position as industry develops. The factors which operate thus are regional factors of location. If industry, however, is brought together at certain points by price reductions due to agglomeration itself, whether it be the more economical use of machinery or merely the advantage of being at a place where auxiliary trades are located; or if industry is driven from such congested places by the high rent; industry is agglomerated or spread within its geographical network according to certain general rules which are quite independent of geography. The factors which operate thus are agglomerative or deglomerative factors.

A third distinction which ought to be made is that of natural and technical factors on the one hand and of social and cultural factors on the other hand. This distinction (also made in terms of the effects of the factors) cannot be fully made, however, for reasons to be considered shortly. It has the following meaning: The advantages which draw industries hither and thither may be given by nature. In that case they could be altered only by changes of these natural conditions, by the extent of the control of nature—in other words, by technical progress. They would be independent of the particular social and cultural circumstances; at least there woud be no direct dependence. On the other hand, the advantages which draw industries hither and thither may be social or cultural phenomena, the consequence of particular economic or social conditions, or of a certain civilization.

For example, all differences in cost which result from the spatial position and climate of different places, particularly all differences of cost of transportation, are locational factors of the natural and technical kind, phenomena of nature which may only be altered by the technical evolution. The differences of the cost of some types of labor may be of the same nature (differences in the hereditary qualities of the population), or they may be the result of a certain cultural environment (differences in the standard of living, or in acquired productivity of labor), and they are sometimes locational factors of a mixed kind. If a different interest rate prevails at different locations of industry, that is something which bears no relation to any natural condition, and represents a purely "social" factor of location.

It is desirable to make a clear distinction between natural and social locational factors. Under our method of procedure this distinction is bound to have considerable significance for us later. For it is apparent that every aspect of locational factors which is not of a natural or technical, but of a social, character cannot be an object of pure theory which is to be independent of particular economic or social conditions. Such aspects must be left to empirical theory. The importance of this classification of locational factors is indicated by the fact that it defines the two large subdivisions of our theoretical analysis.

But it will prove its value later. For the present we shall attempt to build up the "pure" theory without applying the distinction fully or exactly. To be specific, we shall exclude from the purview of the pure theory all locational factors of a *purely* social and cultural nature which our analysis of reality reveals. We shall not even investigate how far the natural and technical factors contain in their present form social and cultural elements which are due to the particular economic and social order, the

particular civilization of today. In order to be exact we ought
to make this investigation and then apply these social and cultural elements in the empirical or realistic theory. But this will
not be done. It will appear that these elements do not alter fundamentally the laws according to which they work; they merely
determine in particular how these laws work out in reality. It
is better to state at once these particular qualifications of the
general rules, and to do so within the framework of the discussions of the pure theory, then to leave them to a special treatment. Accordingly, the analysis of the pure theory will, upon
the basis of the natural and technical factors, be carried into the
ramifications which the modern economic order presents. This
method of treatment will enable us to reach the problem of
reality at our first attempt, and at the same time to verify principles by reference to actual life.   22

Our analysis will be based upon the distinction between general and special factors of location and upon the distinction between regional and agglomerative factors. The distinction between natural and social factors will only silently accompany
our discussion.

III. ASCERTAINING THE GENERAL FACTORS OF LOCATION

Can we survey the several individual locational factors
which are to be found in the various industries? Obviously, a
complete survey could be made only empirically. There is no
method by which one could deduce from known premises the
special locational factors which exist for given industries on account of natural or technical peculiarities. But, after all, this is
not what we need in order to group the chaos of facts conven-
iently for analysis and theory. We need a knowledge of the general factors of location which are applicable to a greater or lesser
degree in every industry. If we know these we are able to inquire
how far the orientation of industries can be explained by them.
Next, by ascertaining further facts, we can investigate the par-

ticular causes of phenomena not explained by the general factors. These causes must spring from the specific characteristics of particular industries; they are particular locational factors which we do not recognize in advance, and can ascertain only by investigation. We shall attempt only the development of a theory which explains the working of the general factors. This theory can be developed after a survey of the general factors has provided its basis.

We can further limit ourselves with respect to the locational factors needed as a basis for our pure theory by considering only general factors of the regional type. If we know these and their working, we can abstractly construe the geographical framework which is created by them (cf. above). We can put in as one single force all the agglomerative and deglomerative factors and general causes of orientation not yet analyzed. They tend to create a certain number of agglomerations of a certain size— agglomerations which are not due to geographical influences. This single force may easily be imagined to be the resulting force which is invariably derived from the counteraction of agglomerative and deglomerative factors. We need only to analyze the importance and the working of this resulting force. The factors composing it we do not need to know.[2] In short, the pure theory may be based solely on the knowledge of the general, regional factors of location which control industry.

We have a simple method of ascertaining them. We can find all general factors of location controlling industry (with the exception of the agglomerative and deglomerative factors) by analyzing some isolated process of production and distribution. These general factors must be at work in any such process, and may therefore be discovered by analyzing it. The agglomerative factors are excepted because they are at work between industries, and therefore cannot be found in an isolated process.

[2] More regarding this point in the chapter on "agglomeration," below.

But we are not looking for them, anyway; we are looking for the 24
regional factors, and they may be found in the way indicated.

We have to find, obviously, those elements of cost which
differ according to the location of the productive process. If we
can secure them, we have the regional factors of location of a
general nature. "Locational factors" are, according to our definition, "advantages in cost." They depend upon the place to which
industry goes, and therefore pull industry hither and thither.
This idea is decisive for our entire further procedure.

Abstractly considered, an industrial process of production
and distribution contains about the following steps or stages:
(1) securing the place (real estate or ground site) of the location
and the fixed capital[3] for equipment; (2) securing the materials
(raw and auxiliary materials as well as half-finished products),
and the power and fuel materials, (coal, wood, etc.); (3) the
manufacturing process itself; (4) the shipping of the goods. In
each of these steps a certain expenditure of natural resources
and labor is invested. In some cases this expenditure has already
been taken care of to a greater or less degree, as in the case 1 or
2 of fixed capital or half-finished products. In other cases, as in
3 and 4, it falls entirely within the stage of production which is
under observation. Each of these expenditures precipitates itself 25
into the price *(Warengeldpreis)* which is secured for the product
on the market. The expenditures of 3 and 4 are primarily labor
costs; those of 1 and 2, primarily material costs. In analyzing
the price of industrial products we meet again in the guise of
monetary elements all those elements of cost which grow out of
the expenditure of goods and labor in the productive process.
We have to ascertain, first, which of these monetary elements
(in so far as they are elements of cost) differ according to the
location of the particular industry. These are the general regional factors of location. We have to discover, second, which

[3] For this use, cf. Palgrave, *Dictionary of Political Economy,* article on
"Capital."—EDITOR.

of them are expressions of a particular economic order (*Wirtschaftsform*) and which are expressions of every economic system. The latter will be the general regional factors of industrial production, even though they appear in the forms of the modern capitalistic order.

We shall have to base our theory upon these factors in their modern capitalistic form, which is the only one practically available for analysis. Nevertheless we work with the elements of the abstract economic order (*reine Wirtschaft*) and accordingly formulate a theory which applies to this abstract order also.

The following remarks should be made concerning the foregoing analysis of the "natural" industrial process as transformed by the capitalistic economic order. All expenditures of labor and goods which constitute the process become monetary advance payments upon the future price of the product. By monetary advance payments we mean that the entrepreneur of each state of production makes advance payments in the form of wages and salaries to his employees, and in the form of prices paid for materials and machines to the entrepreneurs of the previous stage. The monetary outlays of a certain stage of production are nothing but the sum of all these advances which its entrepreneurs must make. It should be remarked, however, that each stage adds two things to its advance payments: the interest on the capital it uses for these advances, and its "profit." In each successive stage these "additions" appear as increases of the cost of materials. Thus the monetary costs are advance payments covering not only expenditure of goods and labor but also of interest and profit of the preliminary stages as well. These remarks may suffice to clarify the nature of the process which we are about to analyze. What form does this process take if observed in connection with the "natural organization" of a stage of production as shown previously?

1. The first step in the natural process of production was the securing of the real estate for the location, and the securing

of the fixed capital. This becomes cost of rent so far as the securing of real estate is concerned, and cost of money [interest plus brokerage charges plus taxes—Ed.] so far as the securing of fixed capital is concerned.

The real estate is not consumed; the fixed capital is consumed but gradually. Both appear in the final price of the product as the interest rate of the sums spent on them.[4] In addition, the fixed capital appears with a monetary rate of amortization proportionate to the time required to consume the fixed capital.

2. The securing of the materials and power which constitutes the second step in the "natural" process of production is divided into the monetary cost[5] at the place of their production and the cost of transporting them[6] to the place of their consumption. We shall not analyze the costs of transportation for the present. The total price (*Anschaffungspreis*) paid for the materials and power supplies plus the interest resulting from the advance of funds used for buying them enters the market price (*Warenpreis*); so do the costs of transportation.

3. The third step, the process of transforming the materials, entails the consumption of the materials, the depreciation (*Abnutzung*) of fixed capital (*Stehendes Kapital*) and the utilization of human labor. The first two elements of cost have been considered already. The last one enters into the market price (*Wa-*

---

[4] It is, of course, of no significance whether this capital enters into the process as loans, so that the interest rate is stated by contract, or as the entrepreneur's own capital. It must always be there, it is always consumed, and its interest rate must be provided for. The stipulated interest rate is, as is well known to theory, nothing but the expression of the interest on capital, becoming apparent under certain circumstances. Resting in principle upon Böhm-Bawerk, although in a somewhat more narrow sense, it is important for the analysis of cost as given here that I interpret this general interest on capital (*Kapitalzins*) as the price paid for goods enabling one to overcome time (*Zeitüberwindungsgüter*). This advanced capital (*Vorschusskapital*), then, makes possible all the advance payments which compose the monetary costs as explained.

[5] I.e., the price to be paid for them.—Editor.

[6] I.e., the price to be paid for transporting them.—Editor.

renpreis) as wages; but again, of course, plus the interest on the advance of funds involved.

4. The fourth step, the shipping, is represented by the costs of transportation which further increase the price by their full amount plus the interest on the funds used.

It should be noted here that in all these stages an additional element of cost exists which is called today general expenses, i.e., expenses of the general management, taxes, insurance, etc.

If we group all these elements of cost according to their character and if we add as the last element of the price the profit of the entrepreneur, we get the following elements composing the price *(Warenpreis):* (1) Profit. (2) The interest rates of the fixed and operating capital *(Anlage und Betriebskapital)* of the different stages. (3) The rate of amortization of the fixed capital. (4) The cost of securing materials and power. (5) The wages. (6) The cost of transporting: (*a*) the (raw) materials 28 and power, (*b*) the finished products. (7) The general expenses.

Of these we can eliminate two, namely, 1 and 7, from further consideration. Let us take up first the general expenses (7). To the extent that they are artificial enhancements of the expense of production by political or other agencies (taxes, insurance), they do not belong in the field of "pure" theory. To the extent that they are "natural" costs (general management, etc.), the local differences determined by geographical conditions which might make them regional factors of location are not sufficient to make them worthy of consideration in the general theory.

As for profits (1), they can never (at least not in the last stage of industrial production) become locational factors because they are not elements of price, but its result. They can become an element of cost only by entering into the cost of materials, etc., of succeeding stages as profits[7] of earlier stages. As

---

[7] It has often been observed that English political economy has not separated profit from interest and wages of management. But Weber separates them

such an element of cost they may become a locational factor for the later stages because it is conceivable that profits will vary from region to region and thus affect the "natural" price of securing the materials (cf. Böhm-Bawerk). To give an illustration: If a coal-trading association today fixes prices which vary from district to district and, not contenting itself with the same profits in all districts, collects higher profits in a "safe" district by manipulating (*Normierung*) the price, then local differences of profits will become regional factors of location for all stages of industrial production using coal. Thus, differences of profit may become locational factors. Nevertheless we can eliminate the varying rate of profit from consideration, for it is, like profit itself, not an element of the "pure" economic order, but rather one of the capitalistic order. It does not concern us in pure theory. It is one of the alterations which the capitalistic order produces in the pure order. 29

The remaining elements of price (2–6) which are relevant for pure theory we may group more simply, i.e., more in accordance with the "natural" process of production. The second element, the interest rate on the capital employed, depends apparently upon two factors, the interest rate and the amount of capital. The amount of capital employed is apparently determined by the prices of the various other elements of production (real estate, fixed capital *(Stehende Sachkapitalien)*, materials, wages, transportation rates). From this it follows that we may enumerate as (cost) elements of price the following as important for us:

1. The cost of grounds.

2. The cost of buildings, machines, and other fixed capital costs *(Stehende Sachkapitalkosten)*.

---

clearly. It is necessary to keep this difference in mind for this discussion in which wages of management and payment of risk are part of the cost of production and not part of the profits. Weber is here, as throughout, concerned with the "pure" or "static" system of economics. Cf. above, p. 10.—EDITOR.

3. The cost of securing materials, power and fuel.

4. The cost of labor.

5. The cost of transportation.

6. The interest rates.

7. The rate of depreciation of fixed capital.[8]

Which of these elements vary according to the location of the place of production and thus represent general regional factors of location? Let us begin with the last one.

1. The rate of depreciation (and therefore of amortization) of the fixed capital (7) is obviously on the whole independent of geographical situation. Only the climatic conditions may be of importance, for example, by causing a greater amount of rust upon the machines due to greater humidity of the air. But these would be special, not general regional factors, and do not concern us here.

2. The interest rate (6) does not have locational significance in connection with the process of production in the territory of an economically uniform state which we use as the theoretical basis of our "pure" theory. The interest rate varies, of course, according to the quality of the enterprise as well as the management; thus the interest rate may certainly be higher as the *consequence* of a location which has been poorly chosen and yields a questionable return. But it does not vary according to regions within a given country as it doubtless does for different countries on account of different security, different wealth, etc.[9] It can never be the cause of regional choice of location in the pure economic system. In fact, it does not even show significant general differences between city and country, (i.e., between scattered and agglomerated industries) within such a political system as the German

---

[8] It was only for the sake of thoroughness that we did not present this grouping at the outset.

[9] This aspect must be kept very clearly in mind in dealing with locational problems in the United States. There is good ground for the assumption that these elements differ from state to state.—EDITOR.

Commonwealth. It therefore does not even require consideration as an agglomerative factor which might operate within a given regional distribution of industry.

3. The cost of land (1) varies in the case of industrial locations according to the amount of local agglomeration, but not regionally—at least not sufficiently to constitute a regional factor of location. In the case of land used for agriculture the price of land may exercise a regional influence. The prices of all other types of land have significance only in connection with agglomerations, for they represent nothing but results of agglomeration and deglomeration. The price of agricultural land may be in one part of the country about $50, in another, $150, in a third even $250 or $300 per acre, depending upon the density of population. This will be a matter of great importance in determining the kind of agricultural production;[10] but for the choice of industrial location it does not greatly matter, as it influences the price in much too small a degree. For example, if a modern spinning mill, which requires a great deal of space, needs $2\frac{1}{2}$ acres for an annual production of 1,200 tons of yarn, it is almost negligible whether $100[11] or $500 will have to be paid for this area. The additional $40 interest per annum cause an additional 3.3 cents for each ton of yarn, the total value of which is from $240 to $800. This is such a small fraction that it is not important as a locational factor. Even industries with a low-priced product and very large space requirements (such as iron works) are insensitive to these regional differences in the cost of land. Suppose, for example, a Thomas steel works which may be estimated to require 250 acres for an annual production of 300,000–400,000 tons[12] has to pay $250 instead of $50 per acre, and thus

[10] Cf. the classical treatment of Thünen, *Der Isolierte Staat*, Vol. I, which deals with this problem.—EDITOR.

[11] Since this is an example only, dollars and cents and acres have been substituted for *Mark, Pfennig*, and *Aar* on a rough average.—EDITOR.

[12] Cf. Heymann, *Die gemischten Werke im deutschen Grosseisengewerbe* (München, 1904), p. 25.

has on its books an item of $62,500 instead of $12,500 for land. The difference in interest on $1,250 per acre[13] causes a difference in cost of $0.005 per ton of product. Since this ton has a value of about $25, the difference amounts to two-hundredths of 1 per cent. This difference is much too small to exercise any influence upon the location.

The situation becomes quite different if local agglomeration enters into the picture and suddenly creates those towering rises to $5,000, $10,000 and even $50,000 per acre.[14] Such rises, of course, put the price of land among the relevant elements of cost of industrial production. For the Thomas steel works, for example, they would mean an increase in the cost of production on account of rent *(Preissteigerung durch Grundzinskosten)* amounting respectively to $0.125, $0.25, and $1.00 per ton. These are amounts which certainly may be important, and on account of which the rent will codetermine the location for products of this kind. It is a locational factor within the agglomerative tendencies. But it need not be considered for the regional factors.

4. The cost of building, the cost of machines, and other equipment (2), and the cost of materials and power supplies (4), represent nothing but the results of the price-making of: (*a*) the production of raw materials and power supplies; (*b*) the previous and auxiliary stages of industrial production.

Regarding *b*, they are for purposes of our reasoning fundamentally the same thing as the particular stage of production which we have chosen for our abstract analysis. Their costs may be broken up into the same elements into which we have resolved the costs of that stage. The previous stages contain no

---

[13] Why Weber should use an interest rate of 2.5 per cent in this instance when he used 10 per cent in the previous one is not clear from the text. But the reasoning seems to hold good, even if the difference amounted to as much as 0.08 per cent, as it would if an interest rate of 10 per cent were used.—EDITOR.

[14] Cf., for example, Andreas Voigt, *Bodenbesitzverhaeltnisse, etc., in Berlin,* regarding the rise in real estate values in Charlottenburg.

new elements of cost, and thus no new and unknown locational factors.

Regarding *a*, there remain, then, as new elements of cost for our consideration the prices of raw materials and of power, and they in fact represent not only a new, but apparently a geographically varying, element of cost, that is to say, a regional factor of location. The price at which the same material or power can be acquired may be and will be different at its various places of production, depending upon the nature of the deposit, the difficulties of its mining, etc. Depending upon which particular "deposit," as we shall call it, one draws for his particular manufacture, the costs of raw materials and power materials will vary. It will obviously depend upon the location of the plant whether it profits from the lower prices of a certain deposit of materials. Thus geographically determined differences of cost influence the location. These differences undoubtedly represent the first general regional factor of location.

5. The second regional factor of location are the regionally differing labor costs (5). It goes without saying that their locally different level pulls production to and from certain regions. This is achieved by the costs of the manufacturing process (*Stoffumwandlung*) within the stage of production here under consideration as well as indirectly by the prices of the auxiliary products which are partly determined by such labor costs. It should be remarked, however, that we mean real labor costs.[15]

6. We come finally to the costs of transportation (6) which have to be met in order to assemble the materials and to ship the finished products. It is obvious that transportation costs will vary according to the location of the plant. They will vary according to the length and nature of the road which the materials

33

[15] The German text reads ". . . . dass natürlich nicht die absolute Höhe der Löhne dabei in Frage steht, sondern ihre Höhe bezogen auf irgend eine Einheit Produkt, das was man eben heute meint, wenn man präzis von "Arbeitskosten" spricht.—EDITOR.

have to travel from the place of production, and which the finished products have to travel to their place of consumption. Sometimes the kind of transportation system will make a difference. These costs, then, also are regional factors of location of a general kind.

IV. THEORY OF THE LOCATIONAL FACTORS

The relative price range of deposits of materials, the costs of labor and transportation, then, are the regional factors of location of every industry. Of these, we may for purposes of theoretical reasoning express one, the relative price range of deposits of materials, by another, by differences of costs of transportation. We shall thus simplify considerably the formulation of our theory, since we shall have to operate with only two regional factors.

The different price levels of different deposits of the same material operate as if one had to overcome different distances from these deposits to the place of manufacturing, or as if the "cheap" deposit were situated nearer the plant, and the "dear" deposit farther away. In order to see this clearly, one might imagine an average price as the normal price of each material at the deposit. The differences in the price at this or that deposit will mean the same thing, from the point of view of the individual plant, as if additional costs of transportation had to be paid. This means that the differences of the price of material deposits may be expressed abstractly as differences of cost of transportation. We need not treat them as a separate locational factor, but may introduce them later as a modification of the effect of the cost of transportation, a modification which, of course, will have to be elaborated considerably.[16] Consequently we may work with two general regional factors, the costs of transportation and of labor.

This result is most important for us. Since we learned before

[16] Cf. below, "approximations to reality," p. 74.

that all general locational factors which are not of a regional kind (i.e., all the rest) can only be agglomerative or deglomerative factors, we may treat these latter factors as a uniform agglomerating force, that is, as a third uniform locational factor. We may thus at once construct our entire abstract system of general locational factors and the theory of its dynamics.

Let us start by supposing that all the isolated processes of industrial production will "naturally" at first be pulled to their most advantageous (optimal) points of transportation costs. Let us then regard this as the basic network of industrial orientation created by the first locational factor, transportation costs. Apparently, then, the differences of costs of labor (the second locational factor) represent a force altering this basic network. The most advantageous places of labor costs create a first "distortion" of the basic transportational *(transportmässig)* network of industrial location. We thus gain the conception of a fundamental orientation of industry according to costs of transportation, and of an alteration of this fundamental orientation by "labor locations" *(Arbeitsplätze)*.

Every agglomerating tendency—in other words, the entire group of all other locational factors which we have not so far taken into account—is nothing but a second altering force, another "deviating tendency" which tends to distort the transportational network and shift it to certain other points, the "points of agglomeration." In its net effect this entire group is a "unit" also. And like the other "altering factor," the differences in labor costs, it is a uniform "locational factor." It is competing with that other factor.

This completes the theory of general locational factors and the general survey of the dynamics within which they work, at least to the extent to which this theory and survey are necessary as a basis for the "pure" theory of location. There are no other general factors influencing the location of industry. The only

question is to what extent and according to what laws these three factors control the various parts of the industrial system. To show this will be the task of the pure theory. By introducing the agglomerating factor into the explanation we seek to make an analysis of the general laws controlling the locational distribution of industry, and not merely those connected with isolated
36 processes of production.

CHAPTER II

SIMPLIFYING ASSUMPTIONS

I

The theory to be given here is to explain reality. In the last chapter we have seen how complicated the reality of industrial location is rendered by the interrelated working (*Durcheinanderwirken*) of "general" and "special" locational forces. But this reality is further complicated by the fact that it results from the interaction (*Hin- und Rückwirkung*) of different economic spheres and of different parts of the same sphere. In our theory we shall ignore certain aspects of this situation. We shall assume that some of the facts which are in truth brought into existence by the processes which we analyze are independent of these processes. After having reached an understanding of the facts thus isolated, we shall introduce the full causal mechanism, i.e., we shall bring into proper perspective isolated data and shall analyze the change which is created thereby.

On the basis of this method, industrial orientation will be further analyzed within the limits of the following suppositions:

1. We shall assume the geographical basis of materials as something given. This assumption is in accordance with the facts when we are concerned with materials like stones, minerals, etc., which are simply dug out or mined—which, in other words, exist at different places by nature. The assumption is not quite so correct when the materials employed have to be produced, as is true of agricultural products. The agricultural basis of industrial materials is nothing "given." Agriculture receives its geographical location by a peculiar process which itself depends upon the distribution of its products, that is to say, upon the

orientation of industry. This has been elaborately shown by Thünen.[1]

In placing industry for the time being theoretically into a given geographical ground plan of material deposits, we shall intentionally neglect the retroactive effect (*Rückwirkung*) which industry may exercise upon this ground plan. This assumption will have to be examined and brought into accord with reality later.

2. The geographical nature of the sphere of consumption also will for the time being be treated as a given phenomenon. The situation and size of the places of consumption will be assumed in the pure theory as a given framework of orientation. We shall thus ignore the fact that each locational distribution of industry, merely by distributing the labor forces, distributes consumption of industrial products and of all other products. The geographical distribution of one sphere of consumption, which contains industry and its productive connections, is itself partly created and molded by this industry.

3. Finally, we shall not introduce the mobility of the labor basis of industry. We shall operate with the schematic concept of an area covered by several fixed labor locations *(Arbeits-plätze)* instead of introducing the shifting distribution of human labor characteristic of present-day reality.[2] We shall further assume that the wages of each branch of industry are "fixed," while the amount of labor available at this price is unlimited.[3] Here also we neglect in so doing a part of reality, for of course the locational tendencies of industry themselves create the standard of wages by codetermining the local demand for

[1] Johann Heinrich von Thünen. *Der isolierte Staat in Beziehung auf Land-wirtschaft und Nationalökonomie* (Rostock, 1842). Cf. p. xix.—EDITOR.

[2] This is the point of attack of Sombart. Cf. *Der Moderne Kapitalismus,* Vol. II, 2 and above, p. xxv.

[3] The details regarding these suppositions and the reasons for them, may be found in chap. iii, sec. I, toward the end.

labor. Moreover, we disregard for the time being to what extent 38
the local distribution of labor, i.e., the situation and size of labor
locations, is generally influenced by the other locational tendencies of industry. We evade all these problems for the moment by
assuming a given basic distribution of labor. It should be said at
once that it will become apparent that this third assumption cannot be eliminated within the scope of the "pure" theory; the dynamic relationship between the local distribution of labor and the
locational tendencies of industries can be explained only by the
realistic theory.

Other assumptions and simplifications will appear necessary
from time to time, but all of them will accompany us for but
short distances. Only the three simplifying assumptions just
mentioned are permanent and constitute the matrix within which
the pure theory will be found.

II

As the foregoing analytic examination of the locational factors shows, we assume in our theory that all industrial production is dependent upon the use of "materials," which are either
raw materials, half-finished products, or power supplies (wood,
coal). We speak exclusively of the use of "transportable" materials. In fact, however, not only materials enter into production, but "forces of nature" as well. They are used as live energy:
either given by nature, like water power, or transformed, like
electricity. The question is whether a theory which employs the
concept of transportable materials only can include the locational effect of those other forces as well. The answer is that
apparently it is possible to treat these forces of nature with regard to their locational influence, as if they were especially cheap
coal deposits. If that is done—how it has to be done is shown in
the last sections of the chapter on transport orientation—we 39
shall get rules determining the locational importance of these

forces. These rules modify only slightly the general rules which apply when transportable materials are employed.

Thus no specific effect which could not be fitted into the theory remains. This theory, then, embraces in its simple mold industry in its entirety, with all the materials and forces which it 40 absorbs into itself.

CHAPTER III

TRANSPORT ORIENTATION
(Transportorientierung)

SECTION I

ANALYSIS OF TRANSPORTATION COSTS

The problem to be solved is how transportation costs influence the distribution of industries, assuming that no other factors influencing the location of industry exist. To what places will industry be attracted? It is clear that it will be drawn to those locations which have the lowest costs of transportation, having regard both for the place of consumption and the place of the deposits of materials. Where are these places? At first we shall locate them in very general terms, and to that end we inquire: On what basic elements do transportation costs depend?

The fundamental factors which determine transportation costs are the weight to be transported and the distance to be covered. Since these two factors may readily be defined in mathematically exact terms, they provide a definite basis for an abstract theory, leading possibly to mathematical formulas. We shall, at the outset, treat these two factors as the only determining factors. This procedure is justified because we are thinking of costs in an economic sense. There are, of course, two kinds of 41 "transportation costs:" transportation costs in the sense of political economy, and transportation costs as understood by the business man paying for the shipment of goods. The former costs are the total amount of goods and labor that are absorbed in effecting such a shipment. The latter costs are the monetary payment made to those furnishing the transportation.[1] If we speak

---

[1] This, in English terminology, would commonly be termed the rate or the price of transportation. Cf. also Emil Sax, *Die Verkehrsmittel*, 2d ed. I, 76 ff. The

of weight and distance as the fundamental factors determining transportation costs we obviously have in mind the costs of "pure" political economy.

Our further discussion is based upon the possibility of expressing in terms of weight and distance all other factors which contribute to the cost of transportation, limiting our consideration to an area with a uniform system of transportation. Because of this possibility we are able to reduce the other factors theoretically to these two.

What this means and why it is the case requires a brief explanation. In this connection it should be noted that the transportation system analyzed here is the railway system prevailing today and the particular rate structure existing in Germany. The railroad system has been chosen for our analysis of the causal relationship between the cost of transportation and the distribution of industries over a territory because the railroad is today the chief means of transportation by land. As a device for simplifying our problem, we shall proceed as if it were the only system existing.[2] The significance of the relationship between carriers subject to different principles of cost determination will be examined later when our abstractions are brought into accord with reality.

It is clear that the cost of transportation depends upon the following factors, besides weight and distance: (1) The type of the transportation system and the extent of its use; (2) the nature of the region and its kind of roads; (3) the nature of the goods themselves, i.e., the qualities which, besides weight, determine the facility of transportation.

problem of joint cost is discussed by F. W. Taussig, "A Contribution to the Theory of Railway Rates," *Quarterly Journal of Economics,* V, 438, and A. C. Pigou, *The Economics of Welfare,* p. 266–68.—EDITOR.

[2] The same analysis could be undertaken for any other rate structure and any other system of transportation, but it is not necessary, because the principle is the same everywhere.

TRANSPORT ORIENTATION 43

Taking up the first point, it hardly needs to be explained that the type of the transportation system and the extent of its use produce great differences in cost as among the different systems. A given weight is carried a given distance today on railroads for one-quarter to one-tenth of the rate prevailing when carriages had to be used. The costs must have dropped correspondingly. However, different systems of transportation do not concern us for the present, since we are assuming a uniform system.

But even in a uniform system the different parts of the system are used with varying intensity, and this varying intensity causes differences in the cost of transporting a given weight a given distance. The shipping of one hundred tons of coal costs more on a road when a special freight train must be made up for the purpose than when an existing train can carry an additional hundred tons. Similarly the costs will be higher when there is no return freight than when return freight is always available. So also the costs per ton-mile vary, even on the same road, according to the volume of traffic. These are well-known facts. It is also known, however, that it is so difficult[3] to calculate individually the resulting differences in the cost of shipping individual articles, that these differences are disregarded in the rate-making of our present uniform railroad system, and the rates are fixed uniformly per ton-mile for all lines. Since, in making its rates, our system of transportation disregards these variations from a cost caluculated according to weight and distance, they may be disregarded in our theory. But if in fact such variations of rates should exist, the problem arising should be solved by assuming that lines with higher rates are prolonged in proportion to the higher rate; and similarly, lines with lower rates should be assumed to be shortened. If, for example, on certain lines a one-and-a-half rate per ton-mile is collected instead of the normal rate of one, such lines should be regarded as one-and-a-half times as long as they really are in applying to them a theory of location

[3] For this point, cf. Taussig.—EDITOR.

which assumes uniform rates. In Germany conditions do not, on the whole, call for this method of treatment.

There is, however, another aspect to this matter, an aspect in which the interest of the carriers in the greatest possible utilization of their facilities is reflected in the rates. Higher rates per mile prevail generally for small shipments and for shipments over short distances. This is not the place to show how and when these adjustments result from the necessity of increasing the density of traffic, nor to show how they relate to the lowering of general operating expenses per unit carried. Since such adjustments do exist, the problem they place before us is this: How may they be disposed of in treating cost of transportation merely as a function of weight and distance?

No serious problem is raised by rates which decrease as the distance increases. The same theoretical principle as before can be used here; the distance can be thought of as varying according to the percentage of the decrease whenever such scales apply. Geographical distances should not be measured by their geographical length, but in proportion to the decreasing rate scale.[4]

The problem raised by the difference in rates between parcels, half-carloads, and full carloads, is best solved by regarding those charges which are made on full carloads as the normal ton-mile rates. Then those goods which are charged higher rates because they are shipped in small quantities can be regarded as possessing an *ideal* weight in addition to the real weight. For instance, if the normal rate for full carloads is 6 cents, the rate for half-carloads 6.7 cents, and the rate for parcels, 11 cents, goods not shipped in full carloads may be regarded as having an addi-

---

[4] If, as in the case of parcel rates in the general class in Germany, a rate of 11 pfennig is charged per unit of weight for 50 kilometers, 10 for the next 150, and 9 for the next 100, and so on, a stretch of 100 is counted as = 50 + (50–50/11) = 95.4 km. We may say, then, that the geographical distance is corrected in proportion to the rates; an operation which, by the way, the present German rate structure fortunately spares us to a large degree. It provides a graded scale of rates only for some of the parcels and for a few bulk goods.

tional "ideal" weight amounting to 1.1 per cent and 83.3 per cent respectively of their real weight. Similarly, the weight of goods shipped on special reduced rates may be thought of as being reduced in proportion to the reduction in rates.

In this way it seems possible for theoretical purposes to express in terms of weight and distance all variations in rates, and thus to fit them without difficulty into a theory based on weight and distance alone. The general principle of this approach to the matter is clearly based on the fact that the effect of all elements of cost will appear as increase or reduction of the rate per ton-mile. This justifies operating theoretically with weight and distance, the two basic elements of the cost of transportation.

In passing we may apply this method to the other two most important instances of variations of cost as mentioned before.

The second factor upon which cost of transportation depends, aside from weight and distance, is the *nature of the locality,* influencing the road bed (see p. 42). On the one hand the nature of the locality determines the cost of road construction, and on the other hand it affects the cost of operation. Obviously, these local increases or decreases of cost, reflected in ton-mile rates, may be expressed by prolonging or shortening the sections in question proportionally. They therefore offer no particular difficulty for our theory. Moreover, the management of modern railway systems operated under consolidated control usually ignores these differences in cost. For instance, rates in Germany are uniform, regardless of the special cost both of construction and of operation of different sections of the system. In our later inductive examination of location we are not dealing with mountains and valleys, but with a mathematically flat plain where the mountains are razed, the valleys filled, and the swamps covered. The rate structure of the German railroads realizes the "ideal"; we shall utilize it in our work and thus simplify our deductions.

The third factor affecting cost of transportation, aside from weight and distance, is that of special qualities of the goods transported. Bulky goods require more space, and thus increase the cost by requiring more rolling stock. Perishable and explosive goods necessitate great care, not only in loading, but also in carrying them. All such qualities result in higher rates per ton. Moreover, certain kinds of goods are given higher rates, which, because of the high value of the goods, do not increase costs particularly. Indeed, there exist systems of rate-making which, disregarding weight, take for their basis value and distance. In fact, however, all so-called value rate-schedules (*Werttarife*) are really based on weight, even though disguised by scales of value. But it does not concern us here whether scales based on value are justified, since the transportation of an object requires the same cost whatever the value.[5] Suffice it for us to know that such scales exist. They do not cause us any difficulty. An increase in

47 the rate per ton-mile, no matter for what reason, means added "ideal" weight, a decrease means subtracted "ideal" weight; that is all.[6]

All the foregoing is perfectly simple. We have not only demonstrated clearly the principle in accordance with which the important factors determining cost may be expressed in the two basic factors of weight and distance, but also the practical execution of this principle for all cases important in the making of railway rates today. The only question that might be raised is

[5] Cf. for this discussion, Sax, *Verkehrsmittel,* p. 76 ff. and 100 ff., and particularly F. W. Taussig, *op. cit.;* also J. W. Clark, *The Economics of Overhead Costs.*—EDITOR.

[6] The German railway freight tariff assigns to "bulky goods" one and one-half times their actual weight, and we may consider them as having this weight. In the German system, value is taken into consideration when certain commodities of low value are shipped at lower rates than is usual. Thus certain parcels of low value are shipped at 8 pfennig instead of 11, and carloads of certain goods of small value at 4.5, 3.5, and 2.6 instead of 6 pfennig. Here again, subtractions in weight may be made in our calculations corresponding to these reductions; for instance, coal, which is shipped at 2.6 pfennig instead of 6 pfennig may be rated as if it had lost 56 per cent of its real weight when we come to applying our theoretical findings to German reality.

whether the deviations from the uniform rate based on weight and distance and the adjustments resulting therefrom are not so large (particularly in other transportation systems) that it is impractical to express theoretically all transportation costs in weight and distance. In answer to this we may say two things:

First, weight and distance are not only the basis of railroad rates but are the predominant factors in the cost of transportation, and hence of rate-making in any system, since they largely determine how much labor is necessary. This labor, regardless of its nature, is the essential factor of cost, and consequently of rate-making. An abstraction based on it is accordingly in no real 48 danger of giving a distorted picture of reality through being distorted by the influence of other factors.

Second, the rate structure as it exists in Germany today approximates closely the abstraction just made. The German railroads use the ton-mile rate as the general basis, calculating rates according to weight and distance. The whole country, as has been said before, is regarded as a mathematically flat surface. They employ merely "ideal" weight additions (*Gewichtszuschläge*) for half-carloads and parcels, as well as for bulky and explosive goods; and on the other hand they employ "weight reductions" (*Gewichtsabzüge*) for the large and important classes of goods of low value. They employ special rates modifying the uniform ton-mile rates only for certain sections, and, as mentioned before, a restricted use is made of decreasing scales with increasing distance for parcels and a few bulky goods of low value.

Reality, then, will not be too greatly distorted by our abstraction. It seems quite admissible to work with weight and distance in theory as well as in practice; in short, to work with the ton-mile rate as the basic scale of transportation costs, at least in a territory with one uniform system of transportation. The justification in both theory and practice for this simplifying assumption of the existence of a uniform system of transportation may be taken for granted for the time being, for we shall show later on that the more complicated situation of several co-operating transportation systems can also be explained in accordance with the theory here developed.

SECTION II

THE LAWS OF TRANSPORT ORIENTATION

If weight and distance are the only two determining factors, evidently transportation costs will draw industrial production to those places where the fewest ton-miles originate during the entire process of production and distribution; for with production at these places the costs of transportation will be lowest.

But how will the places of minimum ton-miles actually distribute the production? That is the real question to be answered.

In order to answer it, the simplifying assumptions of the whole theory set forth in the last part of the preceding chapter must be kept in mind. We are to regard as given the location and the size of the places of consumption of each kind of production; and we are to regard as given the location of the available material deposits. Furthermore, for the time being (up to chap. vi) we proceed upon the assumption that each product will be produced in one stage of production, the raw material being turned into the finished product at some single place of production.

I. THE LOCATIONAL FIGURES AND THE KINDS OF INDUSTRIAL MATERIALS

Let us then imagine ourselves stationed at some *one* of these given places of a given amount of consumption. Clearly, viewed from this place, there must be for every kind of product consumed at this place certain deposits of materials (raw materials, power materials) the use of which will result in the lowest transportation costs.

By no means will these deposits necessarily be those located nearest to the place of consumption. It is possible that in the case of certain materials a position near deposits of other materials is more important (bearing in mind the cost of transportation resulting from the whole process) than a position near the place of consumption. In such a case that position will be chosen which is optimal. In any event, viewed from each place of consumption, there doubtless exists for each kind of product a most advantageous location of each material that is utilized in making the product. Obviously, the deposits thus most advantageously located will be employed for such production as is necessary to fulfil the demand at the particular place of consumption. The

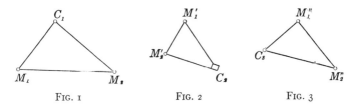

FIG. 1   FIG. 2   FIG. 3

location of the place of production must be determined somehow in some relationship to the place of consumption and to these most advantageously located material deposits. Thus "locational figures" are created, one for each place of consumption of each product. This locational figure is formed (as indicated above) by the place of consumption and the most advantageous material deposits. Each product will somehow select its place of production (location) in terms of this figure.

Let us suppose, for example, that we are dealing with a product composed of two materials which are to be found in scattered deposits. In such a case the "locational figures" would be represented by triangles. One corner of each triangle would be the place of consumption, and the other two corners would be the two most advantageous places of material deposits, as shown in figures 1, 2, and 3.

Assuming that nothing but the cost of transportation influences the selection of the location, it is evident that these loca-

tional figures must give the only possible mathematical basis of orientation. This presupposes, however, that location could be divided, as a matter of analysis, into just as many parts as the locational figures contain. We can presuppose this because we are disregarding for the present all agglomerating and deglomer-
51 ating factors.

These "locational figures" therefore represent the first and most important basis for formulating (*vorstellen*) the theory. We shall apply these figures to the most complicated sets of facts because through their use the outstanding elements of the structure of orientation are laid bare.

How is production oriented in terms of these locational figures? A general observation must be made before proceeding to answer this question. The main features of the orientation of production must be the same in all individual locational figures, no matter what the industry may be. For in all of these figures the main features of the orientation of production depend upon, and are determined by, the nature of the transportation needed for the particular industry. It follows that in order to find the principles according to which one may locate the theoretical point where transportation costs are lowest, it is sufficient in a theoretical analysis to deal with a single locational figure.

Then, too, before we can go on we must introduce some new terms. They refer to the nature of the materials employed by industry: (*a*) the nature of their deposits, and (*b*) the nature of their transformation into products. It will become apparent that the "transportational nature" of various industries depends entirely upon these facts.

As regards the nature of the material deposits, some materials employed in industry appear everywhere; they are, for practical purposes, put at our disposal by nature without regard to location. When the whole earth is considered this actually holds true only in the case of air; but when more limited regions are considered, it holds true for many other things. Brick-clay, wood, grain, etc., are materials available practically everywhere in certain regions. Such materials will be called "ubiquities"; in the former case "general," in the latter, "regional." Naturally they will be available or producible in each place only in limited quantities; nevertheless it is possible that the local demand does not exceed the limits of their supply, and in that case they are practically "absolute ubiquities." If the demand does exceed this limit, they are "relative ubiquities" for the place, the region, etc. Thus, water is a practically unlimited, and therefore an 52 "absolute" ubiquity in many German regions; likewise brick-clay for certain large regions. Grains, on the other hand, are naturally only "relative ubiquities" for all territories which import grains. "Ubiquity" naturally does not mean that a commodity is present or producible at every *mathematical* point of the country or region. It means that the commodity is so extensively available within the region that, wherever a place of consumption is located, there are either deposits of the commodity or opportunities for producing it in the vicinity. "Ubiquity" is therefore not a mathematical, but a practical and approximate, term (*praktischer "Näherungsbegriff"*).[7]

Other materials are not obtainable in the vicinity of a place of consumption (irrespective of where it may lie within the country or the region which is made the object of locational analysis), but only in geographically well-defined localities. Or, if they are technically obtainable, they are in fact mined or are produced by agriculture only in well-defined localities because of economic reasons. We find that minerals and coal, as well as most of the substances which are used for chemical and china manufacture, belong in the former category of technically localized materials, while wood and wool belong in the category of the economically localized materials.

It is obvious that it is not predetermined for all time whether

[7] Regarding O. Engländer's critical discussion of this concept cf. above, p. xxiv, n. 31.

an industrial material is "localized" or "ubiquitous"; this must be determined within each area, country, or region, for the period which is made the object of locational analysis. Let us take for example the southeast of the United States. For that region (perhaps!) cotton is ubiquitous from a practical standpoint; but evidently it is not ubiquitous for the world at large. For Germany cotton represents the reverse of a ubiquity; it is a material which must be brought in from very distant places outside. It is evident also that all relatively ubiquitous materials belong in the sphere of localized materials if at a given place the demand for them or for any of their parts exceeds the amount obtainable at 53 that place. Barley is a case in point in so far as the demand for it in breweries exceeds the production within the "vicinity" of the brewery.

As regards the nature of the transformation of materials into products, a material enters into a product either with or without residues. These residues may be used for another product, but they are refuse from the point of view of the first product. In order to have a term for this distinction we may speak of "pure material" and "gross material." Any ubiquitous material can naturally be either pure or gross. But since this distinction has no significance for location in the case of the ubiquities, the terms "pure material" and "gross material" will, for the sake of brevity, be used only for "localized" materials.

Another distinction may be made regarding transformation of material into a product, as follows: "pure material" imparts its total weight to the product; "gross material," only a part of it. Consequently we may consider fuels (such as wood, coal, etc.) when used for production as the extreme case of gross materials, for not a single bit of their weight enters into the product. They create important chemical and mechanical changes, but their use adds no weight to the product; their entire weight, from the point of view of the location, remains behind—"outside." It is desirable for our purposes that such materials be classified

under the general heading of "weight-losing" materials, together
with the other gross materials which technically play a fundamentally different rôle in production. There are therefore two
kinds of gross materials: the fuel which leaves its total weight as
a residue *outside* of the product, and the gross materials which
leave only a part of their weight. It is apparent that it is very
important for our theory to have covered these two distinct kinds
of materials with one term, for the simple reason that we are
dealing at present with the effects of weight only.   54

The materials used by industry are, for the purposes of the
following analysis, either "ubiquities" or "localized materials";
and these latter either "pure materials" or "weight-losing materials."

2. MATHEMATICAL SOLUTION

I

We have said that production will be oriented, under the influence of costs of transportation, in terms of the "locational
figures" which we have discussed. In view of our explanation of
these figures, this statement means that production must find the
points of minimum ton-miles. These points will be the transportational locations.

How are they to be found? The fact from which we start is
that such a location, wherever it may lie, always shows the following transportational relations: the entire weight of the materials which are used in the production must be moved to this
location from the material deposits; and the weight of the product must be moved away from this location to the place of consumption. This means that this location is connected with the
"corners" of the locational figures by lines along which move the
weights which appertain to these corners (the weights of the
material and the product respectively). Along the lines—let us
call them "components"—of the material deposits run the respective material weights, and along the component of the place

of consumption runs the weight of the product. Let us imagine a process of production which uses two localized materials, three-fourths of a ton of the one and one-half ton of the other being necessary in order to produce one ton of the product. The locational figure shows the weights three-fourths and one-half moving along the components of the two materials; while the component of consumption carries the weight one. (See Fig. 4, p. 55.)

These weights represent the force with which the corners of the locational figures draw the location toward themselves, it being assumed that only weight and distance determine transpor-
55 *tation.* For any movement of the location along a component toward a corner saves just as much as the movement amounts to in ton-miles. And if orientation takes place solely in accordance with ton-miles, the importance of every corner will be proportional to the ton-miles which can be saved by approaching it, i.e., the distance between the location and a given corner will be determined by the weight which attracts along its locational component. It follows as a general principle that *the location will be near the individual corners or far from them according to the relative weight of their locational components.*

The mathematician (cf. Mathematical Appendix I, §2) tells us that the precise location within the figures can be determined mechanically by means of a frame (Varignon's frame; cf. picture in Appendix p. 229). The corners of this frame are to be set up at the corners of the locational figure. Over these corners run threads on rollers, the threads being loaded with weights proportional to the weights of the components. In the inner part of the figure these threads are connected at some point. Wherever this connecting point (which must be prevented from being drawn beyond one of the corners) comes to rest, there is the location. This location point may be in one of the corners, if one of the weights is of the necessary size, or if a peculiar geographical condition prevails; otherwise, it will be found somewhere within the figure.

II

On the basis of the same general concept *(Allgemeinvorstellung)* in accordance with which the location is mechanically determined, "weight figures" can be mathematically deduced for any kind of production. While the locational figures will always be individual or specific for a particular plant, these weight figures are general, applying to all plants of the same kind of production. Such weight figures are formed by line segments whose

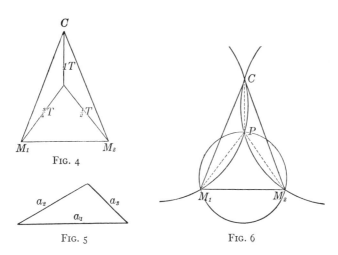

FIG. 4

FIG. 5

FIG. 6

length is proportional to the size of the weights which attract along the components of the locational figure of a particular productive enterprise. If the locational figure is a triangle, and if, as in the previous example the component weights are $1 = a_1$, $\frac{3}{4} = a_2$, $\frac{1}{2} = a_3$, then we can construct a weight figure which looks like Figure 5.

The following propositions regarding the position of the location can be deduced mathematically:

1. If it is *impossible* to form a figure out of the linear segments corresponding in length to the component weights, i.e., if one segment is as long or longer than all the rest together, the location always lies in the corner of this component. This becomes

evident by merely observing the mechanics of the "weights"; for if the one pulling weight is as great or greater than all the rest put together, it cannot be moved by them from its corner.

2. If, however, a weight figure can be constructed, i.e., if no one weight is as great or greater than all the rest together, the locational figure becomes important. If the locational figure is as simple as a triangle, we can discover the location by a simple construction (cf. for the mathematical analysis Appendix I, §4).

The general meaning of this construction is that two "corners of the locational figure" can always be seen from the location at an angle, the size of which depends upon the relative size of the component weights of these corners (in comparison with the component weight of the other corners). If the relative size is large, the angle will be large; and therefore the location lies upon a lower arc connecting the two corners, thus being necessarily *close* to the corners. And vice versa, if the relative component weight of the corners is small, the angle will be small also; and the location lies upon a higher arc connecting the two corners. The location will thus probably lie *far* from both corners, and certainly far from the weaker of the two. This describes in exact terms how the relative size of the weights affect the location with respect to the position of corners.

There is one more remark to be made. The third corner may lie *within* the determining arc which contains the other two, so that the determining arcs intersect each other, not within, but outside of, the locational figure (see Figs. 7 and 8). That occurs either when the component weights of two corners in comparison with the third are small, and the determining arc therefore extends very high over them (Fig. 7), or when the third corner lies near the connecting line of the other two corners (Fig. 8). In these cases the location does not move beyond this inclosed corner, but lies at this corner as in the first case when the weight of this corner entirely preponderates (see Appendix I, §7).

Three cases may be distinguished if the locational figure is a triangle:

In the first case, the weight applicable to one corner is equal to or larger than the sum of the other two weights; then the location always lies at this corner.

In the second case, the weight applicable to the one corner is not equal to or larger than the sum of the other weights, but it preponderates considerably. If this corner does not lie too far away, it is likewise the location.[8]

In the third case, the point where the "determining arcs" intersect is the location. It lies near any two corners, or far from

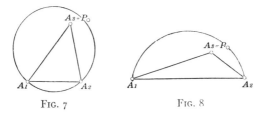

FIG. 7   FIG. 8

them, according to the size of their weights, compared with the weight of the third corner.

3. For all locational figures other than triangles, we do not have any such simple method of determining the location (see Appendix I, §12). The mechanics of the described frame of Varignon offer the easiest way for determining it. We can, however, imagine that the location is pulled toward any two corners of a given locational figure according to the relative size of their component weights, and we can thus apply the general idea gained from the triangle to these more complicated figures; although the pulling forces cannot be so easily expressed mathematically as in the case of the triangle. Although high or low arcs no longer afford a mathematical expression of the location

[8] Under this case comes also the instance of a close geographical proximity of the third corner, but this instance will be disregarded for the present.

being pulled to any two corners, nevertheless the foregoing furnishes a basis for a general picture of where the location lies in
these complicated figures.

III

What follows from these simple mathematical conclusions
as regards reality? Do they cover reality completely?

For all cases in which *localized* materials are employed, the
foregoing obviously furnishes a sufficient explanation as to where
the location will lie. Whether a complicated locational figure
results from the employment of numerous materials, or whether
a simple triangle results from the use of only two materials, or
whether finally the employment of a single material causes this
locational figure to shrink to a "line" which connects the one
material deposit with the place of consumption, the mechanics
59 will always remain the same. The material deposits will pull
with the weight of the material, the place of consumption with
the weight of the product, and the location will be determined
in the manner which has been discussed. The determining mechanics are simplified, however, when the "figure" shrinks into
a line—the only two existing components (that of the one material deposit and that of the place of consumption) coinciding
and thus connecting the two places. Along this straight line the
weight of the material will pull in the one direction, the weight
of the product in the other; and the preponderance in weight of
the one over the other will determine where the location lies upon
the line. This means that the location will be at the "deposit" in
case the material has the larger weight, and at the place of consumption in case the product has the larger weight. In case the
weights are equal, the location will be anywhere on the line.

When localized materials are employed, what will be the result if ubiquities like water are used in addition? This question
arises if any increase in weight of the product over and above the
used weights of localized material results from the use of ubiquities, as was assumed previously. The ubiquities have no defi-

nite deposits which could influence the locational figure; they are, according to their very definition, present everywhere. Their effect seems at first thought to be altogether beyond analysis by locational figures; however, that is not the case. Since they are available wherever production may take place, they will in fact be obtained wherever the location is, which means that they will exert an influence upon the locational figure, not as a material, but only in their manufactured form within the product. They become significant for locational purposes only because they increase the weight of the product. In other words, they affect the locational figure simply by strengthening the component of the place of consumption (which goes from the location to the place of consumption), because they add to this component their weight—a weight which had not previously appeared.   60

When we reflect upon this we see that the theory fully covers reality; it covers the case of both localized materials and ubiquities. Evidently it should be possible to develop out of this theory all variations of reality.

3. MATERIAL INDEX, LOCATIONAL WEIGHT, AND THEORETICAL CONCLUSION

So far as transportation is concerned, we might look upon the process of determining location as a struggle between the different corners, i.e., between the corner of consumption and the corners of the materials. What determines the outcome of this struggle? Perhaps, one might think, the extent to which material is used in the manufacture of a product, and therefore the number of tons of material which are required for one ton of product. Or, what would be the same, the extent of the losses of material, productive processes with many tons of material per ton of product being oriented near the material, and other types of productive processes being oriented near the place of consumption. Judging from our previous conclusions, that is incorrect. The same quantity of coal or other weight-losing factors may be

employed per ton of product in two cases and yet the two locations may lie at entirely different points in the locational figure;
indeed, in one case at the place of consumption, in another case
at the deposit or near the deposits. It depends upon how strong,
relatively, the component of the place of consumption is—possibly as strenghtened by ubiquities.

The determining factor is not the proportion of the weight
of used material to the weight of the product, but the proportion
of the weight of used *localized* material to the weight of the product, all ubiquities being of importance only as they increase this
weight of the product. This proportion of weight of localized
material to weight of product we shall term "material index" of
production. Consequently a productive process which, for example, uses one ton of localized material plus half a ton of ubiquities for one ton of the product has a "material index" of one;
so also has one which uses a whole ton of ubiquities in addition
61 to one ton of localized material (for example, a ton of earth in
addition to one ton of coal); and so also, of course, has one
which uses simply one ton of pure material. Abstractly speaking,
they are all oriented alike.

If we thus call the proportion of the weight of localized material to the weight of the product the "material index" of an
industry, one may say further: the *total weight* per unit of product to be considered for the movement within the locational
figure in any kind of productive process apparently depends
simply upon this material index of the industry. For this material index indicates how many weight units of localized material have to be moved in the locational figure in addition to the
weight of the product. The material index measures the total
weight to be moved. This total weight to be moved in a locational figure per unit of product we shall from now on call the
"locational weight" of the respective industry. It is evident that
this locational weight has the minimum value 1 when the material index (M.I.) has the value 0 (which it would have when

ubiquities only had been used), and rises parallel to the material index: M.I. $= \frac{1}{2}$, L.W. $= 1\frac{1}{2}$, etc.

We now can state the following conclusions regarding the struggle with respect to location between the place of consumption and the material deposits.

First, generally speaking, industries having a high *locational weight* are attracted toward material; those having low locational weight are attracted toward consumption; for the former have a high, the latter a low, material index. In view of our mathematical conclusions, then, *all industries whose material index is not greater than one and whose locational weight therefore is not greater than two lie at the place of consumption.*

Second, with respect to the composition of the material index we can deduce the following: *Pure materials can never bind production to their deposits.* For since they enter without loss of weight into the product, the sum of the component weights of their deposits is always at most equal to the weight of the product, and therefore the material index which they create never is more than one. We shall see the details below. *Weight-losing materials, on the other hand, may pull production to their deposits. For this to happen, however, it is necessary that the material index which they codetermine be greater than one, and that their portion of the material index be equal to that of the remainder plus the weight of the product.* Stated more simply, their weight must be equal to or greater than the weight of the product plus the weight of the rest of the localized materials.

4. CASES

Let us now analyze the various possible cases of reality, and let us attempt to exhaust all possible combinations. The following possible combinations of materials in the various industries are to be considered: (1) use of ubiquities only, (2) use of localized pure materials alone or with ubiquities, (3) use of weight-losing materials alone or with other materials.

1. Ubiquities only.—(*a*) One ubiquity: In this case production will always choose its location at the place of consumption. Our theory shows that the locational figure shrinks into one "point," the place of consumption at which production must occur. It is obvious from the facts; for if production occurs at the place of consumption, there is nothing at all to be transported, while any other location would necessitate transportation after the production. (*b*) Several ubiquities: There appears to be no reason why the location should be chosen elsewhere than in the case of only one ubiquity; the location will lie at the place of consumption.

2. Localized pure materials either alone or with ubiquities.
63 —*a*) If one pure material is used alone, the locational figure shrinks to a "line"; as mentioned before, the line from the deposit of the material to the place of consumption. Along it pull the weight of the material and the weight of the product in opposite directions. In this case the material index is equal to one, since the material enters in its entirety and no further material is added and the two weights are equal. The same weight is to be transported whether production is carried on at the place of consumption, at the material deposit, or somewhere in between. The location is mobile; it may lie at any point along this "line" or at one of its two termini, the place of consumption, or the material deposit.

b) If ubiquities are added the location is affected. The material index is less than one; the component of the material deposit is smaller (just by the ubiquities) than that of the place of consumption; and the location is therefore situated at the latter.

c) In the case of several pure materials alone, the material index is again equal to 1. According to our theory, therefore, the location should be at the place of consumption; for the material index does not pull the weight of the product along one line, but along as many different lines as there are materials. No single one of these components is equal to the component of the

place of consumption; the latter is as large as all of them together. It therefore keeps the place of production at the place
of consumption. This may also be established by another line of
reasoning. The weights of all materials, whether in the form of
materials or in the form of product, have to be moved from their
deposits to the place of consumption. They should not go out
of their way unnecessarily; therefore each material should remain on the straight line leading from its deposit to the place of
consumption. Unless the way of one should lead by chance
through the deposit of another, all these ways will meet for the
first time in the place of consumption. Since their assembly at
one place is the necessary first condition of manufacturing the
product, the place of consumption will be the location. Therefore a productive enterprise using several pure materials alone
is always located at the place of consumption.

   d) If ubiquities are added the location is bound to the place
of consumption more firmly still. The material index, which was
1 in case *c,* becomes less than 1. The component of the place
of consumption is not merely just as strong as all the other components together; it is stronger. That being true, it is quite im- 64
possible to separate the location from the place of consumption.

   3. *Use of weight-losing materials alone or in connection
with other materials.*—(*a*) One weight-losing material alone
gives us again the one straight line to which the locational figure
shrinks. But in this case the location is not mobile, for the component of the material deposit affecting location is larger by the
loss in weight of the material. The material index is by this loss
in weight larger than 1. Therefore the location is at the deposit.

   b) But if ubiquities are added, they strengthen the component of the place of consumption and the choice of the location
depends upon the degree to which they do this. The location
remains at the deposit as long as the material component remains
larger, i.e., as long as the material index remains larger than 1.

As soon as the component of the place of consumption exceeds in weight (i.e., as soon as the material index becomes less than 1), the location moves to the place of consumption. Therefore the choice of the location is determined by the comparative size of the losses in weight and of the weight of the ubiquities.

c) Several weight-losing materials alone make impossible a precise single statement concerning the position of the location. In such a case the locational figures of our theory become operative. The general theorems we have obtained allow us to say: If weight-losing materials *alone* enter into the production, the

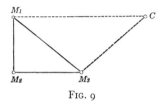

Fig. 9

material index is always more than 1, and the location of production will therefore be drawn somehow towards the material deposits. From our mathematical analysis we know by what arcs running through the material deposits the location is determined in the case of two materials. We know further that the location can lie at the place of consumption only if the latter lies by chance within this arc; and that the location goes in every instance (when two or more materials exist) entirely to one deposit, if the weight of this one deposit is equal to that of all the rest of the deposits plus the weight of the product. This latter fact enables us to realize in what case coal, for example, has the power to attract the location to its deposits; it is the case when its weight is equal to the weight of the product plus that of all 65 other localized materials employed.

If more than two materials enter, Varignon's frame may be used, as we know. We may visualize the geographical region attracting the location which is created by the preponderance of

the material index more distinctly by connecting the points of
material deposits into one figure (Cf. Fig. 9). The triangle M_1,
M_2, M_3 will be the region attracting the location. Its force of attraction will be greater to the degree that the preponderance of
the material index is greater.

d) Weight-losing materials together with pure materials
cause the material index to become smaller, since the pure materials appear again with their entire weight in the component of
consumption. Therefore the tendency toward the material deposits will be lessened. In this case also the location can *never* be
at the place of consumption unless the component of consumption is strengthened by ubiquities. On the contrary, it will always be situated near the deposits unless the place of consumption should accidentally lie upon the appropriate arcs. The
deposits of pure material have no attracting force, however.
Therefore the figure of the weight-losing materials (Fig. 9) can
be used again to see where the geographical center of attraction
of the location lies and how strongly it pulls.[9]

[9] This does not seem correct in view of what has gone just before. To be
sure, the deposits of pure material would not exert the same kind of influence as
the weight-losing materials. But suppose the proportion of weight of the pure
materials were considerable in the particular product and they happened to lie
between the deposits of weight-losing materials and the place of consumption,
like this:

A_1	B_1		A_1 and A_2 are the deposits of the weight-
.	.		losing materials a_1 and a_2;
		. C	B_1 and B_2 are the deposits of the pure
A_2	B_2		materials b_1 and b_2.
.	.		

Obviously, if the weight-losing materials alone determined the location of the production, it would probably be at the point halfway between A_1 and A_2 if we assume a_1 and a_2 to be of equal weight as well as of equal weight loss. But this
would mean that b_1 and b_2 would have to be transported all the way back to that
point. Obviously, then, the place of production would lie somewhere upon the line
connecting C with the point halfway between A_1 and A_2. This point would be
where the sum of the ton-miles of weight losses a_1, a_2 would be equal to the sum
of the ton-miles of b_1, b_2.—EDITOR.

e) If, finally, ubiquities are added also the locational effect should be clear from what has been discussed without further explanation. The material index will decrease exactly in proportion to the extent of their use, and the influence resulting from the loss in weight of the other materials will be counterbalanced. As soon as the losses in weight are actually balanced by the weight of ubiquities, the material index becomes equal to one and the location lies at the place of consumption in spite of the losses in weight. Exactly to the extent to which this condition is approximated as a result of adding ubiquities, the attracting force of the figure of the material deposits will decrease and the attracting force of the place of consumption will increase. If we wish to know whether a productive enterprise using all these different kinds of materials is attracted toward the material deposits or toward the place of consumption, we have to compare only the *loss in weight of its localized materials with the weight of the ubiquities* which it uses. According to which weight is the greater, one or the other attractive force is greater.

All this may serve to make concrete the mathematical theory and to show how it operates when it is applied to individual instances and to show that it covers them. Our construction (or, if the figure becomes too complicated, Varignon's "frame") affords us means of determining exactly the location in every individual case. As the foregoing examination of individual cases has shown, this construction and frame are, however, necessary only when weight-losing materials are used, because only in this case do we get locational figures in which the location does not lie at the place of consumption. In all other cases it is at the place of consumption except: (a) when only one pure material is used; in that case the location is mobile along the way between the material deposit and the place of consumption; (b) when only one weight-losing material is used; in that case the location lies at the material deposit; (c) when ubiquities are used in addition to a weight-losing material; in that case the location lies either at the deposit or at the place of consumption, depending upon the relationship between loss in weight and the weight of the ubiquities.

All this follows from applying the general mathematical theory of minimum points to the combination of facts which the various industries present.

Up to this time we have confined our analysis to examples of the transport orientation within isolated or single locational figures. But it is evident that fundamentally the same reasoning applies in the case of the orientation of an entire industry. For after all this orientation means, as far as transport orientation is concerned, simply the co-existence of a larger or smaller number of independent locational figures which are formed by the various places of consumption and the material deposit. Still, it is well to take up a few more questions.

A. First of all, *How do we get the locational figures appropriate to the orientation of an entire industry?* Which are the most favorably located deposits for each place of consumption? Are they simply and in every case those geographically nearest each place of consumption?

They are in fact the geographically nearest deposits, assuming a simple condition in which no complicated locational figures of counteracting forces are created. If only one material is used it is self-evident that the nearest deposit will be chosen, whether the place of production lies at the deposit, along the line between the deposit and the place of consumption, or at the place of consumption. It is self-evident also that the nearest deposit will be used if several pure materials are employed either alone or in connection with ubiquities, because the location will lie at the place of consumption, and using the nearest deposit will facilitate bringing the non-ubiquitous materials to the location. And finally, it is self-evident that likewise the geographically nearest deposit will be chosen if weight-losing material is combined with other materials without the existence of a complicated locational figure—in other words, when ubiquities are added to only *one* such material. As we know, the location in this case may be either at the deposit of that material or at the place of consumption.

But in the case of an actual locational figure, the deposits which form the figure need not necessarily be the deposits geographically nearest to the place of consumption. The following may serve as an example: Let us assume that GM is the deposit

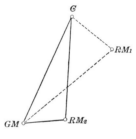

Fig. 10

of weight-losing material in a wide territory and without competition. Two deposits of pure material, however, compete with each other, and of these RM_1 is nearest to the place of consumption, but farther from GM than is RM_2, as the figure shows. Let the location be near GM on account of the preponderance of the loss in weight. It is evident that not RM_1, the deposit nearest geographically to the place of consumption, but RM_2, the deposit nearest geographically to GM, will be used in the productive process and will therefore form the "figure." Obviously, if the location lies near GM, pure material obtained from RM_1 would have to make a long trip first down to GM and then back again to the place of consumption; while this trip is saved if RM_2 is used.

Stated generally, this means that the factor which determines whether a given deposit will be used in forming the locational figures is the index of transportation costs of the figure thus resulting. The figure which has the lowest index of transportation costs triumphs in the competitive struggle, and for that reason is to be looked upon theoretically as the one really applicable. Thus the deposit that will be utilized is possibly not at all the one of its kind geographically nearest to the place of consumption. If the location does not lie in the vicinity of the place of consumption, but rather in the vicinity of a deposit (i.e., if the materials, or indeed *one* of them, predominates), geographical proximity to the place of consumption will be decisive only in the case of this *one* material. But in the case of the other materials, proximity to the deposit of the predominating material will be the significant factor in determining which particular deposits will be used in the productive process, and will in consequence determine the locational figure. In those modern industries, for example, in which coal represents such a predominating material, the geographical proximity to coal deposits, and not to places of consumption, decides whether particular deposits of the remaining materials will be utilized. To be sure, in these instances the production will be oriented in locational figures which are formed by coal deposits, which are in geographical proximity to the respective places of consumption; but this having been taken into account, the locational figures are formed by the material deposits which are as near as possible these coal deposits. Such figures therefore have a narrow base at the coal deposits and a long point extending to the places of consumption. Material deposits lying very near the places of 69 consumption but far from the coal deposits remain unused.

It should be clear theoretically now how these locational figures are created when numerous deposits are available—as is true in practical life. The exact mathematical method to be used in determining these figures in case the optimal deposit of *one* material is definite and a second material is then introduced is offered by Mathematical Appendix I, §10, Fig. 52.

In Fig. 52 A_1 is the place of consumption, A_2 the deposit of the one predominating material whose deposit is definite, A_3 (which is assumed to be mobile) representing the still undetermined deposit of the second material. The lines of equal transportation costs, which are drawn for the location figures arising from various possible positions of A_3, indicate which of the several deposits of the second material will actually be used for the locational figure. Naturally that deposit will be chosen whose use entails the smallest transportation costs. This will be the deposit within the lowest lines of transportation costs as drawn in Fig. 52.

B. Two more aspects of the orientation of an entire industry should be mentioned:

a) It is not necessarily the case that but one single place of production exists for the supply of every place of consumption. Firstly, it can and will happen that several locational figures with equal or approximately equal transportation cost indices exist. If, for example, one material lies nearer the place of consumption in one locational figure while the other material lies nearer the place of consumption in the other locational figure, the two figures have equal transportation costs indices. This results in equality of competition and makes possible the use of the places of production of both figures. This might be the outgrowth of natural conditions; but it may also happen that an appropriate tariff policy might equalize the transportation costs indices. Secondly, and more important still, it can and will happen that the normal output of the material deposits of the most favorable locational figures may not be sufficient to supply the demand of the place of consumption. In that case less favorable locational figures appertaining to the use of other material deposits will of course be brought into play. As a result large centers of consumption (especially the modern metropolis) will often be supplied by a multitude of places of production which belong to locational figures with different transportation cost indices. These places will, as they grow, continuously bring to life "dead material deposits," and they will bring into existence new locational figures whose place of consumption they represent. As a result they will create new places of production.

b) Just as the possible output of a material deposit may be smaller than is necessary for the supply of the place of consumption to which it belongs locationally, so the possible output may

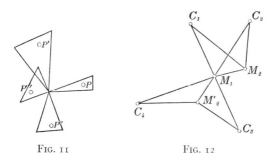

FIG. 11   FIG. 12

be greater, very much greater. That will be the case for all materials localized in large masses. The result is that such a material deposit is used, not only for that first place of consumption, but also for all other places of consumption for which it gives better transportation cost indices than do other deposits. Such material deposits will accordingly appear as the center of locational figures grouped about them. If they quite definitely predominate in attracting the location, these deposits will become the center of a production whose products are distributed in all directions. All this should give a sufficiently clear idea of the orientation of an entire industry so far as transportation costs are concerned, not merely an idea of the orientation of an individual plant. Of course, this is only a theoretical statement; how the orientation of industry will look in actual cases cannot be stated abstractly. The factors, however, upon which the orienta-

tion of an industry depends calls for a discussion with a view to
determining how they change under the influence of the actual
71 development of the economic system.

6. THE FACTORS OF THE TRANSPORT ORIENTATION

Theoretically speaking, the only factor upon which the
choice of the location of an industry depends, so far as transportation is concerned, is the *material index* of the industry and the
composition of that index. The fact should be emphasized that
nothing else can determine or change the fundamental transportational network of orientation except this factor; and this factor is determined wholly and exclusively by the temporary technical situation in the various branches of production. We shall
see later how the extent of the deviations from this fundamental
network (deviations produced by other causes or factors of orientation) is determined: first, by further factors related to the
nature of the various branches of production; second, by general environmental conditions, such as the "density of consumption," the resulting "density of production" and the existing general "rate level" of transportation. In molding the fundamental
transportational network of industrial orientation these factors
amount to nothing. The increasing "density of consumption"
may necessitate the utilization of new material deposits because
of the insufficiency of those already used; it may thereby bring
into existence further locational figures and places of production, and thus cause a further evolution of the fundamental network. But the rise or decline of the general "rate level" does
not change anything at all in the whole picture. It does increase
or decrease the "cost index" in all locational figures, but it dis-
places thereby neither the location within these figures nor the
interacting conditions of their formation. Paradoxically, the
fundamental network of the orientation of industry, which one
thinks of as being under the exclusive influence of costs of transportation, is independent of the general level of these costs.

In fact, however, the transportational orientation of industry which seems so exclusively determined by the relations of materials depends, on account of these relations, upon two factors. These two factors determine the "material index" of every industry (which is, as we have seen, the theoretical expression of the determining relations of the materials). One is the size of the weight losses of localized materials during the process of production, and the other is the weight of the ubiquities used. [72] Every increase of the weight losses in production increases the material index; and every increase of the use of ubiquities decreases it, and vice versa. And it is important to observe that these are the *only* two things which are able to increase or decrease the material index; they therefore determine it and thus settle the question (which depends upon the material index) whether an industry is more attracted toward materials or toward consumption. In any given industrial process it is the proportion of the weight of the ubiquities used to the weight losses of localized materials which gives the basic answer to the question whether the particular industry settles at the places of consumption or moves to the material deposits.

7. TENDENCIES OF DEVELOPMENT

What significance has the foregoing statement for the development of transport orientation? How do these two conditions change in it, and with what result? This is the situation: In reality, development generally means in good times a continually increasing control of nature and a continually progressing concentration of population. Development, thus defined, produces the following changes in the conditions of transport orientation:

In the first place, the development will, as it concentrates population, produce an ever-increasing demand for the available amount of ubiquities. In consequence, unreproducible ubiquities will be used up at certain places, and reproducible ubiquities will be in such demand at many places that the demand will exceed the local output. In both instances this will eliminate the ubiquities from the production at these places; in the first instance entirely, and in the second instance for that part of the production whose demand can no longer be supplied locally. And this elimination of ubiquities will, with the progress of development and an increasing concentration of population, assume ever greater proportions. This process can, practically speaking, go so far in regions of concentration of population that 73 the manufacturing of materials which might in themselves (i.e., technically) be producible anywhere becomes in fact a manufacturing of materials which must be obtained from other places, (i.e., localized materials). This means that the development, in so far as it signifies concentration of population, continuously diminishes the share of ubiquities in production and substitutes localized materials in their place. This constantly lowers the weights of the components of the place of consumption. This is one effect of the general development.

In the second place, development, in so far as it signifies an increasing control of nature, will influence the amount of the *losses in weight* of the localized materials thus increasingly used in production. One could describe what takes place (on account of the increasing control of nature) as a continued further transition from the use of materials which nature offers to man ready for use—examples being wood, clays, etc.—to the use of materials, such as minerals, chemical substances, etc., which can be wrung from nature only by means of industrial processes. This means that increasing losses in weight will take place in production. For the processes which yield the new materials are ordinarily burning processes, and therefore, as a result of the use of fuel material, they are processes of considerable weight losses. Moreover, the new materials themselves, because they must be isolated, entail heavy losses in weight and leave behind "residues" which are on the average greater than the residues of the old materials like wood, clay, etc. Consequently the more such new materials enter into production the more losses in weight will be incurred by the "materials" used in that production. Furthermore, the control of nature leads quite generally to "mechanization" of production. Since this involves the use of fuel material, it results in transforming every mechanized process into a "process of weight loss," and in generally increasing the losses in weight. The development thus increases greatly and in many ways the weight losses in production, and therefore it tremendously strengthens the material components in addition to weakening the components of the place of consumption by displacing the ubiquities.

74

In consequence, industry must shift decidedly and continually from the places of consumption toward the material deposits. And in fact this view of the general development enables us to understand the fundamental features of the large industrial revolution which we have witnessed during the nineteenth century. The rapid concentration of population and the rapid technical development with its mechanization of production and its transition to the use of metal both tended to destroy (and just as rapidly as they took place) the condition which had prevailed up to that time, the condition that industrial location, in so far as it was determined by transportation, coincided with the places of consumption. This removal of the location of industrial production from the places of consumption implied the destruction of the crafts, for the crafts presupposed that industrial location and the place of consumption coincided. Here we have, as far as locational theory is concerned, a general basis for understanding the inevitable collapse of this kind of industrial organization. Of course the crafts were undermined by many different forces, almost all of them strong. It is certain that the change of locational conditions which has been pointed out was not the weakest of these forces.

APPROXIMATIONS TO REALITY

Let us now, for the completion of our theory, leave the abstractions with which we have been working up to this time and modify our conclusions in order to fit them into reality. We have to abandon two assumptions. The first is the assumption that weight and distance are the only factors that determine the costs of transportation. This was the fundamental assumption of our entire discussion; upon this theoretical basis the locational figures and the positions of location were worked out. The second assumption was that costs of transportation, however they may be determined in individual instances, are always uniformly for a whole country those of a single method of transportation. This second assumption accompanied the first one in all our discussions. Stated positively, these two assumptions mean that in order to fit our theory into reality we have to consider, first, the existing system of transportation rates, and second, the interaction of several transportation systems.

I. THE EXISTING SYSTEM OF TRANSPORTATION RATES

We have already discussed in Section I (pp. 43 ff.) how the deviations of the actual rate structure from the theoretical calculation of rates according to weight and mileage may nevertheless be expressed in terms of these two elements, weight and mileage. We saw that deviations which increase or decrease the mileage rate (that is, deviations which produce increased or decreased rates for certain kinds of way, individual lines, or certain distances) are capable of being expressed as additions or subtractions of mileage. We also saw that deviations which are variations from the pure calculation of rates according to weight (that is, deviations which produce increased or decreased rates for certain kinds of goods) are capable of being expressed as increases or decreases in weight, as "fictitious" additions or subtractions of weight; this being true whether they affect the various kinds of goods generally, or only under certain conditions. That was the theoretical solution.[10]

The next question is what significance these modifications have for the structure of the transport orientations. How does it change the locational figures, and how does it influence the position of the locations in these figures?

a) *The deviations from the pure calculation of rates according to mileage.*—If certain lines are shortened in mileage by special lower rates, or if long distances are shortened in general by means of a decreasing scale, it evidently changes the relationship of the various points to one another, as they are considered for the locational figures. Viewed from the places of consumption, certain material deposits may be for locational purposes closer or closer together than would be the case in terms of their actual geographical position. Viewed from the material deposits, a similar situation may seem to obtain. Since the distance of the material deposits from the places of consumption and from one another determines, in terms of the lowest transportation cost index (cf. above, p. 67), what locational figure will be created, these rate variations alter the competitive relationships of the material deposits supplying the places of consumption, and consequently the locational figures change. Certain material deposits which would otherwise not be used for forming the locational figures of certain places of consumption will now be used; and others, which would otherwise be used, will now be eliminated. In this way, in fact, entirely different locational figures and places of production may be created for the supply of the places of consumption than those we should assume, considering merely the geographical locations. Within the locational figures, however, the locations of production will be determined exactly in accordance with the rules previously indicated. Expressed differently, the *theoretical position* of the location in relation to the material deposits and the place of consumption will not be

76

---

[10] Cf. p. 46 f., above.

changed at all; only the locational figures within which the location is determined will be changed. Looking at the map, one will perhaps be surprised that this or that location has not used another deposit which lies nearer geographically. One will find no deviation, however, from the general rules determining location when the material deposits actually chosen are used in the cal-

77 culations.

b) *Deviation from the pure calculation of rates according to weight.*—Evidently the commodity which enters into the locational balance with added or subtracted weight influences the locational balance with another than its real weight; it attracts the location either more or less than its real weight would enable it. If a proportional addition or subtraction of weight does not take place in the case of all the materials, and also of the product, and therefore does not alter proportionally the attracting forces of all corners of the figure, a displacement of the location will result within the locational figure, the location being attracted in the direction of those corners which have a proportionally increased force.

If, for example, the industrial product is bulky, such as chairs, vats, or casks, and if materials used in its manufacture are not as bulky, the attracting force of the component of the place of consumption will be one and one-half times the weight of the product, according to the German rates. The attracting force of the place of consumption will, in other words, be not merely the sum of the weights of materials used, as the pure theory would suggest, but one and one-half times that sum. It may thus happen that the location which, if the goods had not been bulky, would have come to lie somewhere between the material deposit and the place of consumption, will lie at the place of consumption now that the weight of the product is in effect one and one-half times as large as the sum of weights of the material. This is certainly in reality not a rare occurrence in the case of bulky goods. Similarly, a raw material, which is bulky (wool) but whose product (yarn) is not bulky, may, of course, pull the location to its material deposit or to the vicinity of that deposit. The same reasoning applies to combustible goods.

We find a corresponding, though reverse, effect when rates are reduced on goods of small value per unit of weight. Such reduced rates will almost always be in effect subtractions from the weight of *materials,* while they leave the *products* untouched except for occasional small reductions; for the products have a 78 higher value than the materials. Reduced rates on goods of small value will therefore almost always mean reduced attracting force along the components of the material deposits as compared with that of the place of consumption, and consequently the location shifts toward the place of consumption. If, for example, in Germany almost all raw materials of very small value, such as clay, ore, and wood, are transported at rates reduced as much as 60 per cent, and coal at rates reduced 56 per cent, it surely means a strong tendency to shift the location away from the material and coal deposits toward the places of consumption.[11] Such low rates, therefore, constitute an attempt to distribute or decentralize the locations of production. Our theory explains to what extent this distributing measure will succeed, and to what points the locations of different industries will be shifted. For the locational figures we need simply to ascribe to such goods as are transported at reduced rates a weight which is reduced correspondingly. When we construct the locational figures we can then calculate exactly where the transportation costs will pull the locations as simply as in the case when no such reductions are made. Whatever alterations are thus created by reducing or increasing the rates of certain types of goods, they constitute important but exactly determinable shiftings of the location within the locational figure. It is to be noted, however,

[11] The situation in the United States is similar.—EDITOR.

that this is their only effect. A change of material deposits does *not* take place, since such special rates will always affect *all* deposits of the same material to an equal degree, but not the mileage. Only a change of these distances can change the competitive advantage of various deposits and thus alter their use within the locational figures. In distinct contrast with the first case (see p. 76), which changed the locational figures themselves, these locational figures now under consideration remain untouched by rate reductions on certain goods, and untouched also on the whole structural foundations of the orientation of production; only the locations themselves shift upon these foundations.

79   The increased rates for shipments in small quantities (less than carloads and piece-goods shipments) ought to be mentioned specially. These rate increases may theoretically be expressed as weight additions. They do not, however, concern certain definite kinds of goods; they concern all goods, whenever shipped in such quantities. They seem to create no factors which can be calculated precisely and generally when determining the location, since we cannot know whether the production of a given product will or will not attain the quantity which is necessary for the normal rates to become effective, and whether transportation will or will not have to take place at the increased rates. The distortions of the "theoretical" locational picture which are thus brought about seem not to yield to general statements, although they can be calculated precisely in every individual case and for every locational figure. We may simply ignore these distortions for the present, for every locational figure has obviously a definite capacity for moving masses within it, which capacity is determined by the size of its place of consumption. In one locational figure, full carloads, in another only less than carload shipments, will be moved. In the one locational figure transportation, and therefore production and consumption, will be cheaper than in the other; but this will influence neither the figures

themselves nor the position of the location within them. Accordingly this modification of the pure calculation according to weight may as a practical matter be omitted from our considerations.[12]

80

2. THE REAL NATURE OF THE TRANSPORTATION SYSTEM

Our theory has thus far assumed the system of transportation to be uniform for the whole territory considered. This does not *need* to be the case; any existing system may be divided into independent parts. The theory has also assumed the system of transportation to be of one kind. This is in reality not the case; there are railways, waterways, and highways. In applying our theory to reality we are confronted with the problem of determining the importance of these differences.

A. A DIVIDED TRANSPORTATION SYSTEM

A few words will suffice to discuss the possible division of the transportation system into parts which, although co-operating technically, operate as economically independent units. If such division results in independent rate-making by the various parts (and only in such event, of course, is it important for transportation costs) it may be expedient to treat each region (with its different rates) simply as a separate territory within which industry orients itself. The decision whether or not to do

---

[12] This modification becomes important when the production of several locational figures is "coupled" by agglomeration with one another. In the resulting combined figures the size of a single place of consumption no longer determines the possible amount of commodities moved; and therefore the rate. The shipping of materials to the "places of the combined production" may be done in carloads and therefore at cheap rates, although the capacity of the individual places of consumption only admits of shipments in smaller quantities, and therefore at higher rates. This condition will have the same effect as an "addition in weight" to the products, and therefore it means a strengthening of the components of places of consumption. It would perforce have in itself the tendency to shift the combined location toward the places of consumption; if not, other shiftings would take place in the case of such combined locations—all of which makes it seem inadvisable to analyze this tendency further at this juncture (cf. *infra,* pp. 134 ff.).

so will depend upon the extent of the differences in the rates. It would be expedient to do so, for example, when very many additions and subtractions from the normal rates are made in the different regions. In this case a considerably different "theoretical" distinction of the locations would prevail in each of the regions, and it would be better, therefore, to consider them independently.

On the other hand, we may treat the rate variations as *local* modifications of a uniform system of rate-making in a uniform territory of orientation. To do so will be possible and expedient only when nothing but the rates of some unimportant goods vary from one territory to another. This situation exists, for example, with regard to the system of rates within the German Commonwealth, and this fact makes it possible for us to treat the entire German territory as uniform, as far as the orientation of industry is concerned.

B. DIFFERENT KINDS OF TRANSPORTATION SYSTEMS WORKING TOGETHER

When different kinds of transportation systems work together, more complicated problems seem to confront us. But they only seem to do so. If we consider the situation as it is today the problems may be solved.

If we look at the railway system, it appears to be a net which may be illustrated by the diagram in Figure 13. Within this net the existing places of consumption and the deposits of material are located at certain points as indicated in the diagram. This net has been created in order to connect these centers with one another. It connects them, however, not by straight lines, but by lines having many curves, the curves being caused by the presence of other centers and by geographical conditions. The relation of the mathematically straight connections of the ideal locational figures to the actual connections may be somewhat like those indicated in the diagram. The actual transportation depends upon the actual connections, although it may be possible to suggest, and even to bring about, certain improvements in the actual connections as a result of studying the requirements of the locational figures. Anyway, the mathematical lines connecting the deposits of material with the place of production and the latter with the place of consumption will in a real case appear only as curves; that is self-evident. Has that fact any significance for the application of our rules? The answer is:

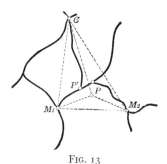

FIG. 13

Yes, in so far as the choice of a location can only be an approximation of the ideal location because the actual location is imbedded into a curved network of transportation. Among the lo- 82 cational points which may in fact be considered in view of the presence of the network of transportation, that point will be chosen which corresponds most closely to the conditions of the ideal location. As is indicated in the diagram, several of the actual points near the ideal location may be considered. One of them, however (P'), will be chosen; because it, although lying geographically farther away from the ideal point, corresponds best with the ideal requirements so far as its position in relation to the material deposits and the place of consumption is concerned.

Having set forth this "deforming" effect of reality, we shall proceed to examine how several kinds of transportation systems work together.

a) *The effect of the waterways.*—Today railways and highways work together. If we treat the railway system as the normal system from which we start in our analysis, we find waterways a somewhat cheaper system and highways a considerably dearer system. What, with reference to location, is the significance of competing waterways whose rates are today in Germany something like half the lowest railway rates, or about 0.25 cents per ton-mile? Let us reflect how waterways and railways are related today geographically. Everywhere we find an extremely dense railway net spanning the entire country, and winding through this net like ribbons, some natural or artificial waterways. These may be connected so as to form a "network" or they may be large unconnected rivers. But even in the case of a network they form a skeleton of such irregularity that they cannot open up all material deposits of the country, and even less can they supply all its places of consumption. As transportation devices connecting cheaply only certain points, they thus traverse the railway system which does open up all material deposits and does supply all places of consumption, and therefore actually carries the orientation of industry. Along the railways the largest part of the places of production and of the material deposits of the country are situated. The railway net contains therefore the attracting points upon which the locational figures and the fundamental outline of the orientation of industry depend. The waterways which traverse the railway system are in effect nothing but routes with especially cheap shipping opportunities; they may and will be considered as parts of the railway system with especially low rates. Thus they are theoretically fitted into the concept of a single and uniform system of transportation, and consequently into our theory. For within such a system, routes with cheaper rates mean nothing but distances shortened in proportion to the decrease in rates. In forming the locational figures, material deposits which can use these shortened routes will have an advantage over other deposits which cannot use them. The sphere of action of certain material deposits will be enlarged; other deposits will be eliminated; and certain locations will be transferred: these are the effects of the competition of waterways with railways. If we know the rates of existing waterways under discussion it is not difficult to put them as locational elements into our analysis and to determine the resulting locational figure according to our rules. We can

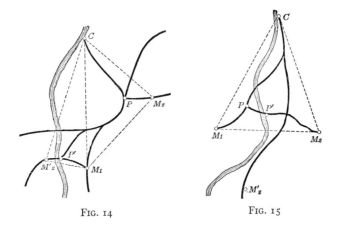

FIG. 14   FIG. 15

make clear their influence by the diagrams as shown in Figures 14 and 15.

Case 1: Elimination of a deposit of material and addition of another through the influence of a waterway, transfer of the locational figure and of the location (compare Fig. 14).

The deposit M_2 is considerably nearer the place of consumption C than the deposit M'_2. If no waterway existed, the locational triangle with the place of production P would be formed for the supply of C. The existence of the waterway may, however, cause the distance separating M'_2 from C to become economically shorter than the distance separating M_2 from C. In that case the locational triangle using M'_2 and the place of production P' will come into effect.

Case 2: Naturally, the effect is not necessarily so far-reaching; it is possible that no change in the utilization of the material deposits is brought about. In that case the locational figure remains the same, and only a displacement of the place of production takes place. Figure 15 will illustrate this smaller effect.

Here also M_2 lies nearer the place of consumption than M'_2, but the locational triangle M_1M_2C permits the use of the waterway. The location P' (which was chosen with a view to using this waterway) should therefore have a smaller index of transportation costs than the location in the triangle $M_1M'_2C$. Therefore M_2 will not be eliminated, and the locational triangle with the material deposits it employed will remain the same as if there were no waterway. However, the location will be realized in P', and not in P, which is the most desirable location if merely roads are used.

These remarks will suffice to make clear the greater or less effect of the waterways, and at the same time to show why the waterways are fringed with places of industrial production. All these locations have, during the process of their becoming established, received a little jolt from the waterways which pushed their position to the right or to the left. Although they now have their chimneys smoking by the water side, they belonged somewhere in the "neighborhood," even if there had been only transportation by land.

  b) *The effect of the net of highways.*—It is well known that the costs of transportation on the highway are on the average four to ten times, and in individual cases twenty times, those of the railway.[13] As a result, freight transportation on the highways over long distances has ceased. Today highways are used only for transporting goods to and from the railway stations. Consequently highways no longer have any independent loca-

---

[13] These sentences were written before the advent of the truck, but the student of this treatise will find it possible to work out the problems created by it if he will use the methods set forth herein.—EDITOR.

tional signficance at all; their function is rather that of a sub-sidiary of the railway system. If we wish to understand the im-portance of this subsidiary, we had best consider each district of collection and distribution grouped around a railway station as a unit with the railway station as its center. As such a unit the district, whether a material deposit or a place of consumption, enters into the total industrial orientation through its railway station. We can disregard for the moment how the district is or-ganized internally under the influence of its street system; this is a locational problem similar to that which asks how industry is grouped in a metropolis under the influence of the traffic fac-tors present there; it is a question of local agglomeration and distribution which will be treated in a later chapter. If such a 86 *railway station unit (Bahnplatzeinheit),* as I should like to call it, enters as a material deposit into the industrial orientation, then not the price at the deposit, but the price at the railway sta-tion, must be regarded as the delivery price of the materials (price at the deposit plus freight charges of road carriage). For obviously it is only on the basis of this price that the material deposit enters effectively into the orientation of industry.

The particular significance of differences in the delivery prices will be discussed in the next section. It may be, of course, (and very often is the case) that the material deposit and the place of consumption are so situated that they do not at all need the railway, since they are in the same "railway station unit." This means, for the orientation of industry at large, that they are located at the same place, and therefore do not come within the scope of our broader theoretical considerations. However, for the local orientation within the railway station unit, with its street net system, exactly the same rules of orientation will be operative in detail which determine the orientation at large for the whole country, with its extensive transportation system. Everything will simply be repeated in miniature.

It has become possible now, in closing, to abandon several other important simplifying assumptions and to consider the importance of certain peculiarities of reality which have been ignored until now. These are, first, the price differences of the materials caused by the local position of the material deposits and the railway stations; and second, the effect of water power 87 upon the process of production. We had said that price differences of the materials (which price differences ordinarily would be an independent regional factor of orientation) may be expressed theoretically as differences of transportation costs of the materials, and thus may be fitted into theory. We had said, too, that water power may be theoretically considered to be a cheap fuel; therefore it may be expressed in price differences of the material, and thus likewise be fitted into the theory. Some very important peculiarities appear, however, when water power enters in. Also the way in which differences in the prices of materials may be expressed as differences in the transportation costs, and the way in which they then affect orientation, need further exemplification. In this exemplification we shall employ the locational rules which we have already discovered.

A. THE PRICE DIFFERENCES OF MATERIALS AND THEIR EFFECT

It does not concern us here from what cause price differences of the materials result; they may be due to differences in the costs of production, or due to artificial price fixing, or due to differences in the cost of transporting the goods to the point where the materials enter the larger traffic (i.e., traffic by rail or by water). We shall consider this point as the "deposit" to be used in analyzing the large locational system, and we shall calculate upon the basis of the price at this point.

Price differences themselves never change the location within the locational figure fundamentally; they merely shift the competitive conditions among material deposits which are equal in other respects. Material deposits with low prices will simply have larger spheres of action than appears from the geographical situation itself; they, rather than deposits more favorably situated geographically, will be used to supply certain places of consumption. In brief, they will operate in the same way as the 88 change of competition of material deposits caused by cheap rates for certain lines which was discussed earlier.

B. THE USE OF WATER POWER

Water power may be used today as a source of power for production in two different forms: directly, under waterfalls, or indirectly, through electrical transmission. Both cases, as former discussions have already shown, are to be treated theoretically as fuel deposits with definite, and on the whole with lower, prices. The horse-power which they produce may easily be calculated in equivalent quantities of coal, and we may then compare the weight of this "white" coal and its price with the quantities of "black" coal which it replaces. This point is simple. There exist, however, peculiarities in the locational effect of these calculated amounts of coal which have to be considered exhaustively.

a) In the case of the use of waterfalls, the calculated amounts of coal can be used only at *one* place, at the waterfall. Locationally, such waterfalls exert an *alternative* locational effect; either the location goes to the place of this locational advantage, or it remains where it is, and in that event it is absolutely untouched by this locational advantage. When does the one thing take place, and when the other? If nowadays the locations remain untouched by this locational advantage it means, practically speaking, the forming of locational figures and the selecting of locations in terms of the most advantageously located coal deposits. We know the locational figures thus created and shall consider them as normal. The use of waterfalls eliminates the use of coal deposits and involves the formation of new locational figures using places with waterfalls. But this means that the locations in the new figures are transferred to a point which may be theoretically new, namely, to the waterfalls. What is theoretically new (as compared with simply eliminating certain deposits of coal by using cheaper or otherwise more advantageous deposits) is the fact that a fundamental transfer of the location in the figure takes place on account of the necessity of having the location at the place of the waterfalls. Therefore in all cases in which the location in the old figures was not at the deposit of the power material, fuel, it will be forced to go to the deposit of the new power material, the waterfalls. From this it follows, formulating our conclusions tentatively, that the locational effect of waterfalls at which power is cheaper and better located than the available deposits of coal will not be as great as if this water power were deposits of coal offering equal advantage. For the effect of waterfalls producing water power is lessened by additional costs of transportation which result when the location deviates from its normal point of minimum transportation costs. The locational revolution, therefore, which will be caused by water power, at the falls will be less than if this water power were correspondingly cheap coal-power. Its influence will remain less to the extent to which the impossibility of transporting water power at falls necessitates a transfer of the location within the figure. This transfer will be most extensive in those cases in which the former location was least influenced by the component of the power deposit.

When will the water power of waterfalls be able to supersede coal deposits and to draw the location to itself? Evidently whenever the cost of power saved is greater than the cost of increased transportation. We shall have to compare, therefore, the relation between the cost of power at its location and the cost of coal at its deposit with the relation between the index of transportation costs of the old and that of the new location. If the sum of the cost of water power and of transportation to the water power location is smaller than the sum of costs of coal and of transportation to the coal location, then the water power is cheaper and supersedes the coal.

90

To give an example, in Figure 16, P is the old location within the locational figure M_1M_2C using coal (coal at M_2); W (waterfall) is the new location in the locational figure M_2WC using water power. We shall have to compare the price of power per unit of product in W plus the index of the transportation costs of W ($a'b'$) with the price (in M_2) of coal used per unit of

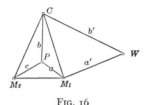

FIG. 16

product plus the index of the transportation costs of P *(a, b, c)*. If the former sum is smaller, the location W supersedes P, otherwise not. This shows that the influence of non-transmittable water power is rather easy to calculate. Its influence is confirmed within the narrow limits which are set by the relationships of cost just discussed. Unless the distances involved are small, the influence of waterfalls will operate most directly in the case of industries which are located at their coal deposits, because in this case the location does not have to shift *within* the figure.[14]

b) Transmissible water power.—First, we shall as before substitute theoretically the amount of coal ordinarily used in producing 1 H.P. for the electrical H.P. here used. The price of this calculated amount of coal (at the water power location) is to be compared with the price of the necessary coal at the coal

[14] As it had to in the above example where the location had to go from a point between the deposit of coal and the deposit of the other material to the water power substituted for the coal deposit.—EDITOR.

deposit. Thus we have expressed theoretically the power utilized in terms of a hypothetical coal deposit which would have a definite, and probably on the whole, a lower, price. Second, we shall consider the cost of transmitting the H.P. used as if it were the cost of transporting the calculated amount of coal. On the whole, we shall find that locations of water power which have good electrical transmission yield an exceptionally low price for the power as calculated in terms of coal, and exceptionally low rates of transportation per ton-mile. The effect seems clear in this case of transmissible water-power, for it theoretically represents deposits of especially low-priced coal which may be transported at exceptionally low rates. The very low price of such water power will, in accordance with our previous discussions, cause its use to a larger extent than its geographical location would lead one to anticipate, and will eliminate as "locational corners" the use of coal deposits more favorably located geographically. The low ton-mile rates of such water power, as calculated in terms of coal, may be expressed in theoretical weight deductions of this "theoretical" coal. They will shift the location in the appropriate locational figures toward the other locational corners—the places of consumption and the other material deposits—much further than would have been the case in the locational figures formed by the eliminated coal deposits. As in the cases when non-transmissible water power was used, we find: (1) The formation of new locational figures results from the use of water power; and (2) a transfer of the location takes place within these figures according to theoretical principles. The situation differs from the previous case, however, because the location is not shifting toward the power material deposit, but rather in the opposite direction—that is, toward the places of consumption and toward the other material deposits. The transfer of the location within the new locational figures is, however, due to the easy transportation of the new power materials, and not to their immovability.

From these observations we may deduce the great and essential difference between transmissible and non-transmissible water power. While in the case of non-transmissible water power the transfer of the location from the point of minimum costs of transportation raises the index of transportation costs, and thereby narrows the "sphere of influence" of such places of water power, in the case of transmissible water power the low cost of transporting the equivalent of 1 H.P. gives additional momentum to the expansion of the sphere of influence already extended by the low cost of production. For it is quite obvious that the 92

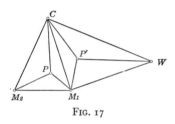

FIG. 17

low rates for transporting electrical current (low ton-mile rates of the "theoretical" coal) mean a lower index of transportation costs of the respective figures, and thereby put these locational figures on a basis which permits them to compete with other locational figures. If the H.P. can be produced and transmitted sufficiently cheaply, *favorably* located water power will cause a great number of locational figures based on coal to be eliminated, and just as many locations to be shifted. On the other hand, even *unfavorably* located water power will not necessarily be excluded from becoming the basis of location and production.

We shall be able to determine, according to our theory, exactly to what extent and with what locational results these stores of water power will enter into modern economic life. Using the diagram of the last example, the location P' (based upon the water power in W instead of the coal deposit M_2) will not be located at W (as in the case of non-transmissible water power), but in the new locational figure M_1WC, and will be nearer M_1

and C than the former location P, based upon coal in the figure $M_1 M_2 C$. Its position within the new figure is determined by the laws which we now know so well from the previous discussions. The weight which has to be applied on the component WP' obviously is the difference between the weight of the "theoretical" coal (water power calculated in terms of coal) which is brought from W and the weight deduction which has to be made along this line corresponding to the lower rate per ton-mile. In order to determine whether the location P' is possible and M_2 should be eliminated, we shall have to add the price of the "theoretical coal" (water power in terms of coal) to the index of the transportation costs of the location P'. This sum has to be compared with the sum of the index of transportation costs of the old location P and the price of actual coal per unit of product (at M_2). If the first sum is smaller, P' is possible; otherwise not. This example is apparently capable of general application. The possibility, then, of fitting water power and its effect into the theory of the transportation orientation is obvious. We may well say that we have succeeded in applying our theory to all modifications of complete modern reality.

CHAPTER IV

LABOR ORIENTATION

SECTION I

THE ANALYSIS OF LABOR COSTS

The labor costs of an industry (in the sense in which we defined this concept in the preliminary analysis of the locational factors) are, in general economic terms, the expenditures of human labor incurred in carrying out the particular process of production. They appear in the capitalistic system as wages and salaries which are paid out in the course of the productive process, and denote the "equivalent" of the labor used. It is obvious, of course, that human labor is not paid for with "wages," because it is something different from a "commodity." However, the economic expression of the energies expended in labor (that is, the "cost of labor" of which we are now speaking) are in the capitalistic economy of today the wages and salaries which are paid out per unit of product. And since we always deal with economic phenomena in their concrete present form—for only thus do they become comprehensible—we shall in our further discussion deal with this sort of wages and salaries, calculated for the "unit of weight" of the product of our previous theoretical discussion.

These labor costs can only become factors in location by varying from place to place. That is self-evident. But it is important to realize that, since we are still investigating the regional distribution of industry, such local differences of labor costs concern us only in so far as they are of significance for this problem. This means that they concern us only if in some manner they are connected in fact with geographically defined points, because only in that event can they attract industry to particular geographical points and thus have an effect on the fundamental regional distribution of industry. Only a part of the actual local differences in labor costs possesses that sort of peculiar geographical relationship. The labor costs of an industry may differ, speaking generally, on account of two quite different sets of causes: (1) because of differing levels of efficiency and of wages of labor, i.e., for more or less subjective reasons; and (2) because of differing levels of efficiency in the organization and the technical equipment with which the laboring force is set to work, i.e., for more or less objective reasons. However, only local differences resulting from subjective reasons have the requisite peculiar geographical relationship—are geographically "fixed." They are fixed differences in so far as they are a function of a given geographical distribution of population, which shows different levels of wages and of performance in its various parts. On the other hand, the differences of labor costs on account of different levels of efficiency of the "apparatus" are, it seems, no more geographically determined than is the use of the apparatus itself. These latter differences may become a factor determining location in a manner that is to be taken up later in the theory of agglomeration; but at the present moment they are outside our discussion.

We do not, therefore, exhaust at present the significance of labor costs as a locational factor; for we deal only with that part of the differences of labor costs which results from local differences in the level of personal efficiency and wages of the population.

What particular circumstances caused these differences of wages and efficiency and the consequent differences of labor costs is a matter of indifference to us and to the whole "pure" theory. Especially does it not concern us that their actual level is, of course, not a phenomenon of "pure" economics, but rather a changing consequence of extremely varied historical and nat-

ural circumstances. All this may be neglected by pure locational

theory which is only concerned with investigating the fundamental significance of such geographically determined differences of labor costs. And for that purpose the actual level of
these costs—and even whether they actually exist—is a matter
of complete indifference. Pure theory conceives them as a "possibility," and investigates the theoretical results of that possibility.

In one thing, however, we must be interested, namely, in the
geographically essential "form" in which these differences of
cost appear. We must know in what general manner the labor
costs, as determined by the different levels of wages and performance, are actually geographically distributed in a country
at a given moment. Are the differences "according to area," so
that one may say this whole region operates more cheaply than
a given other one? Or are they "according to place," so that
they relate to particular towns, or at any rate to more or less
concentrated districts which, in a general way, may be treated
"as a town" (a mathematical point) without committing too
great an error? Whether one or the other of these two possibilities is assumed will be of considerable significance for our
discussion, which is to be carried on by means of mathematical
aids. In the first case we shall have to deal with the mathematical concept of the "plane"; in the second, with that of the
"point."

If in this connection we are to approach the actual situation
without prejudice, we must make various distinctions with regard to the kinds of differences in wage levels.

We will at once recall certain differences in the wage level
according to districts. The higher general level of wages in west-
ern and southern Germany as compared with that of the eastern
part may occur to us as an example. We may think of the familiar tables of average local day wages which can be compiled
from the sickness insurance data; we may remember that, with
certain exceptions, the wage scales fall "like a staircase" from

west to east; and that pointlike exceptions to this regional distribution of wage levels are in general caused only by the large
97 cities. If we think of these familiar facts, the "wage rate" will appear to us as a result of a superficial examination, as essentially differentiated "according to area."

And yet this picture is one of many statistical simplifications which we are always using, and which, though not actually wrong, gives us an idea of reality dangerously inexact in detail.

As evidence for this statement let us cite statistics of wages as given in their annual report for 1901–2 by one of the largest German unions composed mainly of unskilled workers, the Central Union of Trade, Transport, and Traffic Laborers (i.e., janitors, packers, market workers, coachmen, cab drivers, furniture movers, etc.). The figures are best for central Germany where the Union is most widely extended outside the large cities. The average weekly wages of its members in marks show, in the small district in the vicinity of the Harz Mountains, the following variations: Nordhausen, 14.2; Sangerhausen, 12.0; Halberstadt, 15.7; for the district of the southern Thuringian Forest, also not a large one—Sonneberg, 15.7; Suhl, 15.3; Saalfeld, 17.2; Erfurt, 19.3; Jena, 17.0; and for the region on the border of the Saxon industrial area—Zeitz, 17.8; Greiz, 16.7; Plauenscher Grund, 19.4. Here we have in each district differences of from M. 2 to M. 2.70 in the weekly wage, i.e., differences of up to 22 per cent in places very close together. Similar results are seen everywhere. In two adjoining Silesian counties, those of Striegau and Waldenburg, for instance, 12.9 and 15.3 are paid. Hence we find, even for unskilled labor, wage rates differing entirely "according to place," not only in the large towns where wage levels are naturally well above those in the surrounding country, but everywhere else, even in the small places in the country itself. The difference "according to areas" is only the general average of very large local differences.

If it is not permissible to assume a regional distribution of wage level even for that meanest category of labor which may most truly be spoken of as a homogeneous mass, evidently when we study the wage levels of skilled labor our guiding principle ought to be that wage levels will be distributed "according to places." According to the report of the Union of Metal Workers 98 for 1903, pattern-makers (in sand), for instance, earn for piece work in *pfennig* per hour in central Germany: in Hildesheim, 41; Ilsenburg, 27; Thale, 39; Sangerhausen, 34; Gotha, 44—a range of 17 *pfennig*, or 60 per cent, in the small districts around the Harz; in Zeitz, 24; in the nearby Gera, 34—a range of 10, or about 30 per cent; in Bunzlau, 31; Hirschberg, 42; Schweidnitz, 39—a range of 11, or 32 per cent. According to the very complete and careful reports of the Wood-workers Union for 1902, skilled wood-workers (carpenters, turners, etc.) earn on the average per week in *mark:* in Frankenhausen, 13.6; Kalbe, 11.2; Sangerhausen, 16.7; Schkeudnitz, 21; Korbetha, 12; Naumburg, 18.7—differences of 9.8 marks or 86 per cent per week within the small district between the Goldene Aue and Elster-Saale. Similar differences appear elsewhere. The Thuringian Forest shows the following figures: Koburg, 14.7; Weimar, 21; Gotha, 20; Eisenach, 18.2—in other words, differences of 6.3 per week.

All these are local differences in the small towns and in the farming country; if we take the large cities into consideration, the local differences are much larger still. For pattern-makers it is only necessary, for instance, to extend our view from the Harz to Magdeburg and Hanover. There we find average wages per hour of 48–52 pfennig, wages approximately twice as high as those of Ilsenburg in the Harz. Similarly for wood-workers, Leipzig with 23.7 or Halle with 22.3 have twice the wages of Korbetha with 12 or Kalbe with 11.2.

Therefore the wages even for unskilled labor, but much more for skilled labor, form today a rather mountainous terrain with deep gorges and relatively high peaks. So far as wages come into consideration we shall, even when differences of general level form a broad foundation for whole regions, think of variations from point to point.

Now it is well known that differences of wage level do not give an adequate idea of the differences in the level of labor costs. The parallelism between them is disturbed by differences of efficiency. There are two possible cases: A difference in efficiency conditioned by natural and cultural facts (nature of population and environment) may exist at the same wage. This is a local difference. Also the results of the fact, well known empirically to social psychology, that high wages and high efficiency go together may disturb things to a considerable extent. The latter theorem would mean that the rather mountainous picture of *wage* differences would be reflected as less mountainous differences of *cost* of labor. It might even mean a complete smoothing out of hills and valleys; or it might even go beyond that, so that places with high wages would be places of low labor costs. In the empirical theory it will become evident that for industries of a particular sort that may in fact often be the situation. At this time it is sufficient to point out that whether the differences of labor cost run more or less parallel to those of wages, or whether on account of differences of efficiency the two diverge greatly, as a matter of fact today every employer in every industry reckons (as a result of his experience) with this "local," and not with the "regional," nature of the differences in the cost of labor. We have attempted to make clear the local variation of these differences by citing examples of the extraordinarily large jumps of wage rates from place to place, and this explains why, in the pure theory, we do not start from regional, but from local, variations of labor costs. We shall not speak of "areas of labor cost" on different levels, but of *labor locations* with different costs.

As has been indicated in the general introduction, it will be necessary for the present to disregard a number of qualities which these labor locations in fact possess in order to make the effect of their varying levels of costs perfectly clear as a factor in the theory of location. We must neglect the fact that an unlimited supply of labor is, of course, not to be had at any of these locations at a given time at the cost which it offers, and that therefore it cannot attract unlimited numbers of industries simply by virtue of this cost level. We must also leave out of consideration the fact that the cost level of each location is altered by every movement of industry, on account of the change in demand for labor which this movement causes. We must disre- 100 gard these things and imagine the cost levels of the locations to be *fixed,* and the labor supply available at each location to be *unlimited;* for only by so doing can we analyze clearly and to its final consequences the effect which the *differences* of costs will have on the distribution of industry. Only if we conceive the attracting power of each location—which power is based upon these differences of cost—as freed from all limits but those of space, that is to say, only if we conceive it as actually unlimited, can we clearly trace its effect upon location. And it is necessary, of course, to introduce this attracting power as a fixed quantity; otherwise it could not be measured in mathematical terms. Hence we must regard the differences of cost as "given"; and as given with unlimited attracting power.

We shall leave it to empirical theory to eliminate these assumptions and to introduce into the picture the actual environment within which these abstract laws work out, the significant elements of the actual environment being variability of the differences, and the connection of these differences with the competition among industries for what is at any given time only a *limited* supply of labor at each location. Only through recourse to such empirical analysis can the local movements of labor and the general changeability of the ground work of industrial labor cost be taken account of and explained.

SECTION II

THE LAW OF LABOR ORIENTATION

How does this groundwork of labor cost effect the orientation of industry by means of its locations of different labor cost levels?

I. THEORETICAL SOLUTION: THE ISODAPANES[1]

Let us imagine again an isolated process of production and distribution with its raw material deposits and its place of consumption. The point of minimum transportation costs results from this locational figure and from the composition of the well-known material index. What significance will it have for determining whether production will really take place at this point that in the infinite area surrounding it there are perhaps points at which a ton of product can be produced with smaller labor costs?

101   The following is at any rate clear: that every such point of lower labor costs constitutes economically a center of attraction which tends to draw industry away from the point of minimal transportation cost to itself. But the attraction of such a center is essentially not an attraction of a mere *approach;* for an approach to the location with the lower labor costs would have no advantage for the industry. Only a migrating to that place itself would be of use to it; hence there is here the issue of an *alternative* attraction: the question is whether industry should operate at the point of minimum transportation costs or be moved to the labor location.

Under what circumstances will industry be moved to the labor location, and when will it not?

Every change of location away from the point of minimum

[1] Isodapane is a new technical term introduced by Alfred Weber. It is constructed in analogy to the geographical term "isotherm." Similar words are current in scientific literature. Isodapane contains besides the well-known root *isos,* "equal," the word *dapane,* which means "expense," "cost."—EDITOR.

transportation costs to a favorable labor location means, in terms of transportation, a "deviation" which lengthens the transportation routes and raises transportation costs above those prevailing under the most advantageous conditions. The changes of location can therefore take place only if the rise of cost per ton of product which it causes is compensated, or more than compensated, by savings of labor costs. A location can be moved from the point of minimum transportation costs[2] to a more favorable labor location only if *the savings in the cost of labor which this new place makes possible are larger than the additional costs of transportation which it involves.* It is necessary to understand this general theorem precisely, and to analyze its consequences.

To understand precisely its theoretical significance we must bring it into organic connection with the general mathematical concepts which we have hitherto used. The means necessary for this task are provided by what is said in the second part of the appendix about curves of equal transportation cost. The discussion there starts from the assumption that any deviation from the transportational minimum point may take place in quite different directions; and that in any direction in which it may go there will be points at which the costs incurred in such deviation (i.e., the additional costs of transportation per ton of product caused by the deviation) are equally high. From this it follows 102 that there must also be *curves* connecting such points of equal deviation costs which may be drawn around the minimum point at some distance, varying in accordance with the index of materials. These curves, curves of equally high additional cost of transportation, form the conceptual connecting link between the transportational minimum points and the deviation points which represent the labor locations. We shall call them isodapanes (of equal cost), for brevity's sake.

[2] This point is hereafter often referred to simply as minimum point.—Editor.

For every labor location, wherever situated, there must be an isodapane of the respective locational figure. This isodapane indicates how high the costs of deviating the industry from the minimum point of the locational figure to the labor location in question would be.

On the other hand, some isodapane of the locational figure in location will correspond to the index of economies of the labor question in such a way that the deviation costs which it indicates per ton of product are exactly as large as the saving in labor costs per ton of product as compared with the labor costs at the minimum point. Hence it is apparent that, if the labor location lies on a *lower* isodapane than that just discussed, its economies exceed the deviation costs; if it lies on a *higher* one, the deviation costs exceed its economies. That means that a labor location will attract the industry if it lies within the area of this isodapane, because in that event its economies are greater than the deviation costs and the migration to it will cause greater economy than it causes increased cost; and vice versa, it *cannot* attract, *cannot* bring about the migration of the industry if it lies outside of the limits of this isodapane, for in that case the economy is smaller than the deviation costs. With regard to the attracting power of this labor location, this is the *critical isodapane*. To every labor location, no matter where situated with any index of economy whatever, there must correspond such a critical isodapane. The relation of the labor location to this critical isodapane—whether it lies inside or outside of it—determines whether or not such a location will attract the production of the locational figure concerned.

The foregoing analysis has brought the attracting power of labor location (its ability to substitute "labor orientation" for "transport orientation") into the realm of precisely determinable laws, the conditions of which have for the *individual case* been sufficiently clarified by the foregoing.

It remains to introduce into the framework of our general discussion the conditions under which, in the individual instance, deviation and labor orientation can and will occur, and thus to pass on to the general conditions on which labor orientation depends. In this connection we shall ask at once two questions: First, which of these conditions presents characteristics of individual industries; and second, which are conditions applying uniformly to all industries—in other words are "environmental conditions"? We shall see that, in contrast to the basic transport orientation of industry, which through the material index and the "locational weight" depends solely upon "characteristics" of the individual industries, the amount and kind of labor orientation is essentially determined by "environmental conditions."

Let us first deduce the various possible kinds of conditions from the individual analysis we have undertaken. The following are the factors on which the deviation of an industrial production because of labor locations depends: First, the geographical position of the location figures and labor locations. Second, the course of the isodapanes around the minimum points of the locational figures. Third, the indices of economy of the labor locations per unit weight of product.

The geographical position of locational figures and labor locations evidently has nothing to do directly with the general character of the various industries. It is a seemingly "accidental" fact in the situation, independent of the character of an industry. We shall, however, later put this fact into its general context and take it out of the sphere of the individual and accidental in which it seems to stand.

The course of the isodapanes around the minimum points of the locational figures depends upon two subordinate factors. One is entirely implicit in the nature of the given industry, namely, its material index and the locational weight dependent on it. The figures of the Appendix show (what we shall presently discuss more in detail) how completely the distance, and to what degree the form of the isodapane is dominated by this factor. For the distance of the isodapanes from each other, however, a second factor becomes operative, namely, the rates of transportation prevailing at any given time in a region. It is clear that if one draws around a point lines indicating equal additional transportation costs, i.e., lines whose distance from each other is determined by a given unit of additional cost, the actual geographical distance of these lines from each other will be determined among other things by whatever geographical distance the unit rate of costs covers, i.e., by the height of the prevailing rates of transportation. Here we have a further condition of labor orientation independent of the character of individual industries and applying equally to all of them.

3. In order to see upon what the indices of economy of the labor locations per unit weight of product depend, we shall have to inquire how such an economy (for example, of ten marks per ton of product) works out. Evidently, because the labor costs per ton are "compressed" by a given percentage, 5, 10, 20 per cent, etc., the index of economy depends first upon this percentage of "compression." But that is only one factor. How great the total *absolute* economy per ton will be depends also, it is obvious, upon the absolute level of labor costs which are com-
105 pressed. If these costs amount to M.1,000 per ton, a compression of 10 per cent will cause an index of economy for this labor location of M.100 per ton; but if they amount to only M.10, the index will be M.1. This absolute amount of labor costs per ton of product on which the compression is based (and which is in a certain sense the object of this compression) evi⁴ dently pertains to every given industry of a country in a given stage of development in the form of *average costs of labor* which must be applied to the ton of product. We shall call this the *index of labor cost of the industry*. As a condition of labor orienta-

tion the labor costs accruing per ton of product therefore belong to the characteristics of the particular industries.

The percentage, however, by which a given labor location compresses this index of the cost of labor of an industry is not a peculiarity of the given industry but one of the particular labor location.[3] Therefore the actual percentage of compression of the labor cost indices at the various labor locations constitutes a third general environmental condition.

There are thus two general characteristics of industries determining their labor orientation: (1) their locational weight (especially their index of materials), and (2) the index of their labor costs. And there are three environmental conditions determining labor orientation: (1) the geographical position of locational figures and labor locations, (2) the rates of transportation, (3) the actual percentages of compression of the labor cost indices.

3. THE CHARACTER OF THE INDUSTRIES AND LABOR ORIENTATION

Let us take up first the characteristics which we have said to be factors in determining the labor locations of individual industries, that is, let us examine the manner in which the locational weight, or index of materials, and the index of labor costs determine labor orientation.   106

A. ORIENTATION OF AN INDIVIDUAL PLANT

1. *Index of labor costs.*—The significance of the index of labor costs is very simple and really already evident. The formula, according to the foregoing, will run: With a high index of labor costs, a large quantity of labor costs will be available for compression, with correspondingly large potential indices of economy of the labor locations, and correspondingly high critical isodapanes; therefore we shall find a high potential attracting power of the labor locations. And vice versa: low index of labor costs, small quantity of labor cost available for com-

[3] This is certainly true for the labor locations of the same industry.

pression, etc. That is to say, the potential attracting power of the labor locations runs, for the different individual industries, parallel to the indices of labor costs of the industries. The index of labor costs is the provisional standard of measuring the extent to which the industries may be deviated. For many industries it alone decides definitely how they will be oriented; this is true for all those in which the labor costs are so low that they are insufficient to cause effective indices of economy. The other industries are grouped by this index according to the amount of labor they require per ton of product, which primarily indicates to what extent they may be deviated.

2. *The locational weight.*—In order, however, to obtain the actual standard for measuring to what extent an industry may be deviated, we must take into consideration the locational weight and the index of materials.

The locational weight influences the extent to which an industry may be deviated through its effect upon the distance and form of the isodapanes. Speaking first of the distance of the isodapanes, the manner in which the locational weight affects them is theoretically very simple: low locational weight, small mass of material per ton of product to be transported, great distance of the isodapanes from each other, wide extension of the critical isodapane; consequently the industry may be deviated to a large extent. And vice versa. The locational weight represents a standard which further determines the distance of the isodapanes for the particular industry. To the extent that it affects this distance, it simply provides a more precise determination of the provisional standard furnished by the index of labor costs in the foregoing formula.

However, the locational weight affects not only the distance between the isodapanes from each other but also their forms. It does so through the size and composition of the material index on which it rests, as the figures of the Appendix show. It can also tell us that the tendency of a given industry to deviate from the minimum point is not necessarily of equal force in all different directions. So far as we can set up a general rule, only industries which have components of equal strength determining their location (and hence having a centrally situated location) have a tolerably equal tendency to deviate their location from the minimum point in all directions (approximately circular form of the isodapanes). An industry having components of varying strength, and hence an eccentric minimum point (i.e., with a minimum point near one corner or in it), will more easily deviate in the direction of the strongest corners of the location, and the stronger its components are, the more it will do so. Expressed in terms of the use of materials, the industries having a very small material index (very little localized material and hence preponderance of the consumption-components) and industries having a very high material index (a great deal of localized material and hence preponderance of some material component) will deviate unevenly (deviation in the direction of the enlarged corners being easier). Industries, on the other hand, with a medium index of materials (for instance of the size of 2), particularly if it is also evenly composed (1:1), will deviate more or less evenly in all directions.

All this, however, is not of very great importance. It is of significance only for deviations over short distances, really only for deviations which lie within or in the immediate vicinity of the locational figures. For all greater distances the isodapanes approximate (as the figures of the Appendix show) the form of a circle, *whatever* the size and composition of the material index. And this is quite to be expected, for the situation of the location resulting from the material index becomes a matter of indifference for great distances, for which the locational figure approximates more and more a "point." The deviation represents more and more transportation back and forth on the same line, and will therefore be equally expensive in all directions. The material index of an industry, through the form which it gives to the isodapanes, besides its effect upon the distance, becomes geographically significant for small deviations by altering the "direction" in which such deviation would turn under the influence of the index of labor costs; by thus altering the "direction" of possible deviations, the material index affects the shape of the isodapanes, besides determining their distance from each other. But this influence disappears for greater distances. And since the geographical difference of direction is, as the figures show, none too great even for the short distances (for the isodapanes even then approximate rather closely the form of circles), it is permissible for the broad purposes of our theory to ignore the material index in so far as its significance is based only upon the non-circular form of the isodapanes. The theory should be allowed to proceed as if all isodapanes were circular; in which case only the distance *resulting* from the absolute quantity of material used remains for determining more precisely the real deviating significance of the index of labor costs of the labor locations through the locational weight.

3. *Locational weight and coefficient of labor.*—To determine more precisely through the locational weight the real deviating significance of the index of labor costs measured (it will be remembered) by the number of tons of product, we have to bear in mind that every increase of the locational weight diminishes (by contracting the isodapanes) this real significance, while every decrease of the locational weight increases the significance. The real deviating significance cannot be measured by weight of product (as has been done by the index of labor costs so far), but only by locational weight (weight of product plus weight of localized materials). Expressed differently, the amount of labor costs connected with the locational weight of a given industry in the *coefficient of labor,* as we shall call it, constitutes the general characteristic determining labor deviation of the industry.

Indeed, it is quite clear that if the form of the isodapanes (i.e., the different degree of deviation in different directions) may be disregarded, it is the locational weight that has to be moved if a deviation is to take place. This locational weight, therefore, is the only factor which balances the actual deviating influence of the labor costs as they are being compressed. But if 109 the varying degree of deviation of industry in various directions, and if the *qualitative* determination of its deviations by the locational weight and its composition are matters of indifference, then the locational weight may be contrasted with the amount of labor costs simply as a *quantitative* measure of the extent of its deviating ability, and thus be made the basis of calculating this deviation.

The concept of the "labor coefficient" does this. It might be well to point out in this connection that these labor coefficients will be fractions, like 100/3 (i.e., M.100 labor cost per ton of product to three tons locational weight). It will be useful, however, to get the labor coefficient of different industries on a fully comparable basis. We shall therefore reduce it so that the locational weight becomes one. In other words, we shall ask how much labor cost will arise in each industry for one ton of locational weight to be moved. We shall always speak of the labor coefficient of an industry in the sense of its labor costs per ton of weight to be moved, per locational ton, as we may call it.[4]

Using the term labor coefficient in this sense, we shall henceforth say that the *labor orientation of industries, so far as it depends on their general characteristics, is determined by their labor coefficient.*

To illustrate the significance of this theorem we shall give a few examples. The manufacture of corsets has a labor coefficient of about M.1,500; the pottery industry, of about M.55; the production of raw sugar (from beets), of M.1.30. According to these coefficients, 10 per cent of labor cost saved at any place means respectively M.150, M.5.50, and M.0.13 saved per loca-

---

[4] Every such locational ton must be thought of as composed of amounts of product and materials corresponding to the composition of the locational weight.

tional ton. If we assume a ton-kilometer rate of 5 pfennig, we find that the corset manufacture might deviate 3,000 km., the pottery industry, 110 km., and raw sugar production, 2.6 km. The entire—and immensely different—manner of orientation of these three industries is explained by these figures.

110

B. ORIENTATION OF AN ENTIRE INDUSTRY

We have spoken hitherto of the location of isolated individual productive units which are being deviated. It is not difficult to visualize the evolution of the orientation of an entire industry under the influence of the labor coefficient and of its compressibility. It is quite easy to get a picture of this orientation. We should, first, consider how far the individual productive units of a given industry may deviate from the minimum points of the individual locational figures, this being determined by the particular labor coefficient. And we should, second, remember that theoretically each attracting labor location will influence all the locational figures of an industry, wherever they may be situated, and that each attracting labor location has a tendency to attract production from all sides to itself. From these two considerations we get the picture of production piling up at the labor locations, coming from various directions. It is important to observe that the number of locations where they will pile up is related to the extent of the deviation. This last shading of the picture may also be seen by combining the two considerations. For if the attraction of the labor locations of an industry, affecting as it does the locational figures from all sides, is effective over large areas, this will mean an effective competition of the various labor locations with each other. Some labor locations of the same industry will compress the labor costs more, and therefore some will exert a stronger attraction than others. Those which attract more strongly—which attract with the larger percentage of compression—will eliminate those which attract less strongly. Within the radius in which they are effective (depending on the character of the industry) they will draw production to themselves from all sides. This power of attracting industries from all sides, of eliminating the "weak," will be proportionate to the effect of the labor locations of a given industry, and this effect depends upon the extent to which an industry will deviate. The result will be that industries deviating to a high degree will agglomerate in a small number of labor locations, while industries with a low degree of deviation will remain distributed over many locations.

As a result of our consideration of the labor coefficient we can state the following rule about the orientation of an entire industry: *Since the deviation of an industry depends on the size of its labor coefficient, the industry will be concentrated at a smaller number of labor locations, will tend to be more strongly oriented according to labor, the higher its labor coefficient is.*

All this is clear, and would have been accepted as true even before the idea of orientation as a whole had been set forth in detail as we have just done. We could now leave the subject of the orientation of an entire industry if there were not still one point relating to the "concentration" which should be clarified. This point concerns an alteration in the attracting power of the labor locations which takes place through *(hindurchgeht)* an alteration in the costs of transportation in the process of concentration. Let us, for example, imagine the simplest case in which the production of two locational figures is concentrated at one labor location, as is shown graphically in the Figure 18 shown on p. 115. The labor location to which the industry is attracted would draw each of the raw materials which it needs from a different material deposit (the first materials from M_1 and M'_1, and the second from M_2 and M'_2, and if the industries of more than two locational figures were attracted, it would draw from as many material deposits as there were locational figures present, assuming that the industry of each of the locational figures had its own material deposits. It is clear, however, that

for each of the materials used there is one deposit which is most favorably situated in relation to the labor location. And it is quite evident that, assuming a sufficient productivity of this most favorably situated deposit, the industry when removed to the labor location will no longer need the less favorably situated materials which it made use of in the individual figures. It will therefore "close down" those deposits and cover its needs from
112 the one most favorably situated. In our case this will mean that M_1 and M'_2 will be closed down, and the whole demand for raw materials will be supplied from M_2 and M'_1. A labor location which has attracted plants will be connected with all the individual locational figures of the industry only through the markets for which it produces, and not any more through their material deposits; and it markets its goods "all over the world" (as we can daily observe), while it uses only the nearest deposits of sufficient productiveness for its raw material.

The closing down of raw material deposits which is the characteristic feature of this phenomenon takes place for the purpose of saving unnecessary costs of transportation. Its result is that in every locational figure whose industry is diverted the total deviation costs of the old locational figure are no longer set up against the labor economy which the diverting labor location offers; from these deviation costs the amount of transportation costs saved by using the most favorable deposits is now to be subtracted. In our case the economy which A offers is no longer contrasted to the full deviation costs of $M_1 M_2 C$ or $M'_1 M'_2 C'$; since so far as the deviation of the first triangle is concerned, these deviation costs are to be lessened by the transportation costs saved by substituting M'_1 for M_1; and so far as the deviation of the second triangle is concerned, by the economy which the substitution of M_2 for M'_2 offers. These economies of transportation are evident from the different length of the lines to the deposits. Cf. Fig. 18 on next page.

Now in order to make this tendency even clearer we may

express the matter the other way around. We may say: to the economy which the labor location offers through lower costs of labor is added that which it gains through replacement of the material deposits. Therefore in order to make clear the actual attracting power of a labor location in relation to any given locational figure we shall have to set against the deviation costs of this locational figure, not simply the index of labor economy of the location, but also the economies gained through the replacement of material deposits. Only in this manner shall we gain a

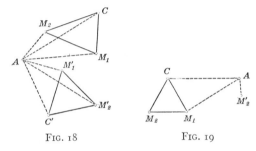

FIG. 18   FIG. 19

measuring rod for the attracting power of the labor location, first, in its effect upon each individual locational figure, and second, in its compound effect upon all locational figures which fall within its circle of influence. And only thus do we gain a correct 113 theoretical picture of the orientation of an industry as a whole, and of the magnitude and form of its concentration at the labor locations.

It may even be that new deposits of materials are called into play by such a deviation. This opening up of new deposits, as well as the replacement of material deposits, may have essential significance with respect to the competition of the labor locations with each other, and may codetermine the deviation of industry. It is obvious that new deposits may be brought to light by the deviation. For the utilization of material deposits naturally need not be limited to those originally connected with the locational figures, but may obviously include deposits hitherto not used, which lie in the vicinity of the labor location. Figure 19 shows a very simple case. The larger or smaller chances of making use of favorably situated new deposits (as in general the possibility of replacing those situated far away from the labor location by similar deposits nearer at hand) is of course a factor in selecting the labor locations. Locations which have material deposits in their neighborhood and have an opportunity to bring about effective replacements in case of deviation will eliminate such others as do not have such opportunity precisely to the extent to which the attracting power of their index of economy is increased by economies of transportation costs.[5] As we have seen from the preceding discussion, only the possibility of replacing material deposits limits the real amount of deviation. It is clear that such replacements influence the choice of the labor locations, and thereby the *concrete picture* of deviation.

114   The general extent of the deviation of the industry depends upon its labor coefficient. The higher this coefficient is, and the greater the distance over which deviation takes place on account of it, the greater will be the distances which the replacements will cover, the more effective will be the economies in transport, and the more will these economies strengthen the attracting power of the labor locations. The attracting power of labor locations of an industry will not increase precisely parallel to its labor coefficient, on account of the increasing replacements; it will increase more than proportionally. The general rule that the coefficient of labor determines the divertibility of an industry may be more exactly formulated. Coefficient of labor and divertibility of an industry may be compared to two rising lines, the

[5] Of course we can calculate precisely how the attracting power of one labor location in comparison with that of another will be affected by this possibility of replacement. We need only compare the distances of the labor locations from their nearest material deposits. By precisely the amount that the distance from one labor location is shorter than the distance from another, the economy in the case of that labor location will be greater than in the other. A proportionate amount is to be added to its index of economy.

rise of one depending upon that of the other; although the rise of the deviation line exceeds that of the labor coefficient line. We may explain this fact by saying that the divertibility is not a phenomenon simply parallel to the labor coefficient, but a more complex functional phenomenon. Industries with really high labor coefficients will therefore at the same time be very strongly agglomerated.

4. THE ENVIRONMENTAL CONDITIONS OF THE LABOR ORIENTATION

Two environmental conditions of divertibility seem to be quite accidental and to defy statements in terms of a general rule: the mutual distance between locational figures and labor locations, and the indices of economy of the labor locations.[6] This appearance is borne out by the facts to a certain extent. For, whatever general rules we may formulate, the actual situation of a given locational figure in relation to the given labor locations will always be different for each instance, and the actual percentage of compression of labor costs will remain a specific one for each location. From that, however, it does not follow that these conditions do not take place within the limits of a general rule, for in fact they do. Both the mutual distance between locational figures and labor locations are, in general, dominated by the same pair of internally interrelated facts, the density of population and the level of civilization.

It is clear that in sparsely populated regions having markets of consumption widely apart from each other the locational figures with their minimum points will be distributed at great intervals over the country; similarly "labor locations" will be more thinly scattered over the country than in densely populated regions. Therefore the average distance between the locational figures and the labor locations will be large. On the other hand, a dense population will mean that one locational figure

---

[6] This statement involves: (1) the distance between the locational figures, (2) the distance between the labor locations, (3) the distance between the locational figures and the labor locations.—EDITOR.

will lie closer to another, one labor location beside another labor location, and hence that a short average distance between locational figures and labor locations will prevail. The ranges of deviation to be overcome will thus vary according to the density of population. An increasing density of population will always mean that shorter distances have to be overcome, and that therefore more and more favorable conditions for deviation will result. That is the general rule to which this seemingly accidental and unrelated point is subject.

With a rather extensive claim to general validity we may further say that thinly populated regions will be culturally backward, or better, culturally "undifferentiated." The efficiency of labor will not be very different for different locations; and likewise the wages will not vary greatly. The differences of labor costs will hence be small and their relative percentages of compression low. Vice versa, the differentiation of labor costs and the relative percentages of compression of the labor costs will increase with an increasing density of population. That is the general rule to which *this* condition is subjected.

Both together (the distances between locational figures and labor locations, and the indices of economy of labor locations) will be influenced by the density of population and the accompanying rise of civilization in such a way as to facilitate increasing labor orientation, since increased percentages of compression, like lessened ranges of deviation, of course facilitate the
116 removal of production to the labor location. It may therefore very well be that in sparsely populated regions industries are predominantly oriented according to transportation facilities, whereas in more thickly populated regions they are predominantly oriented according to labor.

Finally, the significance of the third environmental condition, of the transportation rates, is very simple. Whenever the rates per ton-kilometer decrease, the isodapanes indicating deviation costs go farther apart and the indices of economy of labor locations are lowered proportionately. As a result, labor locations much farther away will effectively attract; or in other words, orientation according to labor will influence a larger and larger part of the whole body of industry, measured quantitatively by units of production. It will concentrate the production of diverted industries more and more at the most advantageous labor locations by extending the sphere of attraction of these locations. That is the general rule to which *this* environmental condition is subjected.

We may look upon a good part of the struggle between handicraft and large-scale industry in the second half of the nineteenth century as a proof of this rule concerning the results of decreasing transportation costs. It has already been indicated how far the decline of the handicrafts means the disappearance of production from the markets of consumption, due to changes in the material index of the industries. Now we may say that this decline was hastened by the fact that the railways facilitated the deviation of industry toward the most favorable labor locations. Local differences of the indices of labor costs (which had been rather veiled, so to speak, by costs of transportation) became suddenly apparent and of practical significance when railway rates began to decline rapidly. Thus good labor locations have collected around themselves large masses of industry which had formerly been oriented transportationally; that is, had been situated near the market and could therefore be organized on a handicraft basis. In the second part we shall show to what industries this applies particularly.[7] But at this time we may ask what has removed products like furniture, baskets, casks, etc., away from the places of consumption (where they used to be produced by handicraft) toward the best labor locations where

[7] As has been pointed out, this second part has never been written by A. Weber; but studies of individual industries by some of his students have been published under his direction by J. C. B. Mohr, in Tübingen. See also Introduction.—EDITOR.

their manufacture takes place for purposes of marketing them on a large scale, though often the conditions of manufacture are 117 technically not greatly changed. We shall find that this change has been caused by the lower transportation rates.

5. TENDENCIES OF DEVELOPMENT

All changes of *environmental conditions* have the tendency to promote labor orientation. For the general course of development is apparently in normal times not only in the direction of decreasing transportation costs but also in the direction of facilitating deviation by increasing the density of population and the differentiation of culture.

On the other hand, the same technical developments which diminish the costs of transportation change, *pari passu*, the general character of the industries by mechanizing the process of production. This decreases the labor coefficient of the industries, altering simultaneously both its factors, the amount of labor used and the amount of material used per ton of product. Obviously, it increases the amount of material used through the use of coal and of weight-losing materials; at the same time it renders manual labor superfluous and thus diminishes the amount of labor used. In consequence there is less and less labor necessary for a greater and greater locational weight. The result is a tendency continually to convert labor-oriented industry into transport-oriented industry. If we wish by means of our theory to make fully clear the whole meaning of this tendency toward integration, it can be done by keeping in mind on the one hand the convergence of the isodapanes which is a consequence of the increase of the index of materials and which represents the "difficulty" of deviation, and by realizing on the other hand how the decreasing compressible quantities of labor costs per ton of product reduce the economy values of the labor locations, thus pushing the critical isodapanes of the labor locations more closely toward the minimum point, and again diminishing the possibility of deviation. If we think of both these things together, we can see that the integrating tendency which results from the mechanization of the process of production must be very strong.   118

Whether it will be stronger than the "disintegrating tendencies" discussed earlier, which also lie in the historical development, cannot be determined in abstracto. For only two of the opposed integrating and disintegrating forces (namely, the decreases of transportation costs and the increase of amount of material used) may be set in relation to each other abstractly and their net effect evaluated by means of more or less well-known facts. For the purpose of a provisional understanding of the tendencies of the development as a whole it will be worth while to investigate the relationship of these two.

An increase in the use of raw materials means an increase in the amount of weight which, in case of a deviation from the minimal point, must be transported. Decrease in the rates of transportation means increase in the amount which can be transported at the same expense. If the amount of material used by an industry should be doubled, but the rates of transportation should be at the same time reduced by one-half, the effects would balance and everything would remain as before as far as the divertibility of the industry is concerned. The position of the isodapanes would remain the same. The tendency to push them apart (decreases in transport rates) and the tendency to draw them together (increases in the material index) balance each other. Starting then from this generalization, we may after all say something about the total effect of the integrating and disintegrating tendencies during the second half of the nineteenth century. The gigantic cheapening of transportation caused by steam has reduced the rates per ton-kilometer to one-fourth, one-tenth, even one-twentieth of what they were formerly. Now there are probably not many industries in which the mechanization of the process of production (however greatly it may have expanded with the aid of steam) has increased the weights to be transported to quite that extent. That, however, would have been necessary in order to balance completely the general tendency of the isodapanes to expand when transport rates decrease. Hence on the whole they must have been widened, for some industries more, for others less, according to the extent of their mechanization, but on the whole in all industries to a significant extent.

119

From the unchecked widening of the isodapanes to four and ten times their extent (as was bound to happen in all sections of industry not yet affected by mechanization) we get a picture of the revolution in the locational conditions for these even now rather large sections of industry—a revolution due to the enormously extended spheres of attraction of the labor locations in them; and we get a picture of the extent to which, for instance, the struggle between handicraft and manufacturing industry may be conceived simply as a consequence of this increased power of attraction.

That the widening of the isodapanes is impeded in those industries which are being mechanized leads us to the following considerations: In so far as such widening occurred—and as we have seen, that was predominantly the case—a loosening of industries and a strengthening of the labor orientation must have taken place. Since, now, a decrease in the indices of economy of the labor locations means a pushing of the critical isodapanes toward the minimum points, we get the following picture applicable to the development of the mechanized parts of industry: the isodapanes are pushed apart (widened) and at the same time the critical isodapanes are pushed back farther toward the inside of the concentric rings formed by the widening isodapanes. Only in the cases in which, as a result of both these movements, the pushed-back critical isodapane was farther from the minimal point than it was prior to the mechanization and decrease in transportation costs has there been any loosening up. It is part of the empirical study to show whether that was in fact the case for large portions of industry, and whether transport or labor orientation has on the whole progressed farthest, and furthermore, which of the two is still progressing today.

With this final application of these questions to concrete reality it is now possible to take leave of the laws of labor orientation so far as pure theory is concerned. To determine, on the basis of the rules we have discovered, to what extent industry is labor-oriented and to what extent transport-oriented will be seen to be one of the principal tasks of the study of the empirical material. It will be evident that this empirical study is one of the best means of checking up the correctness of our theory by an appeal to the facts. For the general criterion here set up of the ability of industry to orient itself toward labor, its labor coefficient, is a clear characteristic of industries, not very difficult to ascertain in reality. It ought to be possible to verify the significance of the labor coefficient of any industry for the deviation of its industrial location from the minimum points.

CHAPTER V

AGGLOMERATION

Costs of transportation and costs of labor are the only two factors in location which work regionally. All others work, as we have seen, only as part of the agglomerative or deglomerative forces contributing to local accumulation or distribution of industry; and so they operate only within the general framework formed by the regional factors. Our present task is to introduce the effect of these factors into the general theory.

SECTION I

ANALYSIS OF THE AGGLOMERATIVE AND DEGLOMERATIVE FACTORS

I. OBJECT OF THE ANALYSIS

The first thing which must be done at this point is to show that in principle the theory does not need to interpret agglomerative and deglomerative factors as two groups, but as one group, namely, as agglomeration. All deglomerative factors are by their very nature nothing but counter-tendencies resulting from agglomeration. But if that is what they are, theory may disregard them as *independent* factors and treat them as the opposite of agglomeration. For the theory is not concerned with the dynamic interaction of operative tendencies toward agglomeration and resultant contrary tendencies toward deglomeration, but rather with the final effect of this process, since only this final effect alters the locational situation.

122 However, this final effect may be that the agglomerative tendencies are completely paralyzed (in which case there is no alteration of the locational picture we have already gained), or it may mean that there is a permanent excess of the tendency to agglomeration (in which case theory has to introduce this factor

of agglomeration as one which may possibly change our previous picture). Theory has, therefore, as a matter of fact to deal only with possible agglomerations—agglomerations which are a resultant of complicated processes.

Nevertheless it would be desirable if the abstract theory were able to analyze into its component parts the dynamic interaction of agglomerative and deglomerative factors which create this "resultant," if it were able to dissect each group and (as in the cases of costs of transportation and costs of labor) determine to what degree each individual industry is under the influence of each factor.

Unfortunately this cannot be done by pure deduction. Both of the hitherto considered causes of location were simple quantities which could be deduced from the known facts of some isolated industrial process, and their degree of influence upon each industry could also be deduced from these facts. The groups of locational factors now to be considered are, on the contrary, distinguished by the fact that they result from the *social* nature of production, and are accordingly not to be discovered by analyzing an isolated process of production. And in the case of these social factors of concentration it is absolutely impossible to say *a priori* whether production costs would be lower or higher. There is no complex of known premises from which such a proposition could be deduced. We have only empirical knowledge of individual facts to tell us that certain elements of industry become cheapened in the process, others more expensive. Since we cannot know within the compass of general theory the groups of special locational factors composing the agglomerative and deglomerative tendencies, it is of course impossible to discover by deduction definite general characteristics according to which we could determine the extent of the influence of these agglomerative and deglomerative factors upon the individual industries.   123

Thus the task of general theory is here of necessity much more limited than in the preceding sections. Speaking precisely, eory can have only the task of finding quite general rules concerning the *manner* and *extent* of the effect of the agglomerative tendencies upon location; it must rely upon empiricism to discover individual agglomerative and deglomerative factors and to apply the general rules of agglomeration to the various industries.

It is, however, worth while to give a certain foundation in fact (without claiming completeness) for our discussion. Accordingly there follows a short survey of the more essential factors known to work in an agglomerative or deglomerative manner. As the discussion proceeds, it will become clear that it is possible to make at least a beginning of a preliminary grouping of industries, and this as a matter of pure theory.

2. DEFINITIONS

An agglomerative factor, for purposes of our discussion, is an "advantage" or a cheapening of production or marketing which results from the fact that production is carried on to some considerable extent at *one* place, while a deglomerative factor is a cheapening of production which results from the decentralization of production (production in more than one place). In the case of each concentrated industry the interaction of agglomerative and deglomerative factors must always result in certain *indices of costs* per unit of product, indices which are a function of the amount of concentration. If these indices of costs are smaller in case of great concentration than they are in cases of little concentration, they clearly become for the industry in question indices of economy. They point out that with a certain degree of concentration the costs are smaller *on account of concentration.* They are smaller by a certain amount per unit of product than they would be in the case of complete dispersion of the industry, or than they would be in a case involving less concentration.

We shall deal with these indices of economy by making use of the expression *the function of economy of agglomeration,*

or more briefly the *function of economy* of an industry. The 124
expression *function of agglomeration* might be used if it were
not better to reserve this latter term for another relation which
will become important when we try to establish a precise arith-
metical determination of the quantities of agglomeration (cf.
Appendix III, §2).

The function of economy is composed of individual indices
of economy (per unit of product) which correspond to each stage
of concentration. If there are several such stages of concentration, each of which results in an additional saving in costs per
unit of product, the industry has a true function of economy. If,
on the other hand, the saving results from a particular definite
amount of concentration, and does not continue to increase in
case of further concentration, then that industry has merely a
fixed index of economy of agglomeration. It is obvious that for
a complete understanding of both these concepts the effect of
the deglomerative factors must be taken into account. For the
present, in order to explain the origin of either this function of
economy or this fixed index of economy, we shall need to analyze
the various agglomerative and deglomerative factors.

3. AGGLOMERATIVE AND DEGLOMERATIVE FACTORS

A. *Agglomerative factors.* 1. We may in the first place, as regards the *agglomerative factors,* distinguish between two stages
of agglomeration at which these factors are operative. The first
and lower stage is that of the concentration of industry through
the simple *enlargement of plant.* Every large plant with a round-
ed out organization represents necessarily a local concentration
as compared with production scattered in small workshops over
the neighborhood. The well-known economic advantages of
large-scale production as compared with small-scale production
(*n.b.,* not the advantages of the large *enterprise* as compared
with the small enterprise; we have nothing to do with that) are
effective local factors of agglomeration. A certain minimum of

agglomeration makes the application of a given technical appliance in the plant possible with a certain percentage of saving; a further minimum of agglomeration makes possible a particular form of labor organization in the plant,—this also with a certain percentage of economy; and finally a certain minimum of agglomeration enables a plant to enter into the economic relationship which makes possible cheap large-scale purchasing, cheap credit, etc. These agglomerative factors combined create the large-scale plant of minimum efficient size for the industry in question. The coefficient of economy of the large plant as compared with the small (index of large-scale production) is also the coefficient of agglomeration of each industry, as far as this stage goes.

2. Whether an industry will agglomerate because of only this tendency to concentration through extension of plant, or whether it will come under the influence of a further tendency to concentration, depends upon the extent of the advantages resulting from close local association of *several* plants. In order to get a preliminary systematic survey ("preliminary" I again emphasize) of this *social* agglomeration, let it be noted that the local aggregation of several plants simply carries farther the advantages of the large plant, and hence that the factors of agglomeration which create this higher stage of social agglomeration will be the same as those which created the large-scale plant. As essential factors of this higher stage of agglomeration we again list the development of technical equipment, the development of labor organization, and a better adaptation to the economic organization as a whole.

a) *Development of the technical equipment.*—The complete technical equipment which is necessary to carry out a process of production may in highly developed industries become so specialized that minute parts of the process of production utilize specialized machines and that even quite large-scale plants are not able to make full time use of such equipment. Such specialized machines must then, together with their own parts of the process of production, be taken out of the single large plant and must work for several of them, i.e., become the basis of independent auxiliary industries. In theory, the workshops of such aux- 126 iliary industries may be separated from the main plants for which they work, and hence need not lead to local concentration of the main plants. As a matter of fact, however, they form one technical whole with the main plants for which they work. And this technical whole naturally functions best if its mutually dependent parts are locally concentrated, because then all the parts remain "in touch" with one another. The development of such specialized machines and of the auxiliary machines belonging to them establishes therefore a technical minimum of agglomeration, and this technical minimum, as soon as it leads to a social concentration of plants, extends beyond the minimum of plants previously considered. It thus becomes a factor of agglomeration.

And a quite similar influence (which yields the same result) is exerted by a second factor which we often find adduced as a cause of social agglomeration, namely, the better opportunities for replacing and repairing machinery. The workshops for replacement and repair are a part of the technical equipment—in a certain sense its "physician." The highly specialized development of this aspect of production is again possible only in connection with a large total technical equipment which exceeds the size of a single plant. In this case also a scattered location of the plants which are to be worked for, "country practice," is possible; but the best and cheapest service is to be secured "in town." The development of these specialized technical functions accordingly becomes a factor of social agglomeration.

b) Development of the labor organization.—A fully developed, differentiated, and integrated labor organization is also in a certain sense equipment. This equipment also has parts which are so specialized that, as a rule, they are not adapted to the conditions of a single large-scale plant. Hence they also tend to form specialized auxiliary or partial industries; and just as in the case of the technical factors discussed before, these trades based on "division of labor" lend to social agglomeration. It is not necessary to repeat the reasons for this.

c) *Marketing factors.*—The last group of factors—those creating a more effective marketing situation—will also be found at the stage of social agglomeration. The isolated large-scale plant is more effective than the small one because it can buy and sell on a large scale, thus eliminating the middlemen. Being a safer investment, it can get cheaper credit. Grouped large-scale plants gain still further economies, especially in purchasing raw materials and in marketing. In purchasing raw materials the concentrated industry develops its own market for its materials, and from this market it takes these materials in the necessary qualities and quantities at the time of demand. The isolated enterprise, on the other hand, is forced to buy its materials in advance and store them. This means a loss of interest for the individual enterprise, and hence an increase of money outlay. In economic terms it represents a wasteful temporary tying up of capital which could otherwise be actively utilized. Then too, in marketing the product, social concentration permits economies because the concentrated industry produces a sort of large unified market for its products. It is even possible that the whole marketing organization of the manufacturer can be dispensed with. Visits and direct buying at the place of production may develop, replacing the traveling salesman. This represents, not only an individual, but a general economic or social saving as well, since in the process "labor" or social energy is saved.

d) *General overhead costs.*—If for the foregoing and other reasons the best adaptation of industry to the general economic environment becomes, at the higher stage we are now considering, a general factor of agglomeration, it should be pointed out also that the diminution of "general overhead costs" which play a part at the lower level of agglomeration (i.e., in the case of the large as compared with the small plant) reappear on this stage; gas, water mains, streets, the whole "general apparatus" will become cheaper for the individual enterprise at the high level of technical development and effective utilization made possible through social agglomeration.

128

To summarize, if for each industry there is an index of the size of the plant (be it low or high depending upon the condition of technique, organization, etc., attained at any time) which tells us what unit costs per ton of product correspond to each stage in the size of plant of the industry, and which represents its tendency toward agglomeration at this lower stage of concentration, these same factors will possibly—they certainly frequently do— carry the plant beyond this stage of agglomeration.

Therefrom a tendency to agglomeration arises which creates social concentrations. These, taken together with the tendencies at the lower stage, determine the extent of agglomeration at this second and higher stage of agglomeration. This may suffice as a preliminary survey of the active factors of concentration.

B. *Deglomerative factors.* As we have noted, every agglomeration may cause opposing tendencies—increased expenses. The balance between the active factors and these opposing tendencies gives us the actual power of agglomeration effective in a given case.

These opposing tendencies result from the size of the agglomeration as such; they have, in contrast to the agglomerative factors which are related to particular characteristics of each industry, such as technique, level of organization, etc., nothing to do with these characteristics. Their strength and manner of working depends solely upon the size of the agglomeration. All agglomerations of equal form and size are subject to them in the same manner. These deglomerative factors all follow from the *rise of land values,* which is caused by the increase in the demand for land, which is an accompaniment of all agglomeration.

This increased demand increases both the significance of the marginal utility of tracts of land and the discounting of this marginal utility by speculative manœuvers. All deglomerative tendencies start from the increase in economic rent (ground rent). We can describe them all as various consequences of economic rent.

This is not the place to discuss through what various means all these consequences take place; still less is it the place to discuss the kinds and extent of the effects of the various increased expenses of production. We are concerned only with stating the situation theoretically. Developing further what has already been said, we have only to note that all these consequences represent merely a weakening of agglomerative tendencies. If we assume, for instance, that economic rent makes the area of land necessary for an industry more expensive,[1] that means an increase of the general overhead costs, of whose diminution through agglomeration we spoke earlier. If we assume that it increases the costs of labor, it means that part or all of the cheapening of labor on account of highly efficient organization will be absorbed. In either case the existence and increase of the rent of land means, not the operation of fundamentally new factors of orientation, but always only a decrease in the effect of the agglomerative factors. But the growth of these counteracting effects will always run parallel to the size of agglomeration as long as the rent of land parallels the size of the agglomeration, which is generally the case.

From the foregoing there follow the important conclusions, first, that we may think of the importance of the deglomerative factors, even in detail, as a weakening of the agglomerative factors—a weakening which, appearing under certain circumstances, runs parallel to the growth of agglomeration. Secondly, while the factors of agglomeration always have application to

---

[1] Let us assume also that this increase in cost could not be entirely avoided by moving the industry to the periphery of an agglomeration.

separate and individual units of industry or to one or more connected branches of industry, the weakening of the tendencies to
agglomeration (created by the agglomerative factors themselves) is connected with only the size—size as such—of the agglomeration. This weakening therefore comes into existence
even if the agglomeration is an accidental conglomeration of *different* branches of industry, and it follows, since the index of
economy resulting from agglomeration is always in part determined by the extent of the deglomerative tendencies which are
at the same time called into being, that there can exist theoretically "pure" indices of economy in the case of a single agglomerated industry, provided it is agglomerated in isolation. But if 130
other industries are added, the resultant weakening of the agglomerative factors and therefore the size of the indices of economy will in part be determined by the fortuitous circumstance
that other industries are also agglomerating at the same location.
Thus the theoretically pure picture of the orientation of an industry will be distorted by the actual situation due to agglomeration. This alteration of reality we shall, following the guiding
principle of our investigation, for the present leave out of account. We shall deal here with the tendency to agglomeration and
its indices of economy as *pure;* more strictly speaking, we shall
proceed as if the various industries did not disturb each other as
the result of the coincidence of their agglomeration at the same
locations.

From all this it should be clear—and, through our references
to reality, abundantly clear—in what sense we shall speak of the
indices of economy due to agglomeration and of the "function of
economy" as being a composite of these indices (see p. 123). It
should further be evident why we, in abstract theory, think of
this "function of economy" as one whose single indices indicate
further and further economies per unit of product as agglomeration increases; and yet these economies grow more and more
slowly as agglomeration increases. For on the one hand we have

the known facts of experience in the matter, showing that the various agglomerative factors, such as the development of technique, of organization, etc., *in themselves* all decrease progressively. On the other hand this decrease is necessarily accentuated by the weakening to which these agglomerative factors are subjected as the rent of land increases with the size of the agglomeration. Thus we may think of the function of economy as one side of a parabola which approaches more and more slowly 131 a maximum value.

It is hardly necessary, I suppose, to explain more fully that the "fixed index of economy," which knows only one stage of agglomeration and which was on page 123 introduced into the theory, is only a theoretical aid, an intermediate assumption to which no actual situation ever quite corresponds. For it is evident that the factors of agglomeration with which we have become acquainted will always create a series of stages (with attendant growing economies) which range from the stage of absolute dispersion of location to the theoretical maximum of agglomeration; and that neither "absolute dispersion" nor "fixed agglomeration of a given size" will ever exist in reality. The assumption of the existence of this fixed agglomeration will, however, perform rather important auxiliary services to our theory.

SECTION II

THE LAWS OF AGGLOMERATION

The theory of agglomeration deals, according to the preceding discussion, with local concentrations of industry which arise because of the fact that the production of a unit of product can in this concentrated producing complex be more economically performed by a certain definite amount. Hence the theory does not deal with those local concentrations of production which appear as the results of other causes of orientation and hence exist quite independently of whether the agglomeration as such has any or no advantages. If, as is very often the case, transportation facilities concentrate industries near the supplies of raw materials, or at the coal fields, or near the big markets of consumption,[2] that phenomenon does not lie within the field of the theory of agglomeration. The same is the case when the attracting "labor locations" develop in such a way as to form large centers of agglomeration.[3] All these are from our present point of view fortuitous circumstances in which agglomeration does not form a specific element. Our theory of agglomeration has to do only with agglomeration as a necessary consequence of agglomerative factors as such, not as a fortuitous consequence of other causes of orientation; only such part of these other concentrations as may be due to independent agglomerative tendencies interests us. Hence that agglomeration with which the theory will deal 132 will be called "pure" or "technical," thus contrasting it with agglomeration which is incidental to other forces.

132

A. AGGLOMERATION WITHIN TRANSPORT ORIENTATION

The tendency to agglomeration for technical reasons may first be considered in its effect upon production which is oriented solely with regard to transportation and not diverted to "labor locations." What effect would a tendency to agglomeration with a fixed index have in this case?

I. AGGLOMERATION WITH FIXED INDEX

Assuming for the present that the agglomeration is a case of only one unit with a perfectly definite economy, let us put two questions: When will agglomeration take place, and to what extent? And, if it does take place, where will it take place?

a) When does agglomeration take place, and how much?—By means of the concepts of minimum points and isodapanes as they have been used earlier it is very easy to develop the answer to this question. It is only necessary to recall what was said about the indices of economy of the labor locations and their ef-

---

[2] See above, p. 71.   [3] Cf. above, p. 112.

fect. The centers of agglomeration also form, with regard to scattered production, centers of attraction having particular indices of economy. If production moves to these centers, that fact signifies a deviation accompanied by transportation costs higher than those of production located at the points of minimum transportation cost. And naturally this deviation depends fundamentally on the same conditions as those set forth on pp. 112 ff. The deviation costs per ton of product must be smaller than the economies per ton of product. These economies per ton of product are indicated by the index of economy of the unit of agglomeration. The isodapanes indicate the deviation costs per ton of product. For every individual part or unit of the production complex there must be a critical isodapane the deviation cost index of which corresponds exactly to the index of economy of the unit of agglomeration.

If that is clearly understood we can at once see that individual units of production become agglomerated and give rise to centers of agglomeration if their critical isodapanes intersect, and if the quantity of production of each individual unit added to that of the other units which participate in the same overlapping segment reaches the effective unit of agglomeration. For if such critical isodapanes intersect, then for the various individual units some common points exist at which the economy of agglomeration is not absorbed by the deviation costs. And when the quantity of production which can be concentrated at that point reaches the assumed unit of agglomeration, then the agglomeration pays; it can be effectively realized. To state it precisely, the formation of centers of agglomeration and the agglomeration of individual units of production at these centers depends upon two circumstances: first, upon the existence of intersections of critical isodapanes in relation to the assumed unit of agglomeration, and second, upon the attainment of the requisite quantity of production within these segments. When these two conditions are fulfilled, the individual units of production become agglomerated and the concentration affects all parts of the production complex. Whatever the situation and whatever the quantity of output of any indivdiual unit, *if its critical isodapanes intersect with those of enough other individual units to make up a unit of agglomeration, it will be concentrated with these others.*

For a clarification of the two "conditions" it is necessary to note the following, which again is in part analogous to the case of orientation as affected by labor. Theoretically, only those productive units can be brought together in the case of each of which the economies relating to its particular quantity of production exceed the deviation costs, since only for such units does the overlapping segment exist. In fact, however, the agglomeration can (for the purpose of attaining the requisite amount of production) somewhat exceed this theoretical limit and can also attract certain productive units which are somewhat farther away and whose critical isodapanes do not quite reach the segment. This may happen if the ratio of economies to deviation costs for *other* parts of the agglomeration is so favorable that a balance on the side of economy still remains for the agglomerated industry as a whole, even though a part of the economies arising from agglomeration must be applied to covering the negative balance between economies and deviation costs of such "fragments"; for in such a case the attraction of the "fragments" will cause lower costs for the group as a whole. Beyond such occasional supplementing of units of agglomeration which are not quite complete, agglomeration cannot and will not go; because, as will be shown later, the "effective unit of agglomeration" roughly forms the upper limit of agglomeration. Only by throwing together many units of agglomeration could a "surplus" be created sufficient to attract on a large scale productive units whose isodapanes do not reach the segment. Thus this whole matter of agglomeration of units which lie too far away when considered by themselves means no great alteration—only a comparatively insignificant modification—of the two conditions upon which agglomeration depends; the basic proposition still holds that a unit of agglomeration with a given index will bring together all those parts of a total industry whose critical isodapanes as worked out in terms of this unit intersect with each other, if the combined or concentrated production of these parts is sufficient to make up the effective unit of agglomeration.

b) *Where will agglomeration take place?*—And where will the center of agglomeration lie? That also is easily made clear by means of the isodapanes. The center of agglomeration must obviously lie within the common segments of the critical isodapanes, for within these common segments lie the points at which production may be concentrated without prohibitive deviation costs. Every point within a common segment is a *possible* point of agglomeration; for at any such point production under agglomerated conditions can take place more cheaply than at the scattered points of minimum transportation costs. But where will the center of agglomeration actually be located? It will be located at that one of the several possible points of agglomeration which has the lowest transportation costs in relation to the total agglomerated output. (See Fig. 20.)

The various units going into the agglomeration have outputs or production of varying size, and the diversion of a large quantity of output toward a point of agglomeration involves greater transportation costs than does the diversion of a small quantity of output. Within the common segments the agglomeration will become so situated that the larger units of production have changed their positions less than have the smaller ones, for this will keep down the total deviation costs. Stated in other words, the large units of production will attract the smaller units to locations near the former's original minimum points, and will there fix the center of agglomeration.

We can state the result of this dynamic process with great precision in the following manner: All the agglomerated productive units, together with their common location of production (the center of agglomeration), constitute one great locational figure of the type which is already familiar to us. Its corners are the various raw-material supplies and markets of the various constituent units. The position of the location in this figure will be determined by the components of the different corners precisely in accordance with the laws of those locational figures which have already been studied. The precise location of the center of agglomeration will thus be that of the minimum point of transportation cost for this locational figure. It must lie with-

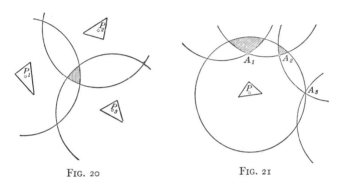

FIG. 20   FIG. 21

in the segment of the isodapanes, and within this segment it may be quite definitely located.

c) *The size of the unit of agglomeration.*—Hard upon the heels of the solution of the question as to the point at which the production in a given segment takes place there follows the problem as to which of several possible agglomerations a unit of production will choose; and this leads to the important rule already indicated concerning the size of centers of agglomeration. If the isodapanes of an individual unit of production intersect in several areas and in several directions with those of other individual units—that is, if an individual unit has several possibilities of agglomeration, it will agglomerate within that common segment in which the center of agglomeration is least distant from the former minimum point of the individual unit concerned. For

thus the smallest additional transportation costs and the largest
136 surplus from the index of economy will result. In this connection
it should be noted that the point of agglomeration is more likely
to be fairly near to the particular unit concerned when the other
individual units are situated close at hand, so that the segments
formed by the intersections of the critical isodapanes are large.
For illustration compare Figure 21. The actual location, however, within the segments still depends upon the relative size
of the quantities of production concerned, as was shown in our
previous discussion. In consequence, even though each individual unit tends to choose the largest possible segment (i.e.,
agglomerates with the other units nearest to it), it will also tend
to choose the particular segment within which the point of agglomeration is nearest to it. Among the segments in its vicinity
it will choose the one in the case of which the smallest possible
additional quantity of production still suffices for the unit of agglomeration which has to be gotten together. Put in a slightly
different way, and using terribly cumbersome abstract terminology (which unfortunately is nevertheless hardly adequate to express these matters), we might say: the isolated units of production will not agglomerate arbitrarily or indifferently with any of
the others near them; but rather they will agglomerate with
those smallest units which just suffice to make up a requisite unit
of agglomeration, and which they can attract farthest to themselves, attracting first the smaller ones and then going upward in
the scale to the larger ones.

This is the theorem which provides the promised insight into
the fundamental nature of this kind of orientation. From the
fact that each individual unit in the process of concentration
selects from those others lying near it the smallest which will suffice for a unit of agglomeration, there follows as a general feature
of agglomeration the tendency not to exceed the size of a requisite unit of agglomeration, and hence the tendency to concentrate
in as many centers as there exist requisite units of agglomera-

tion. This result may also be reached by showing that each ag- 137
glomeration means a deviation with resultant costs; and the
deviation which occasions these costs will not be carried farther
than to form units which just offset these costs. However, it is
important further to demonstrate this by making use of an exact
and detailed analysis of the formation of the individual centers
of agglomeration.

   d) *Modifications.*—We must now (again in strict accordance with our discussion of the attraction of labor locations) introduce the modification of the power of attraction of the centers

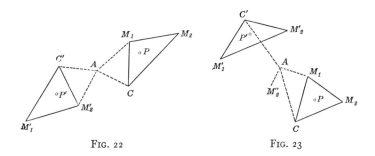

FIG. 22   FIG. 23

of agglomeration resulting from the elimination of material deposits. This modification must be made because of the fact that
in drawing together at one place several units of production more
and less favorable deposits of supply will result for each kind of
material used, the respective advantages of these deposits depending upon the relation of the supplies which were formerly
used by the isolated units to the new site of production. It follows that, as in the case of the "labor locations," the unfavorable
deposits will be eliminated (as in Fig. 22 above, M'_1 and M_2)
and the supply will (assuming sufficient productivity) be limited
to the most favorable deposits of each kind of material.

   In addition to this change, which will take place regularly,
it *may* also happen that the place of agglomeration is by chance
situated in the neighborhood of a material deposit which has not,

up to this time, been used. Then this new deposit will be substituted (in place of all others of the same kind of material formerly used), since it is most favorable for the new conditions of production. Compare Figure 23. Here M'_1 is eliminated as less favorable than M_1; but so also are M_2 and M'_2 eliminated, since both are less favorable than the new deposit M''_2.

138

Both these circumstances will, by saving transportation costs, strengthen the power of attraction of the centers of agglomeration by a certain amount which should be added to their index of economy, an addition which must be the larger the farther the attraction of the original index of economy happens to extend, with the result that more distant units are attracted and the differential advantage between the unfavorable sources of material eliminated and the favorable ones brought into use is greater. All this is similar to what we found in the case of labor location.

But while the position of the attracting labor location is not changed by eliminating certain deposits of material (since this labor location is definitely fixed), the effect of this eliminating process goes farther in the case of agglomeration. In the latter case the geographical position of the attracting place of agglomeration is affected, since this position itself depends (within the segments of the isodapanes) upon the locational figures themselves. If parts of these locational figures cease to operate as effective determinants, the whole basis of orientation will be changed. But it may be stated at once that it is very easy to determine the new position, and that the separation from the old basis is not complete; the old deposits still continue to effect potentially, and in a definite direction, the process of agglomeration. This last point is obvious; for the new deposits might become exhausted, and then it would be necessary to resort to the old ones.

Speaking of the new position, then, (1) the centers of consumption which are to be served from this point of agglomeration and (2) the sources of materials which remain in use are the only factors which need to be considered as the basis of a new locational figure with the corresponding component weights in order to see where the point of agglomeration will lie; it will simply be the minimum point of the new locational figure, according to the laws familiar to us. In Figure 22, A is the minimum point of $C'M_1$ CM'_2; in Figure 23, A is the minimum point of $C'M_1$, CM''_2. As is evident at once, the point of agglomeration will generally remain in the neighborhood of the selected material deposits. For numerous and divided markets which have a relatively weak attracting force will pull against material deposits whose weight is concentrated upon a few strong ropes (using the terms known to us from our Varignon apparatus). In addition, these markets will mutually paralyze each other on account of

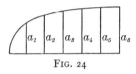

FIG. 24

their necessarily opposed positions. Consequently, the original position of the point of agglomeration in the neighborhood of these (new) deposits will be retained, or at any rate will not be greatly changed.

2. AGGLOMERATION IN THE CASE OF AN INCREASING INDEX

Now to turn to the usual case that, for the unit in question, there is not only a saving for a certain given unit of agglomeration, but there exists also a function of economy because economies continue to rise, increasing while the size of agglomerations increases. Such a function of economy is in point of fact made up entirely of single units of agglomeration, each one having a particular index of economy. The effects (on the distributed or scattered industry) of the tendency to agglomeration can be made clear if one imagines this tendency to agglomeration as being the concurrent effects of all these various units of agglomeration with their different indices. Each of these units will bring together the parts of the scattered industry according to the extent of its agglomerative power, following the laws with which we have become acquainted. Hence we can think of their common effect as a competition of the various units of agglomeration with respect to the form of the agglomeration; while within each of the struggling units the agglomeration takes place according to the rules which have already been developed. The question as to the effect of a function of economy composed of the units a_1 a_2 a_3, etc., is simply: toward which of these units will the agglomeration take place? After that question has been decided all the rest takes place according to the rules already set forth.

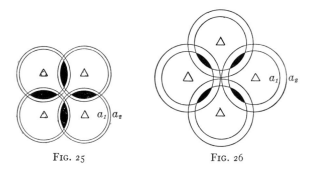

FIG. 25   FIG. 26

Which unit of agglomeration will win out may be deduced rather simply from the standpoint of the individual units of production affected. Around the minimal point of each individual unit of production extend critical isodapanes which correspond to the index of economy of each unit of agglomeration. The critical isodapanes of the higher units with higher indices of economy will lie more distant than those of the lower units; in our example a_2 will lie more distant than a_1, a_3 more distant than a_2, etc. How this works is indicated for a function with two units, a_1 and a_2 in the figures below (25–28). The critical isodapanes of higher units are likely to intersect with more isodapanes of other isolated units than is true of the smaller units. However, these

higher units also need larger masses of production in order to
come into operation; they must bring together a larger number
of isolated units of production. And these higher units will come
into competition with the smaller units. This may best be made
clear by the simple example of two units of agglomeration (a_1
and a_2) competing.

The isodapanes of higher rank (represented in our example
by a_2) may not bring together a larger number of productive
units than do the lower ones, because these isodapanes are drawn

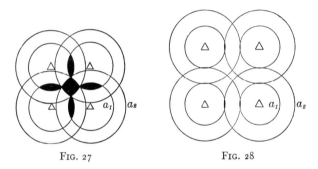

FIG. 27   FIG. 28

around the minimum points at so small an additional distance
from the lower ones that they do not have segments in common
with any more units than do those lower ones (Fig. 25). In that
case the higher units of agglomeration will not be able to compete with the lower units. Or it may be that the isodapanes of 141
higher rank actually include within their segments a larger number of productive units (Fig. 26, where a_2 includes three, and Fig.
27, where a_2 includes four, units, while a_1 only includes two in
each case). Assuming that a quantity of production sufficient
for agglomeration is present, there will be competition between
the two units of agglomeration. The outcome of this competition
will depend upon whether the ratio between the economies of
agglomeration and additional costs of transportation is more favorable in the case of agglomeration toward a_1 than it is in the

case of agglomeration toward a_2.[4] This ratio is accurately expressed by the distance between the isodapane on which the place of agglomeration for the unit in question will actually lie, and the critical isodapane belonging to this same unit. It will be remembered that the critical isodapane indicates the extent to which economies can be gained by means of agglomeration toward this unit. The isodapane on which the place of agglomeration will actually lie indicates the actual additional transportation costs which will have to be assumed in order to effect this particular agglomeration. The greater the difference between these necessary additional costs and the actual economies, the more favorable the situation for agglomeration. Hence it is only necessary (1) to examine from the standpoint of the individual units of production the common segments of the critical isodapane of the different units (in our case the segments of a_2 and a_1) and (2) to ascertain in which of these segments the distance between the points of agglomeration and the critical isodapanes will be greatest in order to know in which segments the agglomeration will take place. Assuming for the time being equally large productive units (which will place the points of agglomeration at the center of the segment), it follows that the distance between the points of agglomeration and the critical isodapanes 142 will increase in proportion to the size of the segments. It is, then, only necessary to look at the size of the segments in order to know toward which units the agglomeration will take place, assuming that sufficient quantities of production are available for the segments of all the units. In Figure 26 agglomeration will take place toward a_1; for, although it seems at a first glance possible that agglomeration might go toward the higher unit (a_2), it will not do so because the segments of the lower unit are larger; they show greater distances between the point of agglomeration and the critical isodapanes, and hence have greater actual economies. But when, as in Figure 27, isodapanes of higher rank lie

---

[4] The text in the preceding paragraph has been rewritten.—EDITOR.

so far beyond those of lower rank that not only do these higher isodapanes include within their segments more production (and sufficient production to make up the greater total quantity required for the higher unit), but also their segments are larger than those of the isodapanes of lower order, then in that case the higher unit of agglomeration will win out.

To sum up the argument in general terms: the agglomeration of higher rank will eliminate the agglomeration of lower rank only when the isodapanes of higher rank surround the minimum point at a distance so much greater that they not only (1) gather within their segments the amount of production required for the agglomeration of higher rank, but also (2) form larger segments and hence offer more favorable points of agglomeration for the individual units of production than do the segments of the critical isodapanes of lower rank.

It may, of course, be that only the critical isodapanes of agglomerative units of higher rank form segments, while those of lower rank do not touch each other at all (compare Fig. 28). In this case the agglomeration of lower rank will be unable to compete. This case is diametrically opposite to that first discussed. In this latter case the isodapanes of higher rank surround the minimum points at much greater distances than do those of the lower rank which cling closely to the minimum points.

3. THE CONDITIONS OF AGGLOMERATION

From the foregoing discussion one condition on which the form of the agglomeration depends should have become clear. It is the *manner in which* the critical isodapanes of the various units *follow each other.* According to the previous analysis, close succession of critical isodapanes indicates that agglomeration will move toward an agglomerative unit of lower rank; whereas wide separation indicates that it will move toward a unit of higher rank; hence agglomeration depends first on the scale of the isodapanes. This scale presents a graphical picture of the rate

at which the economies increase with successive units of agglomeration. It is a diagram of the increase of the function of economy—a diagram projected upon a horizontal surface (compare
illustration below, Figs. 29 and 30). If the indices of economy per ton of product increase rapidly as the agglomerative
units increase, then the corresponding isodapanes (cf. a_1, a_2, a_3
in Fig. 29) are far apart. Vice versa, if these indices increase
slowly, the isodapanes are close together (cf. a_1, a_2, a_3, in Fig.
30). The preceding analysis is thus nothing but an exact formu-

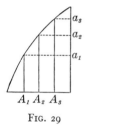

FIG. 29   FIG. 30

lation of the fact that (and in what manner) the size of the agglomeration will be dependent on the rapid or slow increase of
the function of economy. It shows in what manner the function
of economy represents the first factor influencing agglomeration
by determining the number and size of the units of agglomeration.

But on closer examination it shows also what additional factors are concerned. Apart from the succession of the isodapanes,
evidently three other factors must be taken into consideration:

First, The distance according to which the critical isodapanes are fundamentally spaced is to be clearly understood as
something different from their succession in the scale. A given
succession of critical isodapanes may be spread over a widely extended circular formation or over a narrow funnel of isodapanes,
according to whether their basic spacing interval is large or small
(cf. the figures of the Appendix, p. 241 f.). And each will neces-

sarily have its own significance for the agglomeration. We shall
presently discuss that aspect of the matter.

144

Second, The physical distance of the units of production. If
they are spread widely apart, scattered about the country, the
possibility of forming common segments of their isodapanes will
be less than if these industries were already close together.

Third, The quantity of production of the units of production. On this depends the magnitude of the masses of production
which are to be agglomerated within the segments, and this circumstance determines which of the different segments, if any,
have access to quantities of production sufficient for their agglomerative units.

In analyzing these three factors further, the following observations may be made.

We are already acquainted with the first factor from our discussion of labor orientation. We there found that the basic distance of the isodapanes is determined (1) by the locational
weight of the industry (a condition implicit in its character), and
(2) by the general rates of transportation (a general environmental condition). This first factor, therefore, may be separated into two conditions which work independently of each
other.

On the other hand, the second and third factors may be combined, since they depend upon one single condition, that of the
density of industry. For the quantity of production of the several units of production, taken together with their distance from
each other, constitute the density of industry relative to a given
area. It is useful to combine these two concepts into the one concept of the density of industry, since both in reality are a reflec-
tion of the same general environmental condition, the density of
population. Density of population empirically has these two aspects: (1) density of the population of a particular locality=
quantity of production of the units of production; (2) number

of centers of population=distribution of the individual units of production.

As in the case of labor orientation, we find two conditions inherent in the character of the industry, and on these two conditions the deviation to centers of agglomeration depends: (1) the *function of economy* of the industry and (2) its *locational weight*. So also we have two environmental conditions: the *costs of transportation* and the *density of industry* (or, as we may say empirically, the *density of population*). These are the same environmental conditions as those influencing labor orientation.

Let us now first examine more closely the nature of the influence of the locational weight and of the two environmental conditions, and second, work out at least a general picture of agglomeration under the combined influence of all the conditions.

It will probably not be necessary to restate the general way in which the *locational weight* and the *transportation costs* work. It will be remembered that if both decrease, the isodapane will expand; if both increase, the isodapane will tend to contract—in other words, both factors work alike. It is more important to realize that one of the two factors upon which the density of industry depends, namely, the *distance of the individual units of production,* has the same effect. The expansion or contraction of the isodapanes (without altering their order in the scale, to be sure) as caused by a change of locational weight and a change of transportation costs (or either one of these causes) amounts to an augmentation or diminution of the sets of isodapanes. Such expansions or contractions will therefore increase the number of points at which isodapanes intersect, just as bringing the sets of isodapanes nearer together *without altering the size* of each individual isodapane will increase the number of intersections. It is therefore permissible to regard locational weight, transportation costs, and distance of the units of production from one another —to regard all of them as a sort of similar mode of influence which is uniform in its effect.

What does this expansion of unaltered sets of isodapanes mean with respect to the formation of segments, and therefore with respect to the scale of agglomeration? To begin with, it clearly does not mean the same thing as an alteration of the *order* of the isodapanes in the scale—an alteration which results from changes in the function of economy. The expansion of unaltered sets of isodapanes must not be confused with an alteration of the order of the isodapanes in the scale. But, as in the latter case a further extension of the higher isodapanes means facilitating some agglomerations, so bringing the sets nearer to-

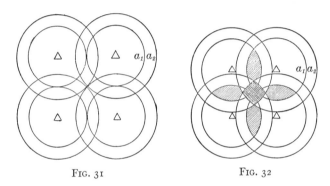

FIG. 31   FIG. 32

gether will have the same effect; because such an approach ob- 146 viously increases the segments and aids in piling up sufficiently large quantities of production within the segments; in other words, the two decisive factors are influenced favorably, and it will cause agglomeration to take place on a larger "scale." This will be evident from the above figures, which are simplified by showing a function of economy with only two stages (a_1 and a_2). The distance of the isodapanes (that is, the function of economy) is precisely the same in Figures 31 and 32; the figures differ only in the distance between the units of production. In Figure 31 the distance between the units is greater than in Figure 32, where they have been brought nearer together by one quarter. In Figure 31 there may be agglomeration only toward

a_1, and even this only on the assumption that two individual industrial units will suffice to make up the required quantity of production. In Figure 32, however, there are (due to the smaller distances of the units of production) possibilities for agglomeration toward a_1 and a_2, if we assume that the total quantity of production of all four units of production is necessary and sufficient to make up the required quantity for a_2. Under that assumption the agglomeration will, in fact, take place in the direction of the higher unit a_2, since the distance between the critical isodapane and the midpoint of the segment (point of agglomeration) is greater for a_2 than for a_1. To sum up: bringing the sets of isodapanes nearer together affects the "scale" of agglomeration. It affects the scale of agglomeration less than varying the function of economy affects it; for if I draw the locational figures a given distance toward one another all isodapanes, including those of lower order, come nearer together. The gross economy, therefore, increases at every step in the scale, but more rapidly in the higher order than in the lower order. If, however, I affect only the rate of succession in the scale—if, in other words, I let the isodapanes of higher order extend farther, then only these isodapanes of higher order within the different sets of isodapanes approach one another and the gross economy of agglomeration increases only with respect to them. The scale of agglomeration will therefore be much more immediately affected. Later it will be our task to formulate more precisely the difference in the measure of effectiveness of the various factors. In the meantime this indication of their different ways of working must suffice.

We now come to consider the second part of the third factor: the *quantity of production of the units of production*. We can only say of this that an increase of it quite obviously facilitates agglomeration, increases its "scale"; while a decrease diminishes it. For if the quantity of production in the individual industries increases sufficiently, the common segments of less widely extended isodapanes will now contain the quantity of production requisite for a unit of agglomeration. Similarly, sets of isodapanes which formerly did not have the requisite quantities in common segments of their higher isodapanes will now possess them. The unit of production may even "by itself" gain so much weight that it represents various degrees of the function of economy even without concentration; and one may imagine the extreme case in which a whole function of economy is realized through increasing the quantities of production of the unit of production without the industry necessarily being deviated. This may suffice to indicate the basic effects of the quantity of production upon agglomeration. It is impossible to give more than this elementary idea here; for the locational figures and their isodapanes fail us as graphic aids in clarifying issues involving the quantities of production of the units of production.

4. THE FORMULA OF AGGLOMERATION

It is, however, possible to get farther by other means in our attempt to explain the significance of all the factors taken together. It is possible to arrive analytically at a precise formulation of the degree of influence of the various factors by assuming that industries are distributed evenly and produce everywhere the same commodity. We may thus get for the entire industry an insight into the orientation which results from every combination of the factors. This is accomplished by the formula of agglomeration as set forth in the Appendix.[5] But it is important to keep in mind the assumption of uniform density of industry throughout a given area, an assumption which will not be valid for any actual industry or any actual country. The formula, so far as it gives us the number and size of the centers of agglomeration arising from any combination of the various factors, has, therefore, only a theoretical value. It gives only a general idea (probably rather far removed from reality) with which

148

[5] Cf. p. 246 f., *infra.*—EDITOR.

we can compare the reality without necessarily expecting to recognize in the reality the picture set up by the formula. The formula is in this respect only an aid to understanding. But that is only one aspect of it. The formula is no doubt more important in so far as it enables us to ascertain with precision the effect which changes in any one of the factors of agglomeration will have upon the agglomeration as a whole. And this service our formula does render, not only theoretically, but also for any given case. Because no matter how many different degrees of density are actually to be found for a given industry in different localities, the factors in question must be operative in each of these localities (and consequently in the whole body of that industry) according to the same *relative* degree of influence which they would have in an industry distributed smoothly and evenly. Such even distribution of industry merely represents *one* of the various grades of density of the real body of industry.

Let us attempt to clarify the result which has been attained in the Appendix and translate its formulas into non-technical language. Up to this time we have dealt only with the *absolute* economies which could be attained per ton of product in each stage of agglomeration. These economies were treated as a function of the size of the agglomeration, the concept "function of economy" being utilized. One may, however, according to the Appendix, inquire into the *relative* increase of economies which takes place as there is an increase in the size of the agglomeration, i.e., the increase of economy which, starting from any given stage of agglomeration, is attained by the addition of another industrial unit. And since this increase of economy depends solely upon the stage of agglomeration already reached—if we imagine the small units as small enough in comparison to the large ones which attract them—we shall recognize a second function which expresses the power of attraction of the various stages of agglomeration. This second function is called in the Appendix the "function of agglomeration." The function of agglomeration $f(M)$ is composed of the additional saving which corresponds to each step of progress from one stage of agglomeration to another. In the Appendix the relation of this function of agglomeration to the function of economy (with which we have previously dealt) is analyzed; it is shown that the two functions are intimately connected, and it is shown in what manner they are connected.

All that concerns us at the present time is the fact that the function of agglomeration expresses with precision the power of attraction which a large unit of industry exercises over scattered smaller units. As the equation *(Bestimmungsgleichung)* for the extent to which a large unit attracts smaller units, we get the formula $R = \dfrac{f(M)}{A_s}$ in which R is the radius of agglomeration as extended, A the locational weight of the industry, and s the transport rate which prevails. Thus we find that the attraction of a large unit of industry is directly proportional to the value of the function of agglomeration, and inversely proportional to the locational weight of the industry and the prevailing transport rates.

So much for the relevance of these three factors of agglomeration. If we wish to get an insight into the actual extension of the radii of agglomeration and to determine the actual amount of agglomeration it is necessary to take into account the thus-far neglected fourth factor of agglomeration, the "density of industry." The density of industry (ρ) determines the length of the radius (R) which is necessary in order to bring together any given quality of agglomeration (M). The formula is as follows: Since

$$M = \pi R^2 \rho ,$$

$$R = \sqrt{\frac{M}{\pi \rho}} .$$

If we introduce this value into the equation of agglomeration, instead of the unknown radius of agglomeration, R, we get:

$$\sqrt{\frac{M}{\pi\rho}} = \frac{f(M)}{As} \ ,$$

150 or

$$f(M) = \frac{As}{\sqrt{\pi\rho}} \ \sqrt{M} \ .$$

The meaning of this formula may be interpreted as follows: Assuming that the locational weight of an industry (A), the rate level(s), and the density of industry (ρ) are known, we must insert into the formula that value of (M), i.e., that magnitude of agglomeration with which some value of $f(M) = \frac{As}{\sqrt{\pi\rho}} \ \sqrt{M}$, if we wish to know which of the possible values of a function of agglomeration $f(M)$ of an industry will become effective, or, in other words, if we wish to know what "scale" of agglomeration will actually become a factor for an industry when the conditions of agglomeration are known. This formula solves the problem. The Appendix shows in a simple manner how one may determine by diagram whether an effective M, which corresponds to these conditions, exists at all, and therefore whether any agglomeration will take place. It shows also how we can determine the value of M. The Appendix brings out further that if we know the size of the individual units of agglomeration we also know the number of centers of agglomeration which will arise in any area with a known total production. We get the number of centers of agglomeration by dividing the total quantity (G) by the value of the single agglomerations.

B. AGGLOMERATION AND LABOR ORIENTATION

What has been considered up to this point has applications to the influence of the forces of agglomeration upon industries oriented at the points of minimum costs of transportation. What will be the result if the forces of agglomeration are considered for industries oriented at the labor locations?

In order to analyze what happens in this case we shall do well to bear in mind that labor orientation is *one* form of deviation from the minimum point; agglomeration is another. When agglomerative forces appear in an industry oriented toward labor, there takes place a competition between the agglomerative deviation and the labor deviation, a struggle to create "locations of agglomeration,"[6] as compared with "labor locations," both being upon the foundations of the transportational groundwork. That one of the two forces which can offer the greater net economies over and above the transport orientation will be the victor.

It might at first thought be held that if we are to consider pure competition between agglom-locations and labor locations we should simply compare the net economies of agglomeration with the net economies of labor. But this is not the correct plan of attack, for a labor location *may,* and, as we already know, in most cases will, itself be a point of agglomeration—accidental agglomeration, we have called it. In connection with this accidental agglomeration economies of agglomeration will occur, and these economies will be precisely in accord with that measure of the function of economy which the agglomeration, according to its size, represents. These economies of agglomeration are separate and distinct from the economies of labor which attract industry toward that particular labor location. These economies of accidental agglomeration must therefore be added to the economies of labor if we wish to know the total amount of economies with which the labor locations compete with the purely transportational locations of agglomeration. The question then is, Which is larger, the economies of agglomeration at such agglom-locations, or the economies of labor plus the economies of accidental agglomeration at the labor locations?

[6] Hereafter occasionally referred to, for brevity's sake, as "agglom-locations." —EDITOR.

That means that all industries in the case of which accidental agglomeration at labor locations creates units of agglomeration as great as, or greater than, pure and independent agglomeration within the groundwork of transport orientation retain their labor orientation. For in such a case the economies due to this accidental agglomeration are greater than those which the agglom-locations can offer. Only those industries in the case of which the accidental agglomeration creates smaller units of agglomeration can *possibly* be otherwise oriented. But this will happen only when the loss of economies of agglomeration (resulting from the smallness of the unit) is not compensated for by the economies of labor which are offered by the labor locations.

It is necessary to keep two things in mind: First, industries with a highly developed labor orientation have a selection of labor locations due to the competition of such locations with one another. This very process of selection causes a considerable
152 accidental agglomeration at the more favorable labor locations; labor orientation itself shows a tendency to agglomerate. Second, the strength of this tendency to agglomerate depends upon three of the four factors upon which the strength of the independent tendency toward agglomeration depends. Locational weight, rates of transportation, and density of population affect labor orientation and its accompanying accidental agglomeration in the same way and just as much as they affect the competing independent or pure agglomeration. Consequently the fourth factor must differ very greatly indeed if it is to prevent the accidental agglomerations due to labor orientation from being so large that (with their economies of labor added) they do not overcome the independent agglomerations. Thus only industries which have a very high function of economy and a very weak labor orientation (and therefore very small accidental agglomerations at the labor locations) can be subject to a successful competition by pure and independent agglomeration. Independ-

ent agglomeration within the groundwork of transport orientation will not eliminate possible labor orientation in any large
proportion of industry.

On the contrary, the addition of economies of agglomeration
to labor economies will in important sections of industry (namely, in all cases in which a large agglomeration is due to labor orientation) strengthen labor orientation as compared with transport orientation. For wherever the accidental agglomerations
caused by the labor locations are larger than any possible independent agglomerations within the groundwork of transport orientation, the balance between the two is added to the economies
of the labor location as an economy not otherwise to be attained,
and this strengthens the power of attraction of the labor location.   153

We can make clear the significance of these influences by
the following example, chosen quite at random: Let us examine
the effect of the following function of economy for a series of
different industries:

No. of tons . .	100	200	300	400	500	600	700	800
Agglom-economy per ton . . .	1	4	6	7	7.5	7.75	7.82	7.88

What will be the effect of these economies of agglomeration
in industries with labor costs of $10, $50, $100, $200, $300 per
ton of product? Let us suppose that the labor economies at the
labor locations amount everywhere to 10 per cent. Let us suppose further that the accidental agglomerations which occur in
consequence of labor orientation amount to 50, 100, 200, 400,
800 tons. The unit of independent agglomeration within the
groundwork of transport orientation which can be attained in
accordance with the aforementioned function of economy is, of
course, the same in all the industries. Let us say it is 300 tons.

Then Table I will show how "independent agglomeration"
and "labor orientation" compare with each other for the various
industries.

We find three groups of industries: First, there are industries with a very small index of labor costs (of less than $50 per ton of product, Group 1) in which labor orientation is in itself so weak that it can only cause small deviations and concentrations. In this case we find a superiority of the independent agglomeration with its larger units of agglomeration and greater economies (5:1); such a state of affairs leads to orientation toward agglom-locations within the groundwork of transport orientation. However, such a type of change in location cannot

TABLE I

	A. Labor Orientation				B. Agglomeration		C. Extent to Which Economies of A Exceed Those of B
	Labor Cost per T. P.* (Dollars)	Economies per T. P. (Dollars)	Unit of Agglomeration (tons)	Total Economy per T. P. (Dollars)	Unit of Agglomeration (tons)	Economy per T. P. (Dollars)	
Group I....	10	1	50	1	300	5	− 4
Group II...	50	5	100	6	300	5	+ 1
	100	10	200	14	300	5	+ 9
Group III..	200	20	400	27	300	5	+22
	300	30	800	37.8	300	5	+32.8

*T. P. = ton of product.

bring with it any considerable movement, since industries which are subject to it have only been slightly deviated anyway. For that reason the movements of this group of industries cannot have very great practical significance.

154

Second, there are industries in which the units of independent agglomeration are larger, to be sure, than the units of agglomeration due to labor orientation (300 as compared with 100 and 200 tons, Group II). But the addition of these economies of accidental agglomeration to the labor economies make the total economies due to labor orientation larger than the economies due to independent agglomeration within the groundwork of transport orientation. Consequently the orientation toward labor locations takes place. (The ratios of economies are 6:5 and 14:5.)

And third, there are industries in which the units of agglomeration at labor locations are larger than those of the independent agglomeration (400 and 800 as compared with 300), and in which the addition of the economies of agglomeration cannot but strengthen the influence of the labor orientation. But granted that these additional economies (due to accidental agglomeration at the labor locations) strengthen labor orientation in general, how will they affect these industries within the groundwork of labor orientation?

In general we may say that they will lengthen the radius of attraction of the labor locations in much the same way as do the additional transport economies resulting from the replacement of material deposits (cf. *supra*, p. 113). We can measure the attracting power of each individual labor location only if we add to the labor economies which it offers, not only those economies resulting from the replacement of deposits, but also all the economies of accidental agglomeration which result from the total amount of production attracted.

This will mean, for the final orientation of the industry, first, that particles of the industry which would otherwise have remained oriented at the points of minimum cost of transportation will be deviated to the labor locations. Due to the additional economies of accidental agglomeration, labor orientation *as a whole* will prevail over transport orientation where it would not otherwise prevail. And it will mean, second, that *within* the labor orientation of the industries the strong labor locations (which by virtue of the large percentages of "cost reduction" which they can offer have already attracted the weaker ones to themselves) get a further "advantage," because the amount of production agglomerated in them represents units of agglomeration having economies of agglomeration. The radius of their attraction will consequently be further extended, and they will attract the production of weaker locations still farther away. The strength of labor orientation itself will be still more accentuated.

The essential effect which the tendencies to agglomeration will have on labor orientation is to increase its inherent tendencies toward concentration at a few locations.

SECTION III

REINTRODUCING THE REALITIES

If we now attempt to fit the results of the preceding paragraphs into the actual development of our economic system we do so because we wish to make the meaning of these results a bit more clear. But we are not concerned with an inductive verification of these results.

I. THE COEFFICIENT OF (VALUE ADDED THROUGH) MANUFACTURE (FORMKOEFFIZIENT)

For this purpose, and only for this purpose, we undertake to discuss the question: upon what qualities of a particular industry does the amount of its agglomeration depend, a question which we had eliminated for methodological reasons. This question causes us to examine more carefully those conditions of agglomeration which depend upon the nature of the particular industry.

There are two such conditions: the locational weight and the function of economy. Of these, the locational weight is a simple and obvious characteristic of every industry, and it contains no problem. We need not stop to discuss it.

But the function of economy is another matter. It is not something visible and tangible, but something quite indefinite; in its way it is merely the product of certain other, more deeply rooted characteristics of each industry. We cannot know by deduction upon which characteristics of a given industry this function of economy depends, and we cannot know by deduction how it depends upon them. Nor would it enable us to determine these characteristics more fully if we could render more explicit the mode by which this function of economy has been created, as has been attempted in the section entitled "Agglomerative Factors." To be sure, it is manifest that there is a connection be- 156 tween the function of economy, the agglomerative factors by which this function is created, and the character of the different industries; moreover, it is manifest that the two most essential groups of agglomerative factors (namely, the development of the labor organization and the development of the technical apparatus of each industry) will create a varying function of economy with varying units of agglomeration. But we cannot deduce definite rules which state what qualities of a given industry will determine the size of the units of agglomeration and their succession, in short, the shape of the function of economy.[8]

If we would secure a general idea of the function of economy and if we would understand its relation to the character of industries we must start from quite another consideration. Only industries with products whose value is to a large degree a result of the industrial (or formative) process itself can possibly have large units of agglomeration with resultant high percentages of compressible[9] costs—an effective function of economy. We may say that such industries show a high "value added through manufacture" *(Formwert)*.[10] The reason why only industries with such a high value added through manufacture will have an effective function of economy is simple. We know it already from the analogous reasoning about the labor value and the index of labor cost.[11] There we said that only where high labor costs per ton of product exist can considerable labor economies per ton of product be effected; and the same consideration holds good for man-

[8] Cf. here the Mathematical Appendix, below.—EDITOR.

[9] Cf. *supra*, p. 106.—EDITOR.

[10] The meaning of this term *Formwert* is best rendered by "value added by manufacture." But since manufacturing is the process of giving "form" to coarse materials, "form-value" may not be an impossible term. A. Predöhl uses it. Cf. *Journal of Political Economy*, XXXVI, 371 ff. Moreover, there is the already established term *form-utility*.—EDITOR.

[11] Cf. *supra*, p. 107.

ufacturing costs in general, including the costs of machinery, etc. These manufacturing costs, speaking generally, appear in the value added through manufacture of a product. They can show high indices of economy through high percentages of compressibility, only provided the costs themselves are high. These general manufacturing costs are the very ones which the effective elaboration of the working force and of the technical apparatus (the two most important groups of agglomerative factors) tend to reduce. They represent the most essential *object of cost reduction* through agglomeration. But even the elaboration of the working force and of the technical apparatus creates, first, large units of agglomeration, and second, high percentages of compression of the large units as compared with the small units; these two developments will be of moment for the orientation of an industry only provided the value added through manufacture of that industry per ton of its product is high. We shall call this value added through manufacture per ton of product the *index of value added through manufacture* of that particular industry or simply 157 *index of manufacture*. If that index rises, equal percentages of cost reduction of equal units represent greater economies per ton of product, and the corresponding critical isodapanes of the locational figures will be farther extended, the attracting force of the unit of agglomeration will increase, etc.

To the extent to which this index of value added through manufacture is the object of all attempts to reduce cost through agglomeration—and we have noted that the two most important groups of agglomerative factors work in that way—this index affords us a rod for measuring the effective tendency toward agglomeration of industries. It must be said, however, that this measuring rod does not tell us anything final concerning the actual trend toward agglomeration of a particular industry, and it does not tell us its actual function of economy; it only outlines the effective tendency toward agglomeration. For this measuring rod does not point out which reductions exist in reality (due

to the elaboration of the working force and of technical apparatus), nor does it tell what is the order of succession of the units
of agglomeration. But since we do not have clear knowledge
concerning the dependence of the function of economy and of
the virtual agglomeration of industries upon the general character of these industries, we may just as well use the measuring
rod which is at hand. This being true, we shall do well to examine this index of value added through manufacture a bit more
carefully, and to relate it to the second general characteristic of
the industries, their locational weight.

The value added through manufacture of an industry has two
main constituent factors: the labor costs expressed in wages
and salaries, and the costs of machinery, the latter to be interpreted in their widest sense, as including interest and amortization of fixed capital and cost of power. We shall distinguish
these two as "value added through labor" and "value added
through machines." Now it is of the greatest importance (if we
are to use the index of manufacture as a measuring rod of agglomeration) to know in what proportion those two factors enter
into that index. To the extent to which the value added through
manufacture results from machines, a factor curbing agglomeration appears. This factor is the increasing use of fuel, which
means a rising material index of the particular industry. We can 158
say that value added through labor is a pure factor of agglomeration, while the factor of value added through machines is to a
large extent paralyzed by a rising material index. This fact does
not prevent us from using the value added through manufacture
of an industry as a virtual measuring rod of its agglomeration, if
only we do not forget to take into equal consideration the second
measuring rod which is contained in the material index and the
locational weight. This necessity of keeping both rods in mind
suggests that we relate the notion of the value added through
manufacture to that of the locational weight and create a connecting concept out of the index of manufacture and of the loca-

tional weight, just as we have previously done in the case of the index of labor costs and of locational weight for our analysis of labor orientation.[12] This is possible by relating the index of manufacture, not to the ton of product, but to the total weight which has to be transported—the "locational ton." In analogy to the term "labor coefficient" used earlier, we shall suggest the term "coefficient of manufacture" in order to describe the value added through manufacture per locational ton. Now we can formulate: *industries with high coefficient of manufacture show strong tendencies to agglomerate; industries with low coefficient of manufacture show weak tendencies to agglomerate; and these tendencies are inherent in their nature.* This formula is comparatively simple, but it must be remembered that a considerable number of assumptions have been made in the process of constructing it.

2. FORMS OF AGGLOMERATION IN REALITY

Let us ask next what will be the practical consequences of this agglomeration whose general rules we have just outlined and whose underlying forces we have characterized in detail. In what forms shall we find it in reality?

It will be remembered that agglomeration may influence both transport-oriented industries and labor-oriented industries. It influences labor-oriented industries simply by increasing their contraction of labor locations (according to rules we have already discussed). Only industries with a very weak tendency to labor orientation show pure and independent orientation within the groundwork of transport orientation instead of showing labor orientation.

It will also be remembered that considerable technical agglomeration occurs only in connection with a high coefficient of manufacture, and this coefficient is composed of value added through labor and through machines. But since value added

---

[12] Cf. *supra*, p. 110.—EDITOR.

through machines is always connected with considerable consumption of material (coal), such value can hardly cause the coefficient to be a high one on account of the resulting high locational weight, unless a considerable increase in the consumption of human labor (value added through labor) occurs at the same time. Consequently industries with a high coefficient of labor will show the strongest tendencies of agglomeration—as long and in so far as machines mean considerable consumption of material. But these industries are strongly labor-oriented and therefore already agglomerated.

The main consequence of technical agglomeration will, under present conditions, be found to be a strengthening of labor orientation. The other consequence, that of altering the transport orientation by creating independent agglomerations, is insignificant in comparison. For in the case of this latter consequence the agglomerating tendency operates generally with a low coefficient of manufacture, and is therefore itself not as strong as in labor-oriented industries.

Two results follow which are important for our examination of reality later on:

First, we shall find the transport-oriented industries somewhat concentrated, and concentrated not very far away from their points of smallest costs of transportation.

Second, wherever we encounter an industry which deviates considerably from its transport orientation we shall be safe in assuming, in case of doubt, that it is an industry oriented toward labor. These results will considerably facilitate our later analysis of the facts, for they enable us to separate industries into two great groups: transport-oriented and labor-oriented industries. This makes it possible for us to approach reality, bearing in mind the simple issue upon which this distinction is based, and to neglect (at least in preliminary studies) all more detailed distinctions.

Which tendencies of development shall we find upon closer examination to operate upon agglomeration in actual life? We know the different conditions of agglomeration from our analysis; they are density of population, rates of transportation, and coefficient of manufacture.

The tendencies and the significance of the first two conditions are clear. It is obvious that rising density of population and declining costs of transportation are evolutionary trends of modern times. They of necessity continuously increase agglomeration. The critical isodapanes of the locational figures are incessantly extended by declining costs of transportation, and this creates effective segments of higher units of agglomeration; quantities of production sufficient for higher units of agglomeration are incessantly created by the increasing density of the population, and this at the same time pushes the locational figures closer together. It is hardly necessary, therefore, to take more time and space for the discussion of these tendencies of development.

But the significance of a change in the conditions which are deeply rooted in the general character of a given industry is not quite as obvious. Such deep-rooted conditions are implied by the coefficient of manufacture, which contains value added through manufacture and locational weight. These conditions also lead in the direction of agglomeration, but not without certain curbing influences becoming effective.

On the one hand the value added through manufacture becomes a cause of considerable agglomeration. For the elaboration of the working force and of technical apparatus during the eighteenth and nineteenth centuries meant, as is well known, the creation of increasingly large frameworks of industrial production. It meant, consequently, the creation of higher units of agglomeration and of more extensive reductions (compressions) of the index of manufacture of various industries in cases in which these higher units of agglomeration become effective. To express these observations in the terms of our theory, this development of organization and technique has given to the value added through manufacture of the various industries that significance which it was necessary for it to have if it was to be utilized in the creation of those high and effective units of agglomeration under whose influence these industries have been ever since. In this way the development of organization and technique has doubtless had an enormous agglomerative effect. 161

On the other hand this development has caused forces to appear which curb these agglomerative tendencies. It has done so by its influence upon the consumption of materials, which consumption in turn influences the locational weight. The creation of those new big frameworks of industrial production has meant to a large extent the replacement of manual labor by mechanical apparatus, and it has meant the replacement of value added through labor by value added through machines. In consequence of all this the weights which must be moved for production are increased, the isodapanes around the locational figures are contracted, and there is an increase of the resistance which the high units of agglomeration have to overcome in order to come into existence at all.

The tendencies of modern development have, on the one hand, given to the coefficient of manufacture a considerably increased significance so far as agglomeration is concerned; but they have, on the other hand, reduced the revolutionary effect of these new units of agglomeration by reducing this same coefficient of manufacture (due to a process of "materialization" of production).

We must keep all these facts in mind if we would understand the part played by agglomerating tendencies in the industrial revolution of the eighteenth and nineteenth centuries. It is obvious from the viewpoint of this part of our theory that the change from handicraft to factory production (which constitutes the most important aspect of this revolution) is a gigantic process of agglomeration. Previous to this development even those parts of production which (due to high coefficients of manufacture) were in themselves capable of considerable agglomeration had remained distributed in individual producing units, which were mostly situated at the places of consumption, because of the low prevailing material index, as has been pointed 162 out. For all these industries the discovery of the fact that their index of manufacture was capable of great reductions within new, highly developed frameworks of production meant their gradual readjustment—the revolution before referred to. This revolution does not appear in its full severity until the rapid rise of population is accompanied by an equally rapid decline of the transportation rates during the nineteenth century. But what will take the place of the old crafts, how far agglomeration will extend, what magnitude of agglomerative units will be developed, at what points the centers of agglomeration will be fixed—all these matters depend quite considerably upon how the material index of industries is changed by the development of technique and organization in these industries. In other words, these matters depend upon to what extent their locational weight increases and their coefficient of manufacture decreases; to what extent the coal deposits enter in; and how far the otherwise prevailing agglomeration at the most advantageous labor locations will thus be interfered with by an agglomeration resting upon transport orientation. All these problems appear in reality as a competition of the labor locations with the coal deposits. The outcome is a selection of the labor locations, with, however, some attention to their proximity to coal deposits. But the inductive part[13] will show that we have usually overestimated the extent to which agglomeration at the coal deposits was necessary; by

[13] Not published. Cf. instead Alfred Weber's contribution to the *Grundriss der Sozialökonomik,* Vol. VI, "Industrielle Standortslehre (Allgemeine und kapitalistische Theorie des Standortes)."—EDITOR.

far the more important part of the effectiveness of modern agglomerative units was the increased concentration of industries
at the labor locations, and this was coming anyway. It will also
show that the concentration of industries at the coal deposits
represents to a large extent a reorientation of industries which
had already been oriented toward material deposits; it is true
that they were different and more widely distributed deposits.
All this agglomeration is accidental from the point of our theory;
it is not technically necessary. Still, we shall find to how large
an extent the new agglomeration at favorable labor locations has
been influenced by the increased emphasis upon the material
aspect of production, and how this fact has influenced, not only
the emergence of the attracting labor locations, but also the extent of agglomeration at these labor locations. It will become
apparent in this connection that only those industries have
reached the highest stages of "technical" agglomeration in which
the change of the proportion between value added through machines and value added through labor does not exceed a certain
maximum.

163

But particularly will this inductive treatment[14] show that
the problem of agglomeration is not exhausted by treating that
accidental agglomeration at extensive material deposits, particularly coal deposits, and not even by treating that technically
necessary agglomeration at labor locations; there exist over and
above these considerations, and exceeding them by far, kinds of
"social agglomeration." This type of agglomeration develops at
the labor locations (largely without any technical necessity)
upon the foundation of certain rules of agglomeration of human
labor. It will be one of the main tasks of the inductive treatment just referred to to show, first, in which particular way this
social agglomeration with its creation of industrial and metropolitan districts develops on top of the simpler and more limited

[14] Cf. the last footnote.—EDITOR.

forms of agglomeration which we have analyzed in the foregoing paragraphs. We shall need to show, second, that this type of
agglomeration does not evolve from causes which belong to a
system of "pure" economics (which we have discussed previously) but that it is the consequence of quite different factors
which are rooted in the particular social structure of the modern
economic system. This type of agglomeration may disappear if
164 the social structure to which it belongs disappears.[15]

[15] This point is more or less well brought out by a number of monographs
published since Alfred Weber's theory appeared. Cf. the series of studies edited
by himself, Alfred Weber, *Ueber den Standort der Industrien II. Teil: Die
deutsche Industrie seit 1860* beginning with Otto Schlier, "Der deutsche Industrie-
körper seit 1860" (1922). For an analysis of recent changes Edgar Salin, "Stan-
dortsverschiebungen der deutschen Volkswirtschaft" (in: *Strukturwandlungen
der deutschen Volkswirtschaft* [1928] edited by Bernhard Harms) should be consulted. Particularly interesting to the American student are two recent monographs by Andreas Predöhl in the *Weltwirtschaftliches Archiv*, "Die Standorte
der amerikanischen Eisen- und Stahlindustrie" (1928) and "Die Südwanderung
der amerikanischen Baumwollindustrie" (1929). Finally attention may be called
to Hans Ritschl, "Reine und historische Dynamik des Standorts der Erzeugungszweige" in *Schmollers Jahrbuch* (1927), and Joh. J. Haurath, "Zum Problem der
hypothetischen und konkreten Standortsbedingungen. Dargelegt am Beispiel der
Grosschlachterei in den Niederlanden," in *Weltwirtschaftliches Archiv* (1926).—
EDITOR.

CHAPTER VI

THE TOTAL ORIENTATION

We have so far built up our theory on the assumption that the activity connected with the productive and distributive process of an industry is a uniform and indivisible thing which can only as a whole be drawn to and from the material deposits and the place of consumption by locational forces, and which goes on entirely independent of the activities of other industries. But this indivisibility of the productive process and its independence of the productive processes of other industries do not in fact exist.

We must now take the following facts into account: First, the productive process of almost every industry consists of diverse parts, which are technically independent of one another and can, therefore, be undertaken at different places. We may well think of the productive process as a heap of little balls which have been rolled together at one place by the (dynamics of the) locational factors we have discussed, but which may be redistributed by those factors. Second, the forces which move those little balls (those parts of the productive process) are not confined within a particular productive process; rather they are aspects of a complex of larger forces resulting from the intertwining of the different parts of industrial production of a country. We shall designate the first set of facts as the organization of the stages of a given productive process or enterprise (*Produktionsstufengliederung*), and the second set as the interlacing (*Ineinandergreifen*) of the independent productive processes.   165

SECTION I

THE ORGANIZATION OF THE STAGES OF A GIVEN PRODUCTIVE
PROCESS

A. THE STAGES OF PRODUCTION AND TRANSPORT ORIENTATION

Let us suppose that an industry is influenced only by cost of transportation, and let us neglect all the deviating influence of labor and agglomeration. What, given such assumptions, does it mean that the productive process does not need to be entirely performed at one location, but may be split into a number of parts which may be completed at different locations?

The only cause which could lead to an actual split and to a resultant transfer of the parts to different locations would obviously be that some ton-miles would be saved in the process. For the reduction of these ton-miles to a minimum is the sole principle regulating transport orientation—the principle which produces the locations we have previously discussed. We must accordingly consider whether the ton-miles[1] are lowered if the locations of the stages or parts of production are separated. If we find that they are lowered, we shall need to determine where the transport locations of the split industry will be situated.

I

Let us take a simple case, an enterprise with three material deposits and one which is capable of being split, technologically speaking, into two stages. In the first stage two materials are combined into a half-finished product (*Halbfabrikat*); in the second stage this half-finished product is combined with the third material into the final product. Figure 33 shows where the location *P* of the unsplit production would be situated according to our earlier locational rules, assuming certain proportions of the weight of materials outside and inside the final product. Let

[1] We shall have to imagine these ton-miles as permeating the entire productive process, of course.

us suppose that possible locations of the split production would be in P_1 and P_2; P_1 for the first stage and P_2 for the second stage. What will be the result if the splitting occurs? Obviously, we shall have two locational figures with three roots instead of one figure with four roots. The first locational figure is $M_1M_2P_2$; it is rooted in the two material deposits of the first stage of production and the place of production of the second stage of production which is also, obviously enough, the place of consumption of the first stage. The second locational figure is M_3P_1C;

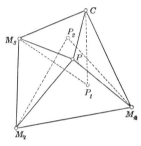

FIG. 33

it is rooted in the place of production of the first stage, and in the location of the additional material deposits, and in the place of consumption of the final product. P_1, the location of the first stage of production is the point of minimum costs of transportation,[2] or the minimum point, as we have called it, of the first locational figure. P_2, the location of the second stage, is the minimum point of the second figure. Thus the problem of the "where" of the locations of stages of production appears to be one which falls within the realm of our analysis. It involves determining the locations of the corner-points of new locational figures. These corner points are the locations of the various stages of production. If we succeed in finding these corner-points, our problem is solved, since these corner-points are the locations of split processes of production. The mathematical

[2] Cf. *supra*, p. 53.—EDITOR.

problem involved is solved in Appendix I, §§ 8–11.[3] We shall make use of that solution at this point. But let us first see whether 167 we can learn from the foregoing *when* this split will occur.

To attack this problem we must alter our question. The problem is not, when does such a split occur? but when does it *not* occur? When does production remain at a single location? If we look at our figures again, we shall see at once that the occurrence of a single location is a particular case among the many possible locations of the separable stages of the process of production. This case is realized when in the locational figure of the first stage the place of production coincides with the place of consumption; and when in the locational figure of the second stage the place of production coincides with the place of production (the deposit) of the unfinished product made in the first stage. If such coincidence occurs, the two locations coincide. In all other cases they lie apart. The problem as to when a split of the location will occur resolves itself into the following question: Under what particular condition does this coincidence of the sites of the separate stages of production occur? We may consider this question first with reference to an enterprise which can be split into two stages only.

One is inclined at first blush to suggest that this coincidence can occur only in case the site of the first stage of production is located (because of the proportions of its weights) at the place of consumption, and only if, furthermore, the place of production of the second stage is (also due to the proportion of its weights) situated at the deposit of the unfinished product of the first stage. If this were true, the non-occurrence of a split would be a very rare exception (assuming that the split were at all possible on technical grounds); and practically all productive processes having several technical stages would have different locations for these stages. But not quite so many conditions need to be fulfilled. It is sufficient either that the production of

---

[3] Cf. *infra*, p. 234.—EDITOR.

the first stage is located at the place of consumption or that the production of the second stage is located at the deposit of the unfinished product. For if, upon the one hand, the production of the first stage is located at the place of consumption, then it will follow *any* location of the second stage which is determined by the proportions of weight within the second locational figure. It will, for example, go to the place of consumption of the second stage, or to one of the material deposits or to any intermediate position. The fact that it will thus follow of course makes 168 the two locations coincident. And if, upon the other hand, the location of the second stage is situated at the deposit of the unfinished product, the location of the second stage will follow the location of the unfinished product anywhere. It will, for example, go to the original material deposits or to any intermediate position. In this case also the two locations are of course coincident.

It is accordingly only necessary that the conditions (weight proportions) *either* in the first *or* in the second stage be such that the location is bound to follow the location of the other stage, and the split will not take place. The following consideration will indicate, however, how frequently this split will take place, provided it is technically feasible. In order for the production of the second stage to run after the location of the first, it is necessary for the unfinished product to enter into the second stage with a locational weight which is at least equal to the sum of the weight of the future product and of the weights of the added materials—all this in accordance with our previous rules. This means that the product will have to lose considerable weight during the second stage. But the second and later stages of industrial productive processes are usually concerned with the working up of pure materials, with little elimination of waste materials *(Materialrückstände)*. These stages will therefore very seldom have such a location unless they are oriented toward coal deposits. So much for that. On the other hand, the production of the first stage must lie at the place of consumption if it is to follow the production of the second stage. This means that there must be no loss of material during the first stage, or at least only as much as will be compensated by the addition of ubiquities. This also will be very rare, since the first stage of industrial production is commonly concerned with bringing into existence the pure material, a process which calls for the elimination of the waste materials. We conclude, then, in either case that the conditions leading to the coinciding of the two locations will not be frequent. We may say, even on the basis of this preliminary

169 analysis: *Single location of production will be the exception and a split of production into several locations will be the rule for productive processes which can technically be split.*

2 [4]

Our next question is: Where will the locations of the productive stages be when production is split? Our answer will make it possible further to elaborate upon the question as to when such splitting will occur.

The locations of the stages it will be remembered, can be fixed as the corner points of the new locational figures in which the split production is carried on. We know the corresponding figures which have to be constructed within these locational figures according to the general locational rules. This is the key by which the unknown corners are discovered, as is shown in Appendix I, § 11.[5] These unknown corners are the locations of the stages of production. I refer to the result found in the Appendix, and I shall here apply it only to a few important cases.

[4] The reader will find quite tiring the reasoning employed in this and the following parts of this section. It is really not intended for those who wish to get the general trend of the main argument; they may omit it. But scientific precision requires that this analysis be undertaken; for it is necessary to show to what extent the mathematical solutions based upon our theory cover the manifold phenomena and problems of reality.

[5] Cf. p. 236, *infra.*—EDITOR.

Let us suppose that the productive process splits into stages —two at first, each of which combines two materials. The locational figures for these stages would obviously be triangles. Since we know the weight triangles of "the two locational figures with one unknown corner," we know the circles upon which the two unknown corners, the two locations, will lie. (They are the two circles over M_1M_2 and M_3C of the following figure.) We know, further, that the two locations will lie upon one straight

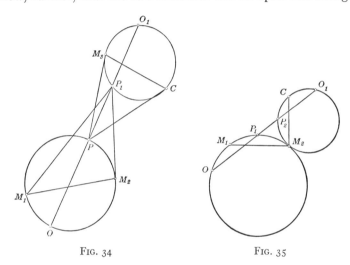

FIG. 34   FIG. 35

line (cf. Appendix I, §§ 9 and 11) which connects two easily constructed points of the two circles (at the points O and O_1 of Figure 34). The points where this line intersects with the circles are the locations of the split production (P and P_1 of the adjoining figure). It will be seen at once that this simple rule is generally applicable.

Let us now assume a productive process based upon two materials so that the entire process will be carried through within one locational figure, and let us assume that it is possible to split the process so that the first stage of production combines the two materials, while the second stage uses one of the ma-

terials (for example, coal) again in connection with the unfinished product, thus completing the product. The diagram which
will give us the location of the two stages is simple enough (cf.
foregoing Figure 35). The circle over the material deposits with
the angle of the first weight triangle as its peripheral angle will be
the general focus of the first location; while the circle with the
analogous angle of the second weight triangle over the second
material deposit and the place of consumption will be the general
locus of the second location. The points O and O_1 situated upon
the circles have to be determined next.[6] The two points at which

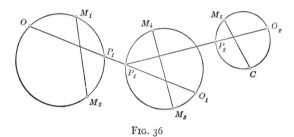

FIG. 36

the straight line connecting them intersects the circles are the
two locations, P_1 and P_2.

Let us next assume a productive process based upon five materials, it being a process which might technically be split into
three stages. The first stage combines the first two materials;
the second stage combines the product of the first with two more
materials; and finally the third stage combines the product of
the second stage with the fifth and last material into the final
product.

The diagram showing how the locations of these stages may
be determined is given in Figure 36.

In principle the diagram of the case when the production is
split into parallel instead of successive stages is quite similar.
Let us take for example car manufacturing. Here the metal

[6] Cf. Appendix, p. 237, *infra.*—EDITOR.

parts are worked up into unfinished products in steel foundries and metal works; other parts are worked up in wood manufacturing processes; and still others are worked up into half-finished products in sundry other establishments and are then united in the final process. The diagram of the productive process and of the locations of its stages appears in Figure 37. In short, we have found a general solution. There is just one significant limitation: our solution holds good only for stages of production which combine two materials only. Such stages have

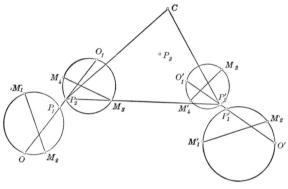

FIG. 37

triangles for their locational figures. This limitation is regrettable in principle, but it is not as important as it might seem. For it will seldom occur that stages of production which involve complicated processes of combination will follow each other. And 172 only where several such complicated stages of production follow one another will there be failure to determine their location by the use of the expedients we have developed thus far. In all other cases we shall always be able to construct the circles upon which the locations of the simpler stages of production lie (cf. the adjoining Figure 38 in which M_4C shows this circle for such an adjoining simple stage of production. This makes it possible to find the line $(P_1-P'_1)$ upon which the location of the more complicated preceding stage of production will lie. We can find this line by using the frame of Varignon[7] for the purpose of moving one corner of the more complicated locational figure along the circle of the location of the adjoining stage in production). Through this method we have a fairly far-reaching general way of determining both locations. A special construction for particular cases can of course be made with the expedients of higher mathematics, even if the complications are much greater. But we shall limit ourselves to the finding of general rules.

3

Another aspect of the foregoing conclusions is of interest here. The simple diagram by which we can generally determine

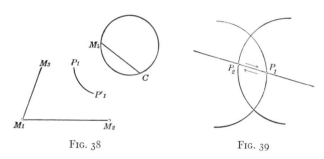

FIG. 38   FIG. 39

the locations of split production also affords us a more precise answer for the question as to *when* this split will occur. The mathematical analysis of the Appendix (cf. Appendix I, § 11) shows that the split will not occur, if the circles determining the locations of the stages intersect and if at the same time the determining straight line goes through that segment.

But this is not theoretically significant, applying as it does 173 only to certain geographical situations; rather, it is the consequence of an accidental proximity of the material deposits of the different stages. Obviously, no split will take place when the intersecting point of the determining straight line is situated in

[7] Cf. Appendix, p. 229.—EDITOR.

the common segment; for the intersecting points go beyond each other (cf. the foregoing Figure 39). The elements of two stages of production remain next to each other after having met. A common location within the segment is the result.

4

It is quite interesting that the construction we discussed before suffices for determining the locations even if the splitting of the productive process involves a change of the material deposits because of the employment of new deposits. Such replacement of old deposits by new ones will always occur when the material deposits of the last stages are situated nearer the place of consumption, or when material deposits of the first stages are situated nearer the deposits of the main materials— nearer than is true of the deposits which would be most advantageous within the locational figure of the unsplit production. The adjoining Figure 40 shows what will happen in these cases. The deposit M'_2 has been substituted in the first stage, while the deposit M'_3 has been substituted in the second stage, because these deposits are more advantageous for the split production than M_2 and M_3, which were most advantageous for the unsplit production. One can see at a glance that the finding of the loca- 174 tions of the separate stages of production is not complicated by these substitutions. We construct in accordance with our former rules, using the new deposits as bases.

This is true even if a material which was formerly supplied for the unsplit production by one deposit is now brought into the production of the different stages from different deposits, inasmuch as it enters into the production at several stages. A frequent example is coal. The splitting of production simply necessitates the substitution of these different deposits, which then become the basis of our constructions, as outlined before. No particular difficulties ensue from that.

Let us suppose next that an industry is oriented toward labor in its productive process or in parts of it. What will be the effect if such an industry is split up and oriented at the locations of the stages of production?

If that industry is already dissolved into stages of production by transport orientation (which is after all the basis of

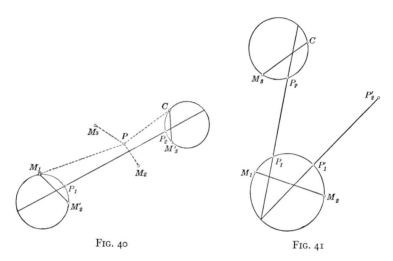

FIG. 40   FIG. 41

labor orientation) the location of each stage may then be regarded as the location of a separate process of production. Location will be influenced by the labor locations of the particular stage according to the rules which we know already. Deviation will occur if the labor location lies inside the critical isodapane of the respective locational figure of the stage, etc. And if deviation does take place, the deviation point is substituted for the transport location. By becoming the location of its particular stage this deviation point will influence the locational figures of the adjoining stages. The construction of the locations of the stages will in consequence be simplified; for a fixed and determined corner will be substituted in the locational figure of the stage for an unknown corner which must be found by construction.

The labor location will consequently alter, not only the location of its own stage, but also the locations of the stages preceding and following. For these are not fixed; they are influenced mutually, each by every other. The locations of the 175 adjoining stages will orient themselves in accordance with the labor location between them, as is indicated in the foregoing Figure 41 which illustrates a productive process having two stages, in which the labor deviation influences the second stage. Due to this deviation, some cost of transportation will be saved ($P'_1P'_2$ is shorter than $P_1P'_2$, which otherwise would have had to be used). This circumstance increases the possibilities of deviation somewhat beyond the scope which could be inferred from the critical isodapane around the locational figure of that stage.

I do not believe it is necessary to discuss further the small alteration which this involves. It is more important to note that in this case also former material deposits may be replaced by others more favorably located.[8] In a split production this may mean the elimination of locations of entire stages of production and their replacement by locations which are based upon entirely different material deposits which happen to be nearer the attracting labor locations. Under certain circumstances this may mean a considerable revolution in the entire set of locations of the stages of production—all due to the labor deviation of just one stage. But this replacement of material deposits does not, of course, create any difficulties of construction. Theoretically its effect is of course exactly the same as that of replacing material deposits within an unsplit productive process: the attracting force of the labor locations will be strengthened in exact proportion to the savings of costs of transportation which result from such replacements.

[8] Cf. *supra*, p. 113 f.—EDITOR.

We ought to mention, finally, that labor deviation itself may cause productive processes to split by causing the deviation of some location which had previously followed the location of the adjoining stage. This may be an effect of labor deviation which is superficially quite striking, but it does not contain any theoretical problem.

C. THE STAGES OF PRODUCTION AND AGGLOMERATION

On the basis of what has been said we may determine what it will mean if we include the factors of agglomeration in our considerations. We are dealing in principle with the same problems which we encountered when dealing with the deviations caused by labor orientation.

A separate function of agglomeration exists for every stage of production and it influences that stage separately. This influence will be exerted according to the general rules of agglomeration.[9] The creation of centers of agglomeration—as is well known—is subject to the creation of segments of the sets of isodapanes of the locational figures of the stages of production which have possibilities of agglomeration.

As in the case of labor deviation, a problem is created by the fact that wherever agglomeration actually occurs there may occur also a deviation of the locations of those stages of production which precede and which follow the stage within which agglomeration has occurred. But what has been said in dealing with this problem in the case of labor deviation holds true also for the case of agglomerative deviation, *mutatis mutandis*. However, this problem will be of much smaller significance than the one created by the replacement of those material deposits which are more unfavorably situated than hitherto unused material deposits lying much nearer the new location created by agglomeration. This is due to the fact that the strengthening of the attracting force of the deviation points is much more important.

[9] Cf. *infra*, p. 246.—EDITOR.

The most important problem which remains over and above those questions which we encountered in the case of labor deviation consists in the fact that the "where" of the point of agglomeration will be altered when the locational figures upon which this point of agglomeration is based are altered. But we have seen before[10] that the center of agglomeration shifts also when the productive process is not split. It will be remembered that this is due to the elimination of bad material deposits. What has been said there holds true here: the center of agglomeration remains determined by the location of the places of consumption and of the most advantageous material deposits, and does not shift very much. Consequently no further discussion of this 177 problem is needed.

This brings us to the end of our theoretical analysis of the nature of orientation as related to the possible stages of a given productive process. Following our usual procedure, our next question is: upon what conditions does this nature of orientation within the productive process depend, and how will the known changes of reality affect it?

D. REINTRODUCING THE REALITIES

I. GENERAL OBSERVATIONS

The fact that the locations of an industry are split is the upshot of its technical nature. The splitting seems therefore to depend solely upon the general characteristics of that industry and to be entirely independent of environmental conditions such as the level of transportation costs and the density of population. Indeed, it is determined by the nature of the productive process; and any changes in that nature will also change the nature of the split. Speaking more precisely, the technical nature of the productive process of an industry and the manner in which it is handled will determine whether that productive process has technically independent parts and what materials are available

[10] Cf. p. 141, *supra*.—EDITOR.

for each of these parts. It will further determine how the independence of the parts and the availability of materials are affected by the general economic development. The several locational figures are created and altered by these facts.

We may say in general terms that the splitting of an industry is facilitated when more materials are used and when these additional materials are used in several independent stages of production. No necessity to split on the basis of rates of transportation will exist for an industry which has a whole series of independent stages of production, of which however only the first stage involves combining several materials, while all the later stages involve only the additional application of labor. The picture in this case will show the location of the first stage near the materials, while the location of all the remaining stages will be somewhere along the way between the location of the first stage and the place of final consumption. As a matter of fact, these remaining locations will almost always be situated at the place of consumption, due to advantages of the market (*Absatz*). In spite of the great number of possible independent stages of production, the productive process will be split into only two stages, which we may call the stage of materials and the stage of consumption. We find this as the typical picture in all those older and simpler industries which are carried on without the use of coal in the higher stages. But if materials enter into one or more of the later stages of production, independent locational figures and fixed independent locations will come into existence. It should be noted, however, that only the entrance of weight materials, such as coal and coarse materials, will really prolong the series of locations. For the entrance of a pure material or of an ubiquity has the effect of pushing the production toward the place of consumption, and consequently does not alter the original picture. The use of coal in the higher stages of production is of necessity the main factor through which the modern development stimulates the splitting of production—if it does so at all.

But it would be a mistake to say that the tendency of a given industry to split increases in proportion to the loss of weight of raw materials within the higher or later stages of its production. For even the slightest loss of weight of an entering material creates the basis for an independent stage of production with a separate location, as far as cost of transportation is involved. The magnitude of this loss of weight does not in principle affect this situation in the least. What it does determine is the extent to which the location of that stage of production will be attracted by the deposit of the material involved. If the material entering the higher stages of production is coal, this attraction may be so strong as to reunite the separate stages at the coal deposit.

These few sentences concerning the extent to which the splitting of production depends upon the extent to which materials enter into the productive process do not exhaust the discussion of the conditions surrounding this splitting process. This splitting will be determined by the nature of the productive process only to the extent that transportation costs enter. But we have seen that splits may also be caused by deviation due to labor or to agglomeration.[11] To the extent to which these devia- 179 tions are possible and occurring, splits are dependent upon the conditions to which these two kinds of orientation are subject. Splitting of these parts of the productive process which have not formerly been separated is dependent particularly upon costs of transportation and density of population, since these two factors as environmental conditions codetermine labor orientation and agglomerative orientation. For example, the manufacture of linen clothes *(Wäsche)*, which was formerly deviated to certain large labor locations, experiences at the present time a split which is moving the intermediate stage of embroidering such cloth (for the German manufacture) as far as Madeira.[12] It is obvious that the split which has occurred in this instance is due

[11] Cf. *supra*, pp. 184 f., 186 f.
[12] Written in 1909.—EDITOR.

partly to the lowering of costs of transportation, a decisive factor. We must say a few words regarding these general tendencies.

2. TENDENCIES OF ACTUAL DEVELOPMENT

We have said before that the technical nature of the productive process and its execution will fundamentally determine whether the various groups of industries are organized into stages of production, and if so, in what manner. Nothing could be more erroneous than to assume that the *technical* differentiation of the medieval trades, from which we shall start in our analysis of actual development, was inconsiderable. There existed that structure of technical stages of production which resulted as a matter of course from the traditional tools which have been the common property of Euro-Asiatic civilizations (*vorderasiatisch-europäischer Kulturkreis*). These tools split the productive process into about as many technically independent parts as it can conceivably contain. For these tools became so specialized that they made it impossible to control more than a very small part of the productive process, and they consequently tore it to pieces technically. The productive process through which the metals, wood, leather, and the fibers, as well as most food materials, had to pass was always long and had many independent stages. It is true, however, that two things are typical of the medieval economic system. First, the economic organization which was superimposed on this technically split production was not split to any considerable extent. The number of successive stages of production which achieved economically independent organization remained small.[13] There were seldom more than two or three. Second, even those stages of production which had become economically independent generally remained together at the place of consumption. No local splits into locations of the stages of production followed the inconsiderable

---

[13] Cf. regarding this point the well-known article of Bücher, "Gewerbe," in the *Handwörterbuch der Staatswissenschaften,* Vol. III.

economic splits of production. It is well known that the preven-
tion of too numerous successive stages of production (as well as
their retention at the market of the town) was a necessary part
of the economic policies of medieval towns.

But what made possible these policies of grouping all the
technically independent parts of production around the market
of the town? Obviously the fact that the technical potentialities
for splitting production did not yet *force* production to split geographically. All these individual and separate parts of the productive processes were largely oriented toward consumption,
just as we found the inseparable units of medieval crafts oriented
toward consumption.

To the extent to which they were *not* oriented toward consumption, the policies adopted for the purpose of concentrating
industries within the town limits *failed*. Indeed, we can completely understand the development of the larger part of medieval rural trades *(Landgewerbe)* only if we conceive of these
trades as "stages of production." The trade policies of the towns
failed with regard to these rural trades because these policies
could not overcome the locational rules according to which these
stages were oriented toward their materials and not toward consumption. Consequently the concentrating policies of the towns
never attempt to inclose within the town walls the foundries;
these have always been oriented toward the material deposits.
Similarly, the towns did not attempt to draw to themselves the
growing glassworks; these were oriented toward the fuel materials. And when later (since the fourteenth century) water power
is increasingly introduced into production and thereby increases
the materialization[14] of initial and intermediate stages of production, then these stages of production—the iron works, the copper

[14] We mean by "materialization" the extent of the use of localized materials which strengthen the components of the materials in our locational figures.
The change from ubiquitous to localized materials means also "materialization."
In view of this circumstance the Middle Ages had little "materialized" industrial
production on account of the extensive use of ubiquitous materials like wood.

works, the rolling mills, and the paper mills—follow those other stages of production which have already been taken outside the towns, and they do so in spite of the concentrating policies of the towns.

181

It is simply the slight materialization of medieval production which causes the inconsiderable locational differentiation of the stages of production.

It is interesting to analyze how further development leads to further splitting of the productive process. From our point of view the large textile industries organized under the putting-out system in the fifteenth and sixteenth centuries represent migrations of industry away from the place of consumption, their large-scale production supplementing or even destroying the old handicrafts' production. Spinning and weaving are separated from tailoring, which remains oriented toward consumption, while the former migrate to locations of lowest costs of labor. Obviously, from the standpoint of our theory changed environmental conditions, and not technical conditions, eliminate the old locational unit of the handicraft production. Those parts of the productive processes which become organized according to the putting-out system migrate to locations which have become more attractive because of the general improvement in transportation together with the increasing density of population—the latter producing local labor surplus with ensuing possibilities for decreasing labor costs.

The third great period of revolution, from the second half of the eighteenth century until the end of the nineteenth century, increases further the dispersion of the locations of the stages of production. This is the time when the old mercantilist industries operated under the putting-out system and the handicrafts themselves were gradually mechanized to such an enormous extent. The zigzag course of production increases when mechanized spinning is torn from mechanized weaving; when the mechanized wood-planing and refining factory pushes itself in between

182

the sawmill and the manufacture of various finished products; when the mechanical manufacture of legs appears between tannery and shoe and boot manufactures; when the manufacture of pulp comes into being as a separate stage of paper manufacture; when the mechanization of the manufacture of metals quite generally puts the factory of half-finished products (of the parts of locks, of watches, of automobiles, etc.) between the production of the raw materials and that of the finished products; in short, when everywhere the mechanization of production creates new stages of production which have independent locations.

There can be no doubt that the mechanization and capitalization of production has done just that during the time of the great industrial revolution of the nineteenth century, thereby creating the impression that the productive processes were increasingly split by division of labor and oriented independently. It is hardly doubtful, either, that this process has served as the basis for the superficial doctrine of the "international division of labor," which is so closely connected with the doctrine of free trade. It will be remembered that by this doctrine we were made to believe that the parts of the productive processes which were given an independent existence by the increasing division of labor would quite freely move to their optimal locations, and that like parts would concentrate at these places, as if no transportation costs were involved which would bind them locationally and which should therefore first be consulted regarding the locational distribution of these parts of the productive processes. Economists observed how the productive processes were differentiated by the division of labor; they made no distinction between specialization and differentiation into stages of production; they observed the independent local orientation of the stages; and since the idea of the division of labor had in general become the great pillow on which all economists went to sleep, we rested (as far as the theory of location was concerned) upon the idea of the geographical or international division of labor, a beautiful idea, perhaps, but rather devoid of real meaning.

At present every glance into life makes us feel that the entire concept of a continual separation of new parts of the productive process—a concept based upon the law of the division of labor— is really explaining a transitory stage which is followed by a

183 quite different and contrary development. We are today face to face with the fact that the capitalization and mechanization of the industrial processes have entered upon the contrary development of concentration. If mechanization has in a certain sense differentiated the productive process into its smallest parts in order to subject these parts to its force and to give them their appropriate form, that same mechanization is now gathering these mechanically well-organized parts into units. Mechanization thus introduces through enormous concentrations a new and quite as gigantic a revolution in industrial locations. These processes of concentration are first of all concentrations of capital. They need not affect the technical and organizational independence of the combined parts of production; they could let the former structure of the stages of production and their locations remain intact. But there exist as a matter of fact many connecting links between the tendencies of capital to concentrate and the tendencies of technique to organize—links the discussion of which would lead us much too far afield at this time. But it can be said at once that the concentration of capital is creating for the concentration of organization and technical process new frameworks which will gather together productive processes which had previously been independent. Everyone knows of the development in the iron industry; the once independent processes of mining the ore, producing and rolling the steel, have been gathered into one undivided process. There are many parallel developments, which are perhaps less striking,

184 but not less effective. The manufacturer of worsteds who acquires a spinning mill and attempts to combine it with his weav-

ing factory, the hardware manufacturer who combines all the different parts of production as they had grown up under the putting-out system; the gun-factory which includes all stages of production from the raw material to the finished product—all these are specific instances of a general development. Everywhere the accumulations of capital stand behind these technical and organizational combinations as their larger framework. The structure of the stages of production is simplified and the split-up parts group themselves together again. New "locational units" are created which sometimes include whole series of industries. These new units must orient themselves anew according to their "locational weight," "labor coefficient," and "coefficient of manufacture" resulting from the combinations. The necessity of an entirely new orientation may remain hidden during the beginnings of the development; certain strong plants may simply attract other stages of production and thus become centers of crystallization. The foundry may attract the rail-rolling mill or the forge works; the iron forge may attract as large a foundry or as large a hardware factory as seems suitable. But even this beginning may mean locational alterations of a very noticeable kind; it may cause the total or partial stagnation of industrial districts which are losing the parts of the productive process in which they had specialized.

But this is not the end of the story. In the long run the movement will not end with such attractions of parts or stages of production to the stronger points of crystallization. That is to say, in the long run the movement will continue until it permeates the entire industry. In the long run, then, there must come about a fundamentally new orientation of the new large units of production which have been created by these combinations. This new orientation may come about slowly, because of the enormous fixed capital which is involved in a dislocation of these industrial giants and which give great weight to their location as it developed historically. But this new orientation must sometime take place if location is at all controlled by economic laws, and it will push the new units to the locations which are determined by their locational weight, their labor coefficient, and their form coefficient. This will complete the locational revolution which was started by the recent development toward concentration. During the entire nineteenth century we were under the influence of a revolution in locations, a revolution which, starting with the unity and simplicity of handicraft organization, eventuated in the extremely chaotic orientation of independently organized large-scale industries of the old style. Today we are at the beginning of a new revolution which may lead us to a new and much more simple orientation, to units of locations of large-scale industries organized in combinations.

SECTION II

THE INTERACTION OF THE INDEPENDENT PRODUCTIVE
PROCESSES

We have proceeded thus far on the assumption that the various processes of industrial production are independent of each other without any relationship to one another. This is not the case. They in fact interact upon one another in various ways. It remains to discuss this interaction. It may be of three kinds:

First, the production of quite different articles may be combined in one plant (*Betrieb*). This is, from our viewpoint, a local *coupling* of independent industrial processes.

Second, the locally separate production of various articles may be based upon the same set of materials and unfinished products. Here we have a connection through materials of the preliminary stages of several different industrial processes.

186

Third, the product of one industry may enter another industry without being, as in the previous case, material or unfinished product, but rather "means of production" or "auxiliary product" (for example, wrapping material). This may be described as *market* connection of one industry with one or several others.

I. THE COUPLING OF INDEPENDENT INDUSTRIAL PROCESSES

If products of different productive processes—and since each product has theoretically its own process, we may simply say, if different products—are produced in the same plant[15] this may be due to either technical or economic reasons. It is possible that for technical reasons several products of different kinds must be produced at the same time, as for example in certain chemical industries. But this technical necessity may be absent. The factory which produces cables, accumulators, and other electrical apparatus, the garment factory which manufactures overcoats, capes, shawls, blouses, etc. at the same time, does so for economic, and not for technical reasons. This difference is rather significant in general as well as for location.

The coupling of productive processes which results from a connection of technical factors makes one location for several kinds of product imperative. It may be regarded as the bifurcation of a unitary process of production at the place of production. Not one, but several, places of consumption influence the location; and from our discussion of agglomerated production we know the influence and significance of several places of consumption. We know that the existence of several places of consumption does not seriously complicate the determining of the location. True, we must take the components of several places 187 of consumption into account when considering the orientation of this type of production. The locational figure which results has several components of consumption, their number depending upon the number of kinds of product. These components must be weighted with the weights corresponding to the kinds of products. That is all. The locational figure of an isolated unit of production will look somewhat like Figure 42 (next page) for plants which combine two kinds of production. The location will then be determined according to the general rules.

---

[15] By plant (*Betrieb*) we do not mean enterprise, since an enterprise does not need to be confined to a local unit of manufacturing.

One might think that the same situation would arise *when the coupling was technically not necessary*. Without doubt the locational figure which is finally created will be quite similar. But it will be created in an entirely different way, and has therefore, locationally speaking, quite another meaning. This locational figure of the coupled processes will always involve a deviation by which those processes will be moved away from the location which they occupied when they were isolated, except in the unusual instance in which the coupled processes have the place of consumption and the material deposit in common. Obviously the coupled productive processes would have had different locational figures and different minimum points if their

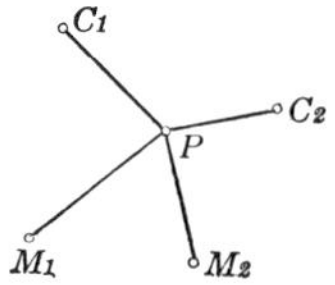

FIG. 42

material deposits and places of consumption were different. If their production is actually coupled, a deviation from those minimum points must have taken place. This kind of coupling, then, will follow the rules of deviation which we have found for the labor orientation and for the agglomerative orientation of industries, and it must be analyzed accordingly. This analysis may be determined by the special nature of labor deviation as well as by that of agglomeration.

It may happen that the coupling of several productive processes at the new location takes place because this location has a labor supply which renders certain savings possible for each 188 of these processes. The particular skill of these laborers may, for example, protect these industries better against the evil effects of business cycles or changes of fashion. This really constitutes no peculiar problem. Such labor locations are points

THE TOTAL ORIENTATION 199

toward which the several processes will deviate; such locations will attract these processes according to the influence which their index of savings has for each process. As we have seen,[16] this influence will be determined by the respective labor coefficients. The elimination of unfavorable material deposits, the increase of the attracting force of large locations, all this will take place according to the rules which we know. The only difference is that each place attracts several productive processes of *different* kinds, and not processes of an identical kind. We need therefore to analyze the way in which these processes are influenced separately. That is simple.

The other case seems more complicated. It may happen that the coupling of productive processes and the deviation which it entails are due to agglomerative forces. Coupling takes place because through such a connection of productive processes it is possible to eke out advantages which are unattainable by divided production. These advantages may be due to organization, to the use of machinery, to wholesale buying and selling—any or all of which the separate processes did not permit on account of their small size. A unit of agglomeration made up of several industries will come into existence. This unit of agglomeration will be determined by a function of economy or a function of agglomeration[17] which is related to several industries instead of being related to one. There is nothing peculiarly difficult about the question of how this function of economy agglomerates the individual productive processes of the industries involved. We merely apply the rules which, as we have found, determine the formation of segments by the isodapanes. The difference—the new element—is that the isodapanes of several different industries are involved.

But the application of the general formula of agglomeration seems to be rather difficult. This difficulty would in turn render difficult the understanding of the final orientation of such com-

[16] Cf. *supra*, p. 110 f.—EDITOR.   [17] Cf. pp. 126, 246.—EDITOR.

bined production. It seems that we shall have to apply the several functions of agglomeration of the several industries. But although this formula is a theoretical makeshift (as we have often emphasized), a solution is not as difficult as may at first sight
189 appear. In our formula of agglomeration we shall have to substitute the $f(M)$ (the function of agglomeration) of the combined productive process and its locational weight (A). If we ask which tendencies of agglomeration does any one of these products follow, the theoretical answer is twofold. If the products are all produced separately, they will follow the tendencies which are indicated by their individual formula; if they are produced in combination or coupled with others, they will follow the tendencies which are indicated by the formula of agglomeration of the combined process.[18] But generally this complicated formula will not be necessary for the arbitrary combination of several different productive processes in the same plant (plant, not enterprise; cf. foregoing) will as a rule be profitable only provided similar kinds of labor, of machinery, or of materials are used for the different products.[19] This means that arbitrary

[18] The meaning of the text is not certain here. It reads: ". . . . Wenn sie alle getrennt produziert werden, den und den, die sich aus der *einfachen* Formel ergeben; wenn kombiniert, mit den und den anderen produziert wird, den und den, die sich aus der *Kombinations*formel ergeben." It is likely, from what is said in this paragraph as well as in previous chapters, that this sentence refers to the following problem: Will a given productive process, under the influence of various agglomerative tendencies, enter an agglomeration which does not involve a coupling of it with other productive processes, or will it enter a unit of agglomeration which does involve such coupling? It must be supposed that some of the agglomerative tendencies referred to issue from a unit or units of agglomeration which do not involve the coupling of the several productive processes which are being attracted; while other tendencies issue from a unit or units of agglomeration which do involve such coupling. The answer to this problem, following as it does from comparison of the two or several formulas, seems to be indicated in the text.—EDITOR.

[19] The situation is of course quite different where coupling is technically necessary. In this case it is quite usual for the products which emerge from the same materials to require quite different kinds of machinery and labor. But it would not be worth while to combine two products which are essentially dis-

combination can take place only if a productive process has the same function of agglomeration and the same material index no matter whether it agglomerates the productive processes of one, or of another, or of several of the products. We do not have to distinguish, roughly speaking, between the agglomerating processes of isolated and of coupled productions. The formula of agglomeration of the one is identical with that of the other.

This consideration of the arbitrary coupling of productive processes yields a rather important by-result. The *density of production,* it will be remembered, must be taken into account 190 in considering the probable extent of agglomeration of a productive process in reality; it must be entered into the formula of agglomeration. This density of production must be determined from the amount of space required by *all the productive processes* within a given area which are *similar to each other* and may be coupled and combined into units of agglomeration. For this amount of space apparently determines which agglomerations either of separate productive processes or of coupled processes will come into existence in reality. That this is true will hardly need further proof after all that has been said; but it is probably the most important result which the foregoing analysis yields, supplementing the general theory of location.

2. CONNECTION THROUGH MATERIALS

Independent productive processes may be connected by the materials which they use, and such connection may be due either to technical or economic factors. Productive processes are *technically* connected if the material of one process is the by-

---

similar in these particulars unless such combination were technically necessary, since neither a more intensive use of the machinery, nor of labor, nor wholesale buying of materials could be achieved—all of which means that the most important savings of agglomeration are absent. As a matter of fact only these two forms exist in reality: Technically necessary coupling of partly differing productive processes, and arbitrary coupling of loosely related productive processes. Concerning by-products, cf. *infra.*

product of the second main product of any one of the stages of another process. For example, the woolen industry is connected with certain lines of the leather industry through its materials, because leather branches off as a second main product of one of the initial stages of the production of wool. Similarly, the dye-stuff industry is connected with other industries using coke, because coal tar (upon which the dye-stuff industry is based) is a by-product of the burning of coke. Productive processes are *economically* connected by their materials, if a given raw material, or a given unfinished product may be used either for the

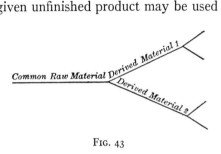

Common Raw Material Derived Material 1

Derived Material 2

FIG. 43

one process or for the other. This case is very frequent. Our modern industrial structure, enormously differentiated by innumerable branches functioning as independent productive processes, is rooted in a few raw materials which it is not very difficult to enumerate. In other words, large parts of this industrial structure are connected by materials, since groups of raw materials, such as wood, metals, soils, leather, etc., may be used alternatively by the different parts.

The effect of these two kinds of connection through materials (technical connection and economic connection) is in no way the same.

Each individual productive process connected for technical reasons with another productive process through a material will at a certain place join the other process (cf. the adjoining schema, Figure 43). If the materials of the different industries as they come into existence at the junction show a distinct order

191

of rank, i.e., if one of these materials is the main material while the others are distinctly by-products,[20] or even waste, the resulting problem of orientation is simple. The process whose material is the main material is the controlling one, and the common initial stage will be oriented toward the location of this process. The resulting location is the material deposit of the other industries which use the by-product. There remains no problem.

But a problem does remain if all the products which are produced at the junction point are of importance from a locational point of view (this being either due to their weight or to their value, cf. the last footnote). In this event this connected stage 192 is a part of several equally important or similarly important processes of production; it has therefore two or more lines of production continuing it. All of these lines of production influence the location of the junction point which is their common initial stage of production. Consequently the location of this junction point is not apparent without further analysis. The solution is the same as in the reverse case, in which two or more different series of productive processes are united into one product by a process of combination. We need only imagine the figure which was given on page 181 to be applied in reverse geographical position in order to see how the common initial location (which is here substituted for the common final location there), and the succeeding locations of the several series of productive processes will influence each other.

[20] They may be by-products, because they are very inferior in weight, although equal in value. In that case they do not have any effect whatever upon the location of the junction point because their determinant is too weak. Thus wool does not appreciably influence the orientation of the co-product, leather, although wool is a second and valuable product of the tannery, or may be such at least. On the other hand, by-products may become trifling influences because they are greatly inferior in value, if not in weight. They *would have* to have an effect upon the location if they would not be eliminated from consideration *for economic reasons*. This is the case of bones in the slaughter-house. The location of the slaughter-house will not be influenced appreciably by the realization of the bones, because the by-product has, comparatively, too small a value.

Much simpler is on the whole the case in which different productive processes are connected by materials on account of *economic* reasons. This case is also much more important because it permeates the entire industrial structure. Theoretically we have to start from the idea of individual productive processes, as that idea has always been used so far. The transport orientation of the individual process, in which materials are used which may be used alternatively in other and different processes, will nevertheless take place according to the simple and well-known rules, without regard to whether the material may be used in other processes. The individual productive process does not need to concern itself—and therefore will not concern itself—about whether its material will also be used in different productive processes, any more than it concerns itself about whether its material will be used in other individual processes of the same kind of industry. It follows that the basic transport orientation within the economic structure (from which we always have to start in our analysis) will be quite indifferent to such connections through materials. The basic transport orientation will not be affected by the fact that iron is today an important raw material in several hundred different series of productive processes and will be supplied to these series from the same deposits.

193 The same is true of wood, leather, etc. The groundwork of locations as determined by the costs of transportation—considered for the time being apart from its alteration due to agglomeration and labor—will not be affected by whether a hundred different kinds of productive processes will use one and the same material from the same material deposit, or whether they will use a hundred different raw materials which happen to come from one and the same deposit. The different processes become internally in no way dependent upon one another because they all use the same raw material; they merely happen to have the same geographical starting-point, nothing more.

The importance of the possibility of such a common geographical starting-point becomes apparent only when we consider that agglomeration and labor orientation influence the transportational groundwork. But no new locational problem is created, at that. Just as agglomeration and labor orientation will create locations of common orientation for the initial stages of the same industry, so they will create such common orientation for those stages of *different* industries which use the *same material or half-finished product*. The result is the same as in the first case. The individual stages of production, which belong to different succeeding processes of production (i.e., belong to different industries), will agglomerate according to the same rules and in the same way as those stages which are the initial stages of the same kind of production. It is of importance for this agglomeration that the different processes be rooted in the same place and therefore lie near one another, but nothing of theoretical significance can be said about it. However, it is probably fortunate that the picture of the originally isolated orientation of the different productive processes connected in fact through their materials and the picture of their agglomeration according to our general rules will render lucid and simple the apparently very complicated problem of how the orientation of these different processes is interrelated within the industrial structure. The entire industrial structure is permeated by such "economic" connections through material; and it seems at first almost impossible to consider the orientation of an individual industry in isolation and to define rules for it, since a great many other industries seem to influence its orientation. Still, such isolated consideration and analysis is seen to be possible and admissible now that we have seen that the "economic" interrelations through materials create only secondary alterations of the groundwork of the transport orientation—an orientation which is built up upon the basis of the isolated processes of production and is quite independent of such economic interrela-

194

tions.[21] These deviations take place according to the same rules that would be operative if the entire industrial organism were one single and uniform industry. I believe that an understanding of these considerations will justify the manner in which our entire theory is built up—using, as it does, an isolating analysis of the individual industries or even of the individual process of production.

3. MARKET CONNECTION

As stated before, the product of an industrial process may enter into another industrial process without being used as material or half-finished product; it may be a fixed means of production or an auxiliary product. The new situation, as compared with the cases studied thus far, is constituted by the fact that the two industrial processes are no longer connected by a common place of production. Instead, they are connected by the fact that the one productive process creates places of consumption for the other; this situation exists where they are connected through some means of production. Or they are connected by the fact that a common market is created (where for example the main product and the wrapping material are brought together); this situation exists where the processes are connected through some auxiliary product. Neither of these situations can be called "a connection of production" since there takes place no transformation of materials which would create new products. No organic connection of the two productive processes takes place. The connection is based solely upon the linking of the market of the one with the other.

This connection may have very important consequences influencing the location at which the means of production or the auxiliary product are produced, quite apart from the fact that the locations of these productive processes are in any event influenced by the places of consumption created by the main

---

[21] These rules have been elaborated for the deviations due to labor and agglomeration, as set forth in chaps. iv and v.—EDITOR.

process. It may be, and often is, the case that the manufacture of the means of production, or of the auxiliary product, will be drawn toward the location of the main process so strongly as to become united with that main process. If this occurs in accordance with our general rules of location (i.e., because the 195 locations within the locational figure of the auxiliary process are situated at the place of consumption, thus following their material index) then this situation contains nothing theoretically remarkable. The locations of the production of the main industry are the locations of the auxiliary industry simply because the former are the places of consumption of the latter. But if the auxiliary process is drawn to the location of the main process for special reasons (for example, because the auxiliary industry needs, on account of the nature of its product, local contact with the production of the main process—which happens for example often in the manufacture of machinery), then a special situation seems to arise. But may it be emphasized at once, no real problem appears. All we can say here is that special locational factors—and such special factors will often interfere with the rules of the theory—will draw the location of the auxiliary industry to the place of consumption although, according to the general rules, it should lie elsewhere. As the place of consumption is definitely given by the main industry, nothing remains undetermined.

It may be well to indicate here that without doubt special locational factors have extensive application to the production of such means of production and of auxiliary products. In fact, these special factors are the very ones which make the nature of these industries as auxiliary industries quite apparent even at a cursory glance. But it should be emphasized that whether or not such a connection of the places of production is caused by such special locational factors, the fact will not at all alter the fundamental locational nature of these industries. An industry manufacturing machines will remain an industry connected with the market or consumption place of its main industry, and this is true whether its locations are drawn to its places of consumption (say, the locations of the main industry) or whether it orients itself within its own locational figure according to the general rules. It would be quite wrong to narrow the definition of an auxiliary industry by requiring the existence of such local contact. Any industry which is connected with a main industry 196 by its market is an auxiliary industry.

The only instance in which such market connection yields anything for our general theory occurs when the location of the main process is affected. This is possible; the necessity for local contact may cause the main process (if at a certain stage it needs certain kinds of machinery) to tend toward the locations of such machinery, for there it would find opportunities for easy and dependable repair and such stimulus to further technical development as would result from local contact. In that case the main process may perhaps deviate to the locations of the manufacture of such machinery. But this type of deviation is known to us already; it belongs in the category of agglomeration. For the machine factories on their part will, for the purpose of local contact, try to find locations in which they are kept fully busy. These locations are the units of agglomeration of the main process. We have seen how this local contact with machine factories (cf. 129 *supra*) is one of the factors which create these units of agglomeration.

Here, as before, it may be a bit difficult to see clearly the dynamic working of these forces. The want for local contact is the reason why the machine industry, to stick to our example, orients itself toward the location of the main process of production. The resulting tendency to come into contact can be realized, but it can be realized only at locations having considerable production of this kind. This tendency also exists in the case of the main process, and means a saving for it; but since such saving appears only in units of agglomeration to which it is linked from the other side, it becomes an agglomerative factor and therefore influences the main industry according to the rules of agglomeration. The manufacture of machines goes to the places where the main industry agglomerates; and the main industry agglomerates there partly because the manufacture of machines goes there.

4. THE TOTAL ORIENTATION

We have given a picture of the connecting links between the different industrial processes which are of importance for locations. Apart from the technical coupling of productive processes and technical connection through materials, they all represent merely secondary alterations, if alterations at all, of the groundwork of industrial orientation as built upon the basis of theoretically isolated branches of industry. All these secondary altera- 197 tions take place according to the general and simple rules of location. These alterations are in fact but certain special aspects of the familiar deviations due to labor and to agglomeration, and they are subject to the well-known rules determining such deviation. The two technical relations connecting productive processes which really do interfere with the groundwork of transport orientation both take place according to well-known rules. They really are but one and the same phenomenon as considered for different stages of production. Their interference in no way destroys the general theoretical basis upon which our analysis of orientation was built.

Thus, this basis and the rules developed from it really embrace quantitatively and qualitatively the final and entire orientation of industry. Quantitatively, because they cover industrial productions of every kind; qualitatively because they include all these productive processes in their theoretically isolated orientation as well as in their final orientation, having regard to all general relations which affect them. We arrive at a complete theoretical understanding of the final orientation if we start with the individual industries, if we then come to a clear understanding of the points of minimal transportation costs for each individual series of productive processes going from the places of consumption back to the material deposits, and if we finally analyze, according to the rules of labor deviation and agglomeration, the ways in which these individual series are connected with each other and are woven together into that seemingly very complicated tissue which the modern industrial structure represents. All this, including the connection between the productive processes of dissimilar products, is theoretically clear and serves to explain the development of the complicated combinations which we so often encounter today in the actual industrial world with its manifold goods.

CHAPTER VII

MANUFACTURING INDUSTRY WITHIN THE ECONOMIC SYSTEM

The question now arises as to what extent our rules as developed so far will determine the local distribution of all the units of industrial production within the definite geographical limits of a country. This question is by no means answered by all that has been said so far. It might be that the rules thus far evolved determine the local distribution of production in all its component parts as dependent upon one another and still leave open the possibility of production grouping itself in very different ways throughout the land.

This is in fact the case. We shall try, therefore, to reveal the limits of the pure theory of location by placing the manufacturing industries in the setting of the whole economic system. It is obvious that our previous discussion can give a definite picture of the orientation of industry only upon the basis of the hypotheses upon which it was built. It will be remembered that these conditions were fourfold, namely, (1) that the location and the size of the places of consumption are given as fixed; (2) that the location of the material deposits is given; (3) that the location of the labor locations is given; (4) that the labor supply at these latter is unlimited at constant cost.[1] If these hypotheses be allowed, the theory as stated so far will positively determine the location of each particle of industrial production.[2]

[1] It will be observed that this involves the assumption of a (only theoretically possible) complete mobility of labor. The foregoing passages have been somewhat changed from the original in order to recall as clearly as possible what has gone before.—Editor.

[2] In the original the following methodological observation is inserted at this point: "It is no flaw in the theory that the picture which is created thereby is dependent upon certain other factors, such as transportation rates, density of

But these hypotheses should now be subjected to analysis. The location and the size of the places of consumption are from the viewpoint of locational theory no more given than are the locations and the wage level of labor. Nor is the location of the 200 material deposits, at least of the agricultural ones, so given. On the contrary, these are matters which are determined to a certain extent, or perhaps completely, by the prevailing locational conditions. For that reason they cannot be presupposed in a theory of location; rather they ought to be explained. We must get behind this assumption that they are given, because it was only justified as an aid in our analysis. An attempt to look behind this assumption will show whether the theory as developed thus far suffices to explain industrial location, or whether it has perhaps gaps which must be filled by another approach.

"To analyze the elements which were assumed as given" involves an analysis of our locational rules as they will actually operate within the living economic system as a whole. There appears at once before our imagination the picture of a circle of forces which it seems hardly possible to break through. The locations of the places of consumption, the labor locations, and the material deposits, which supposedly determine the orientation of industries, are themselves resultants of this very same in-

population, locational weight of the industries, and the indices of value added through manufacture and of labor costs. The introduction of these factors does not detract from the completeness of the theory; for these factors are indeed 'given' from the viewpoint of locational theory. They are subject to rules which are distinct and independent of locational theory. Transportation rates and material indices are a resultant of the general technical development, while the indices of labor costs and of value added through manufacture are partly a resultant of this development and partly a resultant of the general development of economic organization and industrial technique. The density of population and of production also has its roots outside of the locational sphere, at any rate in the general form in which it figures as a determining factor in our theory so far (namely, as the general ratio between the size of the population or of the amount of products demanded and the area). In all these conditions we do not assume anything which the theory itself ought to explain." (This is slightly abbreviated.)—EDITOR.

dustrial orientation. For each particle of industrial production which moves to a certain place under the influence of locational factors creates a new distribution of consumption on account of the labor which it employs at its new location, and this may become the basis of further locational regrouping. Such a particle of industrial production creates a new basis for material deposits which will be used (or, in the case of agricultural materials, even created), which in turn will be partly the basis of further reorientation of industries.

I

In order to break through this circle we might say: each equilibrium of industrial location at a certain given moment is a modification of a previous equilibrium, and this modification has been necessitated by the development of the general conditions of locational distribution. Viewed from the particular period, such an equilibrium would appear as a rational transformation of a historically developed system which had become partly irrational and was therefore transformed. This historical ²⁰¹ system of locations of industrial production, of places of consumption, and of material deposits is the given reality; and by operating upon this basis, our rules will determine the locations according to the development of the general conditions, such as rates of transportation, material indices, etc.

Without doubt such an assumption of a basis as given in time rather than in thought will be a valuable aid for the investigation of industrial locations. In no other way will it be possible, for example, to analyze the locational developments within the German economic system since 1861. But it is obvious that this historical basis is something entirely different from what we are looking for at present. This historical basis is the material, so to speak, which is transformed; whereas we are looking for a basis or theory of this transformation itself. We want to find the general basis upon which the new system orients itself. We have construed such a basis thus far by assuming as given:

places of consumption, material deposits, and labor location. Since nothing is to be assumed as given for the new system which we wish to analyze, we must try to analyze further the whole economic system itself.

II

What is the most general force which connects the different parts of an isolated economic system from the point of view of location? We shall recognize it if we ask ourselves what force determining location would develop if some people were to occupy a new and empty country for the purpose of building up such an isolated economic system. We assume, of course, that its local grouping will be determined entirely by economic considerations.[3]

Under such circumstances "layers" or "strata" of locational distribution would develop. These strata would be interrelated, i.e., they would affect each other. It is obvious that there must be a first stratum of local distribution of industries which will become the basis and the starting-point of all further development as soon as the (supposedly limited) area of settlement is chosen. This first stratum must be the agricultural stratum, whatever may be the conditions in any other respect, and whether or not cities are at once founded; for under all circumstances the settlement of agricultural lands must take place to an extent sufficient to produce the necessary agricultural products for the whole population. In order to achieve this purpose the requisite part of the population must distribute itself over as large an area suitable for agriculture as is necessary for the production of this necessary amount of agricultural products, given the prevailing

[3] These problems have recently been discussed from a new and interesting viewpoint by Hans Ritschl, "Reine und Historische Dynamik des Standorts der Erzeugungszweige," *Schmoller's Jahrbuch* (1927), pp. 813 ff.; cf. also Introduction above, p. xxxii.—EDITOR.

conditions of the natural environment, technique, and organization.[4]

203

This first stratum of local distribution—this settled area with its population, the agricultural stratum—represents the geographical foundation for all other strata. It represents such a foundation first of all for that part of industrial production (the primary industrial stratum, it may be called) which works directly for it. The places of consumption for all stages of this primary industrial stratum are given by the local distribution within the agricultural stratum. If we recall our rules it will be evident that this second stratum of local distribution (this primary industrial stratum) is oriented under the influence of agriculture. Agriculture fixes the places of consumption, the material deposits, and the locational figures.

But there are a number of other large groups for which a place will have to be found in our structure of locational distribution: (1) The industrial population which is engaged in supplying the wants of the primary industrial stratum for industrial

[4] In the original the following observations are inserted here: "It does not concern us for the present that this area may be more or less densely populated and depending upon this degree of density may be somewhat larger or smaller as the further strata of locational distribution (concentration in cities, etc.) develop. Both these developments will take place in accordance with the well-known law of Thünen about the relation of the different degrees of intensity of agricultural production and the distance of that production from the place of consumption [Cf. Johann Heinrich von Thünen, *Der Isolierte Staat*, and above, pp. xix ff.—ED.] It is certain that some relation exists between the number of people who want to live in an isolated economic system and the area which is needed for agricultural production (a certain natural environment, standard of living, as well as a development of technique and organization). This ratio can oscillate only between the limits just discussed. It is of course possible, and occurs frequently, that this area of agricultural production is chosen partly with a view to advantages to other industrial production such as that of raw materials. But that does not alter the fact that the size of this area is the foundation of the whole structure of strata of locational distribution. And this size is necessitated by the wants of the whole system for agricultural products." This is slightly abbreviated, and a footnote of the original text is worked into it.—EDITOR.

goods; (2) the population engaged in circulating the goods produced through trade and transportation; (3) that group of the population which only consumes, like officials, free professions, persons living on their own private means; and finally (4) the industrial population which supplies the wants of these last two strata.[5]

The group of industrial population supplying the primary industrial stratum is determined by it just as this latter stratum 204 is determined by the agricultural stratum. The primary industry creates the geographical layout of the sphere of consumption and thus creates the framework of the locational foundation. It should be noted, however, that in a strict sense this industrial stratum which is oriented under the influence of the primary industrial stratum is not a single whole, but is itself divided into numerous substrata. If we assume that the division of labor is highly developed, we shall find first a substratum which is directly engaged in supplying the wants of the primary industry; next we shall find a substratum which is engaged in supplying the wants of the foregoing substratum; another one which works for this one; and so on. There will be a number of substrata or layers (superimposed on each other and decreasing in size) of which each gets its sphere of consumption and therefore its general locational foundation from the previous one. If we suppose, for example, that 50 per cent of a people are agriculturists while the other 50 per cent are engaged in industrial pursuits (and the country has only the strata which we have discussed thus far), then obviously 25 per cent of the population will suffice for supplying the industrial products wanted by the agriculturists, since 50 per cent suffice to do it for the whole peo-

[5] Offhand it might be suggested that we treat the domestic servants as a special stratum. But from the viewpoint of locational analysis these people are a part of the consuming stratum to which they belong; they do not necessitate separate treatment.

ple.[6] In other words, the primary industrial stratum oriented under the influence of agriculture will contain 50 per cent of the industrial population. For these 50 per cent a further 25 per cent of the industrial population must suffice to supply its demand for industrial products. These 25 per cent are the first substratum of the secondary industrial stratum oriented under the influence of the primary industrial stratum. In turn, another 12.5 per cent must suffice for supplying this first substratum. These 12.5 per cent would then be the second substratum, and for supplying their wants 6.25 per cent must suffice—which would be the third substratum. This example illustrates how the industrial population is intertangled in substrata or layers of decreasing size and how each substratum is the locational foundation of the succeeding one. But we need not concern ourselves further with these interrelations. The whole structure has its foundation in the local distribution of the primary industrial stratum oriented under the influence of agriculture. We shall treat these substrata collectively as the third great stratum, the "secondary industrial stratum" which is oriented under the influence of the primary industrial stratum.

If we now think of this third stratum together with the first two as one whole, we have before us the economic system. The locational distribution of the largest part of the remainder simply leans upon it. The rôle of such groups as have not yet been discussed is simply one of a proportional strengthening of the different parts of this system. 205

This strengthening of the existing structure is illustrated by all those parts of the population which attend to the actual shipping of material goods from one location to another (the retail traders and the transportation agencies),[7] and thus handle the

[6] This seems to presuppose an equal amount of consumption per individual throughout, that is, an equal standard of living as far as industrial products are concerned. Otherwise the foregoing statement would not hold good.—EDITOR.

[7] Cf. Introduction above, p. 4.

process of circulation. Similarly, the large body of officials with local functions represent merely a strengthening of the existing locational distribution. These officials are distributed largely according to the general distribution of population, and are therefore from a locational viewpoint only exponents of it. This whole mass of local tradesmen and functionaries need not be differentiated from our previously discussed strata at all. If one wishes to separate them, however, one may think of them as a local organizing stratum, for purposes of classification.

A really independent stratum is made up of the other parts of the population engaged in the circulating process and the groups which only consume. Of the former this stratum would include all those who are engaged in the general organization and managements of the exchange of goods, whether material or immaterial; of the latter it would include those officials who do not have local, but general, organizing functions—the liberal professions and those persons living on their private means. All these persons show tendencies of stratification totally different from those of the local organizing stratum. They seem to be quite free in the choice of their locations. They appear to be elements of the economic system very little subject to economic causes in their choice of their locations, as in the case of persons living on their private means, intellectuals, artists; or, if they are subject to economic causes, such causes operate upon them in a very complex way and are mixed with other causes (as is the case of officials in the central government and wholesale trad-
206 ers). But be that as it may, what primarily interests us here is the fact that the locational distribution of these elements is something separate and independent. If they are oriented in relation to the economic system at all, they are oriented in relation to it as a whole and as it is created by the three or four previously mentioned strata. Although their stratification is of varying types and subject to quite varying rules, they belong in one group in the sense that their stratification can only take place

upon the foundation of all the other strata we have discussed before. We shall refer to this group under the term "central organizing stratum."

There remain those parts of the population which supply the wants of the last two strata, the organizing strata, as we have called them. These parts of the population will be partly industrial and partly either local organizing strata or central organizing strata. Superimposed on these there are the industrial and other substrata supplying the groups just mentioned, which in turn possess their dependent substrata, and so on. These groups telescoping each other ad infinitum do not need to concern us. For we need only separate out those substrata depending upon the central organizing stratum, since the substrata depending upon, and following, the local organizing stratum will merely contribute to the existing local distribution, for that, as we have seen, is precisely what the local organizing stratum does. But the stratum depending upon the central organizing stratum constitutes the fifth stratum, which we shall call the "central dependent stratum." Its substrata consist of industrial units inter- 207 spersed with local and central organizing groups. But we may ignore the central organizing groups as numerically not important, while the local organizing elements are to be thought of as strengthening further the industrial units. For purposes of practical analysis we may treat this entire group collectively as one single stratum the locations of which are determined by the industries it contains and are dependent upon the central organizing stratum.

We have now found: (1) the agricultural stratum, (2) the primary industrial stratum, (3) the secondary industrial stratum, (4) the central organizing stratum, (5), the central dependent stratum. The local organizing stratum is embraced in the first three as a strengthening element. These strata afford us a systematic understanding of the whole mechanism of stratifi-

cation—an understanding which is sufficient for practical purposes.

The locational forces which connect the different strata play
back and forth from the upper strata to the lower, as well as
from the lower to the upper ones. The location of the centers
based upon the non-agricultural strata creates the places of consumption for agricultural production; around these places of
consumption the agricultural production groups itself in circles,
as Thünen has shown.[8] This formation of circles creates not
only a certain geographical distribution of the kinds of agricultural production, but also a distribution of the agricultural population, since the agricultural population ranges itself according
to the intensity of production. In so doing these circles change
to a certain extent the foundation of the whole pyramid of strata.
This causes one of those rounds of interdependent forces which
make the analysis of economic life such a thorny task. When we
come to the empirical analysis we shall have to take up this problem created by these changes of the foundation of the pyramid
208 of strata and of their quantitative importance. All that I wish to
show now is that these changes do not destroy the theoretical justification of the locational structure which we have erected. It
should be remembered that such changes are after all only a reaction. The formation of such circles can only follow an already
existing and definite stratification of the economic system along
the lines which we have suggested. Speaking more strictly, it
must have been preceded by the choice of some area as the foundation of the economic system. This foundation must have been
chosen as the agricultural basis within which the settlements of
the non-agricultural population are afterward fixed.[9] It is im-

[8] Cf. above, pp. xix ff.

[9] It may be, as was said before, that the economic advantages of these non-
agricultural settlements have been decisive in the choice of the area. But that
does not alter the fact that they are only an incidental factor decisive in choosing
the area as a whole, but not the primary factor in the process of its stratification.

possible to conceive of this "reaction" as anything but a secondary phenomenon, although it is true that Thünen did assume the city as the unexplained basic phenomenon of the distribution of agricultural locations. We, on the other hand, wish to clarify as far as possible just where and how cities develop. For this purpose we must go beyond the reaction of this growth of the city upon the distribution of the agricultural population; we are forced to analyze in the foregoing manner the process of stratification.

III

How far does this locational structure substitute real data for construed ones and thus fix the industries unequivocally according to the rules which we have found? Three construed data had to be replaced with real data: those relating to places of consumption, those relating to material deposits, and those relating to labor locations and their unlimited labor supply at constant cost (equal wage levels).

1. Our entire analysis of the mechanism of stratification is built upon the idea of treating the different strata as spheres of consumption of their successors. The sphere of consumption is therefore throughout these strata something given, although of course variable in the upper strata in accordance with changes in the lower. In most cases this sphere of consumption is given, 209 not as an indefinite geographical distribution of consumption, but rather as very definite places with very definite magnitudes of consumption. Certainly they were treated as definite places in the elaboration of our theory. And the sphere of consumption is in fact given in this definite form for all the higher strata, for which higher strata the places of production of the lower strata, as well as the centers of organization and trade, become places of consumption of a very definite magnitude. And what we have just said of the higher strata holds true even for the primary industrial stratum which is built upon the agricultural stratum. While this is true, it certainly must be conceded that there are

manifold agrarian forms of settlement which make for multi-
farious structural developments of this basis of consumption;
and it must furthermore be conceded that the connection between this primary industrial stratum and the underlying sphere
of agricultural consumption may be very difficult to detect, because the rather scattered agricultural consumption cannot be
supplied except via the agglomerations created by industrial production (cities). All these facts are only extraneous complications which interfere with our perceiving that here also we have
a system (a very complex one) of places of consumption having
a given magnitude. The industries will orient themselves in accordance with this system in exactly the same way (disregarding
the "reaction" we have discussed before) as they do in the higher
strata where the forms of distribution of consumption are more
clearly perceivable.

2. The distribution of the material deposits takes place in
terms of the system of places of consumption according to the
rules which the theory has given for the construction of the locational figures based upon the places of consumption as a starting-point—at least this is true of a large part of the material
210 deposits which exploit deposits already in existence such as
mines and the like. In such cases the choice of the material deposits is all that has to be done, and this has been described in
the theory. But the problem remains of how those material deposits are located which are agricultural in nature, since in this
case the "deposits" themselves must be "created," natural conditions being the only given factor.

If there were no independent forces involved in the distribution of agricultural production, the answer to this question would
be simple. In that case we could say that the natural conditions
of production of the materials are the determining factor, that
the more or less favorable "natural conditions," in conjunction

with their location, would determine the development of such
"deposits" according to the same rules according to which the
more or less favorable location of the already existing mining
deposits determines their employment in conjunction with their
productivity. In both cases these deposits would be given if the
places of consumption were given. As a matter of fact the industrial strata do try to shape their basis of agricultural materials
in a way analogous to their basis of mined materials, as something given by their natural conditions. But industry will be
thwarted in these attempts by the inherent tendencies of agricultural distribution, which tendencies of course affect the development of agricultural production in spite of the fact that it is
the basis of industrial strata. In other words, the economic conditions of agricultural production will become a determining
factor in addition to those which would be decisive if only the
usefulness of agricultural production as an industrial material
deposit were in question. Specifically, this involves its location
in relation to the places of consumption and in relation to the
labor locations as well as its rank among competing material deposits. These conditions are of course the ones analyzed by
Thünen,[10] and as we have seen they are in part secondary phenomena of industrial stratification itself. In this case they touch
the primary foundation. This shows that the actual develop- 211
ment of these agricultural material deposits can only be regarded as given provided this circular process is introduced into our
analysis, i.e., in the empirical analysis. But it is important that
we know these rules and that we realize they do not contain anything problematical. As said before, the interference of the economic conditions of agricultural production means that the rules
as set forth by Thünen become operative. Each agricultural
material deposit is under competition from other agricultural
employments which would use the soil for the production of
different materials. The most profitable use will be the one un-

[10] Cf. above, p. xix.—Editor.

dertaken. For our purposes this fact may be expressed in the following fashion: each industry will have as many potential deposits of the agricultural materials it needs as there exists area which is by its nature capable of producing this material. But it will have these potential deposits at very different "prices at the deposit." At each deposit the "price at the deposit" for a certain material is determined by the necessity of displacing the (according to Thünen's law) next profitable employment. Thus these potential deposits are by this "price at the deposit" placed into the scale of possible material deposits of their own kind much in the same fashion as the deposits of mining materials are. They will be developed as bases of locations and employed for production according to the rules we know.

The places of consumption and the material deposits are given by the locational structure of the economic system as we have analyzed it. The rules which determine them are sometimes quite direct and simple, sometimes a bit more complicated, but in every case they are quite unequivocal. This means that the picture of the orientation of industry would be revealed (within the framework of the locational structure we have analyzed) by the locational rules which we have discovered, if this orientation were independent of the labor locations and of the differences between their wage levels, and were based solely upon costs of transportation and the "pure" agglomeration built upon this transport orientation.[11] For to the extent to which orientation is determined by these forces, only the world of places of consumption and of material deposits comes under consideration as the given geographical basis of the real structure. It would be possible to calculate for each geographical framework and for each stage of general economic and technical development how the locational picture of industry would shape up provided the number of population, the distribution of agricultural settlement, and the main distribution of the "central or-

[11] Cf. pp. 135 ff.

ganizing stratum" were known. There would be no room for the influence which a particular economic system (capitalism, socialism, or some other) could exercise upon the basic locational orientation, since the "pure" rules would fix the locations of industry in a general way, at least. The theoretical task would be completed, and no further "realistic" theory would be necessary.

IV

But what will happen if we take into consideration the deviations due to labor and the labor orientation which rests upon them? The discussion of these deviations has thus far been based upon the assumption that the labor locations were given and that the differences in their wage levels were constant. Does the mechanism of local distribution which we have considered thus far give us any clues for determining the local distribution of such differences of wage levels, for the causes creating the labor locations, and finally for the rules determining their development which have so far been eliminated by the assumption of an unlimited supply of labor at equal cost? Apparently none whatever. This is the great gap in our analysis so far. In the rules determining the creation and the development of labor locations lies hidden the problem which remains for a further theoretical analysis. This problem will have to be solved by the 213 "realistic" theory. For at this point it becomes necessary to consider particular economic systems. I do not wish to assert that the creation and development of labor location can be explained by economic reasons; but if it can be so explained the reasons will be related to the position which the particular economic system gives to labor. For apart from what one calls (according to Sombart) an "economic system," i.e., apart from the particular determining form of organization which the particular social concepts of a given time impress upon all economic relationships on account of which they appear as a part of a social order, all economic relationships are taken into consideration by our general analysis of a "pure" economic system.[12] The further realistic theory must therefore consider how labor is handled in the particular economic system which is studied. If we would exhaust the theory of location of industries of today, if we would explain fully the local grouping of the economic forces and the aggregation of population, we must ask what it means for the local grouping of labor that labor is treated as a commodity. It will be seen that this circumstance determines about one-half of the local distribution of our present social system.

[12] The interested reader may with profit consult Talcott Parsons, " 'Capitalism' in Recent German Literature: Sombart and Weber," in *Journal of Political Economy,* vols. XXXVI–VII, and the literature cited there. Cf. also above, page 10, footnote, on the concept of an economic system.—EDITOR.

MATHEMATICAL APPENDIX[1]

GEORG PICK

Introductory remark.—Upon the suggestion of the author of this treatise I have attempted to outline in popular form some mathematical considerations which are necessary for an understanding of the problem of locations. Regarding sections I and II, I should like to refer to a recent treatise of Scheffers[2] which gives the necessary mathematical aid for the solution of such problems. The formula of agglomeration which forms the main part of Section III is stated in analogy to similar problems in different fields of application. I wish that further formulas, particularly locational figures with more than three points, might be developed. But they still present some real difficulties.[3]

I. THE LOCUS OF LEAST COST OF TRANSPORTATION

§ 1. *The locational triangle.*—In the accompanying figure, A_1 represents the material deposit, A_2 the fuel deposit, A_3 the place of consumption. Let us suppose that a_1 tons of material and a_2 tons of fuel are needed to produce a_3 tons of the product (we shall assume a_3 always to be 1). If the place of production is located in P, at a distance of r_1 miles from A_1, r_2 miles from A_2 and r_3 miles from A_3, then a_3 ($=1$) tons of produce apparently require   226

$$K = a_1 r_1 + a_2 r_2 + a_3 r_3$$

ton-miles of costs of transportation.

For which positions of P are these costs as small as possible? It is obvious at once that as long as P is situated outside of the locational

---

[1] As Mr. Bauer suggests, the whole case corresponds rather strikingly to certain parts of electrostatics, particularly equipotential surfaces. Cf. J. H. Jeans, *The Mathematical Theory of Electricity and Magnetism*, pp. 54 ff.—EDITOR.

[2] G. Scheffers, *Funktionen der Abstände von festen Punkten* (1900).

[3] For an attempted, though unsuccessful, solution of this problem, the reader may consult Launhardt, "Die Bestimmung des zweckmässigsten Standorts einer gewerblichen Anlage." I have given a résumé of the pertinent passage beneath, p. 238.—EDITOR.

228 THE LOCATION OF INDUSTRIES

triangle $A_1A_2A_3$, any approach of P to the side of the triangle next to P must result in shortening all three distances r_1, r_2, r_3 and thus in lowering the costs of transportation. The locus of the minimum point cannot, therefore, lie exterior to the triangle. It lies either interior to the triangle or upon its boundary. We shall begin with treating the first of these two possibilities.

§ 2. *The minimum point in the interior of the locational triangle. Mechanical model.*—The mathematical analysis of the necessary conditions[4] or the point of lowest costs of transportation shows the following

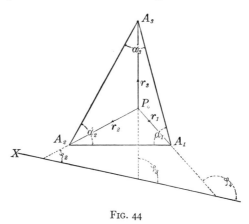

FIG. 44

results. Let us imagine a variable point mass at P which is pulled with the force a_1 toward A_1, a_2 toward A_2, and a_3 toward A_3. The position of P for which these three forces are in equilibrium is the locus of the minimum point.

This suggests that we might demonstrate the position of P_0 (as we may call the point of least cost of transportation) by a mechanical model with an automatic device. This leads us to an old apparatus

---

[4] The necessary conditions of this case may be stated as follows: The function of the locus K has in its minimum point the differential quotient zero in all directions:

$$\frac{dK}{ds} = 0$$

(for each direction of s). This formula gives us two equations for the necessary condition the significance of which is set forth in the text (cf. Scheffers, *loc. cit.*).

which was invented by Varignon to demonstrate the parallelogram of forces. Upon the edge of a graduated circular disk three little rollers with horizontal axes may be affixed. Over each roller runs a thread. The three inner ends of the threads are coupled together at some point, the outer ends hang down and may bear little weights. In order to 227 realize a given case, we shall first place the rollers so that they form the corners of the locational triangle. For this we can use the scale upon the edge of the circular disk. After this we load the three threads with weights proportional to the transport weights a_1, a_2, a_3 for which we

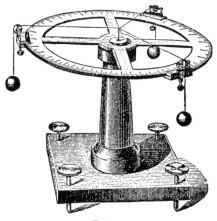

FIG. 45

may substitute the same units of a small weight, e.g., dekagram. The connecting point will move by itself to the position of the minimum point.

§ 3. *Geometrical construction of P_0. The weight triangle.*—Figure 46 shows the forces a_1, a_2, a_3, acting upon P_0 as straight-line segments whose length is proportional to the force. According to the theorem of the parallelogram of forces each of these straight-line segments if laid out from P_0 opposite its own direction will constitute the diagonal of the parallelogram formed by the other two straight-line segments provided a state of equilibrium exists. If one lays out the three balanced forces (straight-line segments) following each other in their proper direction and length, a closed triangle ($G_1G_2G_3$ of the figure) results.

The angles of this triangle $\gamma_1\gamma_2\gamma_3$ are the supplements of the three angles $\beta_1\beta_2\beta_3$ which are formed in P_0 by the straight lines connecting P_0 with the corners $A_1A_2A_3$. This may be seen by a glance at Figure 46. The triangle $G_1G_2G_3$, which is fully determined in advance by its sides $a_1a_2a_3$ shall be called weight triangle. This weight triangle gives us the angles $\gamma_1\gamma_2\gamma_3$, and therefore $\beta_1\beta_2\beta_3$. In order to find the point P_0 we shall have to determine that position of P from which the lines connecting P with $A_1A_2A_3$ form these particular angles, or, as one sometimes says, that position of P from which A_2A_3 is seen subtending the angle β_1, $\overline{A_3A_1}$, the angle β_2, $\overline{A_1A_2}$, the angle β_1.

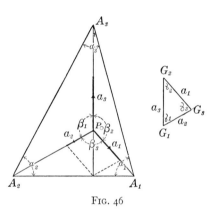

FIG. 46

§ 4. *Continuation. The three circles of construction.*—In order that the angle $A_1P_0A_2$ have the given size β_3, P_0 must lie (according to the theorem about angles at the circumference of a circle) upon a certain arc which stretches from A_1 to A_2. But P_0 must also lie upon a corresponding arc A_2A_3, because $A_2P_0A_3$ should have the given size β_1; and finally P_0 must lie upon arc A_1A_3 because $A_3P_0A_1=\beta_2$. Hence we only have to construct these arcs (two suffice), in order to get P_0 as their point of intersection (Fig. 47).

In order to construct the arc through A_1A_2 we have to apply the angle $(\beta_3-90°)$ to A_1A_2 at A_1 and A_2, so that an isosceles triangle results, with its apex at C. (Fig. 48.) This apex C is the center of the required circle, which may therefore be constructed at once.

Indeed it is $A_2CA_1 = 180° - 2\ (\beta_3 - 90°) = 360° - 2\beta_3$, and consequently the salient angle at C is equal to $2\beta_3$, as was required.[5]

§ 5. *Approach of the position of the minimum point to the boundary or to a corner of the locational triangle.*—When does P_0 lie near one of the sides of the triangle, for example $A_1A_2A_3$? It is apparent that the angle $A_2P_0A_3$, i.e., β_1 will be almost equal $180°$, and that γ_1 will be almost equal $0°$. The weight triangle has therefore one very small angle; consequently the subtending side a_1 will be very small, too, while

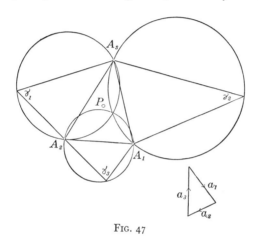

FIG. 47

the other two a_2, a_3, will be nearly equal. If a_1 becomes zero (and $a_2 = a_3$), P_0 lies upon A_2A_3. This is apparent anyway; for A_1 has disappeared; the locational triangle has shrunk to a locational line (Fig. 49).

229

When does P_0 lie near a corner, for example A_1? It is evident that in that case the angle $A_2P_0A_3$, i.e., β_1, will be almost equal to $A_2A_1A_3$, that is, almost equal to the angle a_1 of the locational triangle, while β_1 would be noticeably larger if P_0 were located more in the center of the locational triangle. Similarly, γ_1, the supplement of β_1, is now almost equal to the supplement of a_1 (the exterior angle of the locational tri-

[5] Instead of this construction, we may state the following rule: Erect a triangle similar to the weight triangle upon each of the three sides of the locational triangle. The circles described around these triangles are those required.

angle at A_1) which would usually be considerably smaller. Hence as long as the angles of the weight triangle are smaller than the corresponding exterior angles of the locational triangle, P_0 will lie within the interior of the latter; but if one of the angles of $G_1G_2G_3$, for example γ_1, is equal to the corresponding exterior angle of $A_1A_2A_3$, in this case $180° - \alpha_1$, then P_0 is located at the corresponding corner, A_1.

§ 6. *Position of P_0 in one of the corners. The cases without a weight triangle.*—We shall imagine now that the weight triangle $G_1G_2G_3$ is

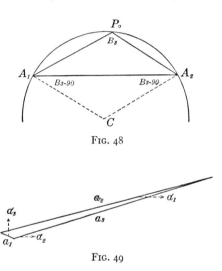

FIG. 48

FIG. 49

undergoing changes, and see what changes of the position of P_0 result from it. a_2, a_3, shall remain unaltered, while a_1 is increasing gradually which causes the opposite angle γ_1 to increase also. We have just seen that P_0 goes to the corner A_1, when γ_1 has reached the size $180° - \alpha_1$. What will happen if a_1 and γ_1 increase further? Apparently P_0 remains in its position at A_1. For if the share of a_1 is already so considerable that the transport from A_1 to P_0 must be avoided altogether in order to achieve a minimum of costs, it will be that much more necessary when the relative value of a_1 increases further.

When the value of a_1 has become equal to a_2 plus a_3, γ_1 has become equal to $180°$, in other words the weight triangle has shrunk into a line (Fig. 50). If a_1 increases further, so that $a_1 > a_2 + a_3$, no triangle can be constructed out of a_1, a_2, a_3, and the weight triangle has ceased to exist. But still, P_0 lies at A_1.[6]

The model described in § 2 shows the right position of P_0 for these cases, provided that care is taken to prevent the connecting point of the three threads from sliding over the rollers.

§ 7. Comprehensive recapitulation. Characteristics of the different cases.—We may, then, distinguish three separate possibilities which may be characterized as follows: First, weight triangle exists, P_0 lies in the interior of the locational triangle; second, weight triangle exists, P_0 lies in one of the corners; third, weight triangle is lacking, P_0 lies always in one corner. But while the third case can be recognized at once

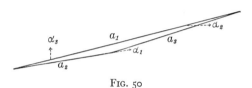

FIG. 50

because of the impossibility of constructing a weight triangle, it remains to give an additional characteristic in order to distinguish the first two cases. Let us recall the circles of construction in § 4. As long as P_0 lies in the center of the locational triangle, these circles intersect in the interior of the triangle, each of them excluding the corresponding third angle. If P_0 approaches the corner A_1, the arc over A_2A_3 passes near A_1, and if P_0 reaches A_1 (because, as we have seen in § 5, $\gamma_1 = 180° - a_1$) this arc passes through A_1 and intersects there with the other two circles. If γ_1 increases further, the arc subtending A_2A_3 will 231 go beyond A_1, so that A_1 will come to lie in its interior. The point of intersection of the three circles now falls entirely outside of the locational triangle. At the same time this point ceases to be a solution of our problem; for P_0 remains at A_1. The second case can be recognized by the fact that one of the circles of construction includes the third (i.e., that corner which does not lie upon its base); in this case this included corner is always the minimum point.

[6] In these instances where P_0 lies in one of the corners, other conditions prevail than those indicated in footnote 4. $\dfrac{dK}{ds}$ is now positive in all directions from P_0, and usually not equal to zero at P_0.

§ 8. *The behavior of P_0 when the weights a_1, a_2, a_3, remain unchanged, but the locational triangle changes.*—We have investigated the changes of the position of P_0 which are caused by changing the transport weights a_1, a_2, a_3 while the locational triangle remains unchanged. We shall now suppose a_1, a_2, a_3 fixed, while we change the form of the locational triangle, and we shall observe how P_0 acts under these conditions. Let us, moreover, suppose two corners, perhaps A_1, A_2, fixed; only the third corner, A_3, shall move.

Let us first take up those cases without a weight triangle, where one of the three weights a_1, a_2, a_3 exceeds the sum of the other two. Ac-

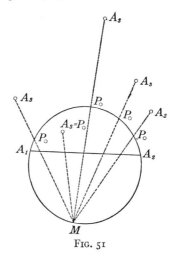

FIG. 51

cording to § 5, P_0 lies at A_1 when a_1, at A_2 when a_2, at A_3 when a_3 is the large weight. Hence P_0 either remains unmovable at one of the fixed corners A_1, A_2, or P_0 participates in all movements of A_3, always coinciding with this point.

§ 9. *Continuation. The center lies upon the circle through A_1, A_2.*—If the weight triangle exists, we can take from it the angle γ_3 and construct the arc over A_1A_2 as was shown in § 4 (Fig. 51). It is necessary to distinguish whether A_3 lies in the segment between the chord A_1A_2 and the arc or outside of it. The first case is identical with the second case mentioned in § 7: P_0 coincides with A_3. If, however, A_3 lies outside of the segment, then the construction shown in § 4 takes place, as we know in advance that P_0 will lie upon the arc A_1A_2 itself. The line connecting P_0 with A_3, together with the lines connecting P_0 with A_1 and A_2, forms (cf. § 3 and § 4) the angles $180° - \gamma_2$ and $180° - \gamma_1$. Its extension backward beyond P_0 together with these lines includes the fixed angles γ_2, γ_1. Wherever A_3 may be, P_0 will lie upon the arc 232 through A_1A_2, in such a way that the extension of A_3P_0 together with P_0A_1 always includes the same angle γ_1 at the point P_0. According to the theorem regarding angles at the circumference of a circle, P_0A_3 will intersect the circle through A_1, A_2 in a fixed point (M of Fig. 51) which can easily be constructed. We only have to apply the angle γ_2 at A_2 to $\overline{A_2A_3}$ downward, and the second side of this angle will intersect the circle in the required point M.

This reasoning is correct as long as P_0 does not coincide with one of the points A_1, A_2. Because in these cases there is no longer any reason why A_3, P_0, and M should lie upon one straight line. Indeed, it is apparent that P_0 lies always and only at A_1, if A_3 lies somewhere in the angular space which falls between the extension of $\overline{MA_1}$ beyond A_1 and the extension of $\overline{A_2A_1}$ beyond A_1. The situation regarding A_2 is analogous.

Let us imagine A_3 approaching A_1A_2 from a great distance along any line going through M. If the straight line upon which A_3 is approaching crosses the line going through A_1A_2 outside of the segment A_1A_2, P_0 lies fixed either in A_1 or in A_2. But if it crosses between A_1 and A_2, P_0 lies at the point of intersection of A_3M with the arc as long as A_3 has not reached the segment of the circle subtending A_1A_2. But as soon as A_3 enters into the interior of this segment, the point P_0 will be taken along and will always be combined with A_3.

While A_3 changes its position in the entire half-plane above the straight line going through A_1A_2, P_0 always remains confined to the interior and the boundary of the segment of the circle subtended by A_1A_2.

§ 10. *Survey figure showing the changes of transport costs when the position of A_3 changes.*—One and the same position of P_0 may correspond to very different positions of A_3, as has just been seen. But total costs of transportation change with the position of A_3. We will 233 get a good view of this situation if we connect by a curve all those positions of A_3 which show equal costs of transportation. These curves show (Fig. 52) a very different shape in the different parts of the half-plane extending above the straight line going through A_1A_2. In the before-mentioned angular spaces at A_1 and A_2 they are apparently concentric arcs around A_1 and A_2 respectively. In the main space lying between these two we have to distinguish again the segment from the exterior. Within the segments we get elliptic curves; but in the exterior one curve results from another if we move its points the same distance upon each of the straight lines through M. At the lines separating the four spaces the curves appear broken.

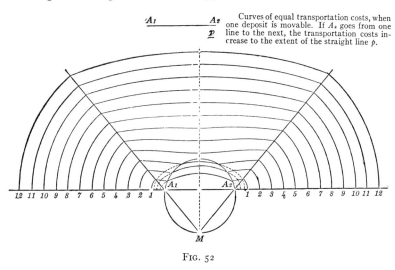

Curves of equal transportation costs, when one deposit is movable. If A_2 goes from one line to the next, the transportation costs increase to the extent of the straight line p.

FIG. 52

§ 11. *Two locational triangles in mutual relation.*—Two locational triangles $A_1A_2A_3$ and $A_1'A_2'A_3'$ shall be related in such a way that A_1' is at the same time the place of production for the first triangle and A_3 at the same time the place of production for the second triangle. In view of this quality we shall designate these points as P_0, P_0'. We shall assume the locations A_1A_2 and $A_1'A_2'$ and the two sets of weights a_1, a_2, a_3 and a_1', a_2', a_3' as given. The points required are $P_0=A_1'$ and $P_0'=A_3$ in such a position that total costs of transportation become as small 234 as possible. Those cases in which no weight triangle exists in one of the two locational triangles are extreme cases. If this is, for example, the case with regard to the first set a_1, a_2, a_3, then $P_0=A_1'$ must lie combined either with A_1 or A_2 or with $A_3=P_0'$. We therefore either have A_1' given at once, or the two places of production are combined, which would mean that one place of production for four given points would have to be found. Separate places of production located elsewhere than in the given points are only possible, therefore, if both weight triangles exist. Under this condition the two segments subtending $\overline{A_1 A_2}$ and $\overline{A_3' A_2'}$ exist as has been discussed in § 9. We get the

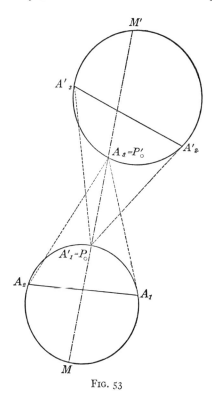

FIG. 53

two points M and M'. If we connect therefore M with M', the connecting line will cut the two circles at the required points (Fig. 53).

But this rule is subject to several limitations. If the segments overlap in part, and MM' traverses the common part, then P_0 and P_0' are combined (according to § 9) and may not lie upon MM'. We get again the case of one place of production with four determining points. If, on the other hand, MM' does not meet one of the segments at all, then P_0 or P_0' will lie in one of the corners A_1, A_2 and A_3', A_2' respectively (cf. Fig. 52); in other words, either P_0 or P_0' are given at once and the remaining problem reduces itself to the fundamental problem. The exceptions are therefore of a more simple nature than the regular case for which construction Figure 53 brings the solution.

235   § 12. *Locational polygons with more than three corners.*—In spite of the fact that generally speaking the essential part of the problem and the principles of its treatment are unchanged in the case of locational figures with more than three corners, it is impossible to give equally simple rules for construction even in the next higher case of the quadrangle. It is worth noting that the mechanical model functions in all these higher cases (if properly adapted). For if we let weights corresponding to the sets of transport weights pull threads at the corners of any locational figure, the point at which these threads are coupled together will automatically go to the minimum point.[7]

[7] Cf. for the contrary opinion, Launhardt, "Die Bestimmung des zweckmässigsten Standorts einer gewerblichen Anlage," in *Zeitschrift des Vereins Deutscher Ingenieure* (1882), pp. 107, 110–11. In this short essay Launhardt is concerned with figuring out the most favorable location of an isolated process of production which uses only localized materials. Although this is a very narrow and limited aspect of the problem of industrial location, it seems desirable to give a short résumé of his geometrical arguments, because they lead him to the conclusion that the construction of minimum points is possible for polygons with any number of corners.

After having arrived at the conclusion that "the kilometric costs of transportation must hold each other in balance at the location of production," he finds the minimum point by constructing a triangle similar to the weight triangle upon the side A_1A_2 of the locational triangle. He then describes the circle around this triangle and connects the third corner O of this triangle with the third corner of the locational triangle, A_3 (it will be observed that this involves the simplifying assumption that A_3 is always the center of consumption, while the reasoning of Pick is entirely independent of the question as to which of the three points is the center of consumption). The point P_0 at which this connecting line intersects the circumference of the circle is the required minimum point. Launhardt calls the point O mentioned above the "pole" of the locational triangle.

Using the theorem of Ptolemy, Launhardt proceeds to analyze locational polygons with the aid of his construction of a "pole" (cf. Fig. 53A). He thus replaces both A_1 and A_2. This substitution of the pole O for A_1 and A_2 becomes the basis of his construction of the minimum point for a quadrangle, $A_1 A_2 A_3 A_4$, in which A_3 is again fixed as the place of consumption. What he does is simply to

Even for distinguishing the cases where the minimum point P_0 lies in the interior from those cases where it lies at the corners of the locational figure, we do not have those simple criteria which we had in the case of the triangle. Suffice it to indicate that P_0 will apparently lie at one of the corners, if the weight of that corner equals or exceeds the sum of all others (Fig. 54).

---

construct a "pole" for A_2 and A_4, and then construct another "pole" for A_1 and O. The line connecting this second pole Q with A_3 will, Launhardt believes, give the minimum point P_0 where it intersects the circle described around the triangle A_1QO.

Launhardt does not attempt to prove his contention. It appears to be wrong. Neglecting the (rather important) circumstance that it is not apparent just on

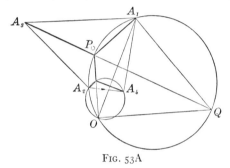

FIG. 53A

what basis these two poles are constructed (inasmuch as in the fundamental case of a triangle they were found by constructing a triangle similar to the weight triangle which does not exist here, since we are dealing with a quadrangle), the obvious objection to it is that it involves a detour, and therefore additional costs of transportation for the materials coming from A_2 and A_4 to P. It is difficult to see how, in view of this fact, it could have escaped Launhardt's attention that he was not really getting a minimum point at all. Moreover, he himself observed that a second and different solution is possible. This, he says, is achieved by constructing first a "pole" O' for the points A_1 and A_4, and by then determining the location P_0 for the remaining points A_3, A_2 and O' through their "pole" Q'. Was this fact in itself not an indication that the real minimum point lay somewhere in between these two? There is, as a matter of fact, still another and third possibility, namely to begin with A_1 and A_2.

It is surprising that Bortkiewicz, in his review of Weber's theory (*Archiv für Sozialwissenschaft und Sozialpolitik*, 1910) should not have noted these fundamental limitations and errors in Launhardt's essay when he, at the same time, asserted that Launhardt had done before what Pick is setting forth in this Appendix.— EDITOR.

II. CURVES OF EQUAL TRANSPORTATION COSTS

§ 1. *The concept of the isodapanes.*—If in any locational figures the transport weights a_n are known and the minimum point P_0 ascertained and still the place of production is not located at P_0, then costs higher than the minimal costs will be incurred. It is imaginable that the place of production gradually moves away from P_0 in any and all directions. In every direction the costs of transportation will rise gradually and may reach any amount, provided only we move the place of production far enough away from P_0. Smaller costs of transportation than in

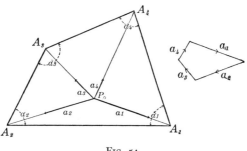

FIG. 54

P_0 of course cannot be found anywhere; but it is obvious that we shall be able to find loci for any amount of transport costs higher than those in P_0, and we will be able to find such loci in every direction from P_0. Consequently there exists not only one such locus, but a closed curve around P_0 which consists of all the loci having equal costs of transportation. Such a curve (curve of equal transport costs, level curve of transport costs, isodapane) will exist for any value of total transportation costs, provided only that such value is higher than the minimum. The totality of these curves gives a clear picture of the way in which the transport costs depend upon the location of the place of production. If the minimum is M ton-miles, we may draw the isodapane for each additional 10 ton-miles; in other words, those curves upon which the costs of transportation would be $M+10$, $M+20$, $M+30$, etc., ton-miles (cf. Figs. 55–58).

§ 2. *Isodapanes for very high values of costs are approximately circles.* —Very high transport costs have loci which are very far away from P_0 and the locational figure too. If this distance is so considerable that the dimensions of the polygon appear insignificant, then that distance becomes the only determining factor. Hence those curves which correspond to very large costs of transportation will not differ very considerably from large circles around P_0 as center. If the radius of such

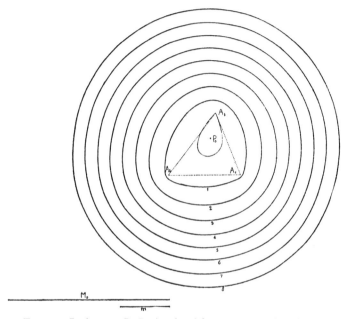

FIG. 55.—Isodapanes I. Ratio of weights: 3, 4, 5. The minimum costs of transportation are represented by M_0, their increment from one isodapane to the next by m.

a circle is R, the transport costs for some location of the place of production upon its circumference are approximately equal to

$$R(a_1+a_2+a_3+a_4 \ldots .) \text{ ton-miles,}$$

because it is admissible to assume without noticeable error that all locations are united in P_0. If we designate the sum

$$a_1+a_2+a_3+a_4 \ldots . .$$

that is the total weight which has to be moved for the production and distribution of one ton of product, as G (locational weight), we can

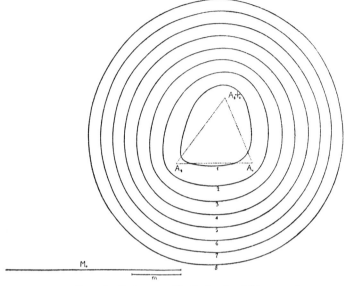

FIG. 56.—Isodapanes II. Ratio of weights: 3, 4, 6

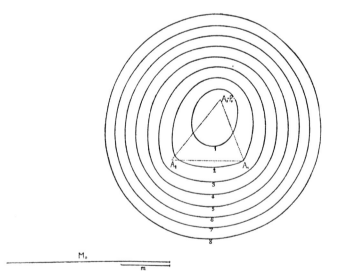

FIG. 57.—Isodapanes III. Ratio of weights: 3, 4, 8

formulate the following rule: The transport costs for places of production very far away from the locational figure are to be found by
multiplying the locational weight with the distance of the place of production from the minimum point: $G \times R$.

If the isodapanes are drawn for a certain gradation of the transportation costs, as indicated in 1, these large circles will lie the closer
the larger the locational weight is. For the larger G is, the smaller is

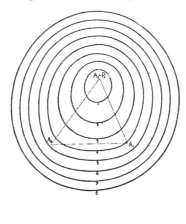

FIG. 58.—Isodapanes IV. Ratio of weights: 3, 4, 12

the increment of R which is necessary for causing the same increase of
$R \times G$. 239

§ 3. *Smaller values of the transport costs. The descent of the transportation costs.*—If we pass now to smaller values of the transport costs, the
corresponding isodapane will run closer round the locational figure. At
the same time the shape of the locational figure and the distribution
of the sets of weights a_1, a_2, a_3, ... between the several corners will
exert an increasing influence upon the shape of the isodapane, which
will differ from the shape of a circle the more, the less the transport
costs exceed the minimum, i.e., the closer the isodapane runs round
P_0. Under all circumstances the system of curves which we have drawn
will show us the following: If we transfer the place of production from
one isodapane to the one next farther away from P_0, we shall increase

the transport costs by 10 ton-miles. It follows that if we leave an isodapane in the perpendicular direction away from P_0, the transport costs increase, and they do so the faster the nearer the next isodapane is to the one left. If, for example, the distance from the next isodapane is 5 miles, these 5 miles cause an increment to the transport costs of 10 ton-miles; if the distance had been 10 miles, we would get the same increment of costs only after 10 miles. In the first instance the additional costs for 1 mile are 2 ton-miles. If we call the amount by which the transport costs are increased when the place of production is moved away from P_0 1 mile in a perpendicular direction, the descent of the transport costs, we can derive the following rule for the determination of this value: Divide ten by the distance of adjoining isodapanes.[8] The closer the isodapanes follow each other, the larger is this descent.

§ 4. *Illustration by a spatial model.* (*Surface of transport costs.*)—Let us imagine that we had raised a perpendicular straight line at each possible position of P in the plane, giving this perpendicular line the length corresponding to the sum of transport costs at the point where it is raised. In this way we shall get above each position of P a point in space, and all these points together constitute a surface. The lowest point of this surface lies above the point P_0; right around it the surface rises, and at a certain distance from P_0 it does not differ very noticeably any longer from a conical surface whose vertical axis goes through P_0, although it shows an irregular shape around the lowest point. If we go along upon this surface in such fashion that the distance above the ground plain remains unaltered, we shall be moving along an isodapane. The steepest ascent at any particular point is given by the line which runs perpendicular to this isodapane. The steeper the ascent is, the faster do the costs of transportation increase if we move away from the isodapane in a perpendicular direction. The steepness gives an immediate picture of the descent of the transport costs.

5. *The picture of the system of isodapanes in the immediate neighborhood of P_0.*—In the immediate neighborhood of P_0 the distribution of the isodapanes, and in connection therewith the shape of the surfaces of transport costs, differ widely, in accordance with the main cases

---

[8] Such inexact explanation of this concept may suffice here. In truth what is involved is the differential quotient (taken with the inverse sign) $\dfrac{dK}{ds}$ of the transport costs in that direction in which K decreases fastest.

given in I, § 7. If P_0 lies in the interior of the locational figure, the first isodapane following P_0 (given fixed gradation, e.g., the 10 ton-mile increment) will be fairly far away from P_0 on all sides, due to the fact that strictly speaking the descent has the value zero in P_0. The same is true when P_0 is located in one of the corners, as long at least as the corresponding weight does not exceed the sum of the others considerably. But it appears at once that the first isodapane, in so far as it runs outside of the locational figure, runs much closer to P_0 than it does in the interior. But if the weight attached to the particular corner becomes very considerable, the first isodapane approaches the point P_0 correspondingly from all sides, so that it surrounds it closer as the

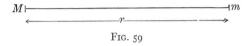

FIG. 59

weight of that corner increases as compared with the sum of the others. The surfaces of transport costs will in the first case have the shape of a very shallow depression which in the case of location in the corner will be somewhat steeper outside than inside of the figure. In the case of considerable weight at one corner, however, the surfaces will exhibit a more or less steeply funnel-shaped depression. The Figures 55–58 will give a clear idea of all these aspects, since they correspond to our different assumptions.

III. AGGLOMERATION

§ 1. *The function of economy and its diagram.*—A large unit of production having the daily quantum of production M will absorb (agglomerate) a small unit of production of the same kind having the daily quantum of production m and lying at the distance r, if the economies resulting from the agglomeration are greater than the resulting increase of costs of transportation. The latter is easy to calculate. If A is the locational weight of production, the additional costs for one ton of product apparently amount to Ar ton-miles. The total additional cost amounts to Arm ton-miles, or $Arms$ money-units, if s is the transport rate.

The economies which result from agglomeration depend upon the kind of production. For each species we may imagine that we had set down in a tabular form the economies per ton of daily product which

241

occur for each and any amount of agglomeration. Such economies are caused by the quantum of agglomeration M; they are a function of M. We shall call it the function of economy $\phi(M)$. Instead of giving it in the form of a table, as just mentioned, we may present it very clearly by a geometrical figure. Let us lay out the values M from the point of intersection of two axes perpendicular to each other. These straight line segments M are called abscissae. Then we raise a perpendicular at the extreme point of each abscissa and give it the length of the corresponding function of economy $\phi(M)$. These lines are called ordinates. By this operation we get points in the plane which together

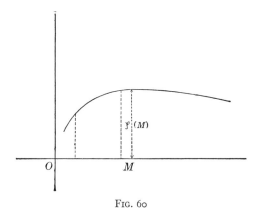

FIG. 60

constitute a curve, which presents the total course of the function of economy.

§ 2. *The basic formula of agglomeration. The function of agglomeration.*—If M is the quantum of a large unit of production, the economies produced by agglomeration will be $\phi(M)$ for each unit of product, and therefore

$$M \phi (M)$$

242 for the daily product.

If the small unit of production having the quantum of production m is combined with the larger unit, we shall get total economies amounting to

$$(M+m)\phi(M+m) .$$

Accordingly the increase of economies due to agglomeration is

$$(M+m)\phi(M+m)-M\phi(M) .$$

As long as this value is larger than the increase in costs of transportation, $Arsm$ (cf. above), the agglomeration will actually take place. We get therefore the following equation for calculating the largest distance R to which the absorbing force of the large unit of production extends:

$$ARs=\frac{(M+m)\phi(M+m)-M\phi(M)}{m} .$$

The right side of this equation contains M as well as m. If m were at all considerable, it would indeed have an influence upon the magnitude

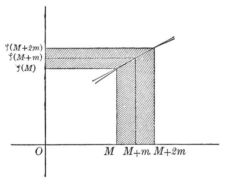

Fig. 61

of R. But the nature of the problem under discussion involves that m is a very small quantity as compared with M. In view of that the right side of the equation becomes quite independent of m, it becomes a function of M alone; but let us imagine for once that the equation contains first the value m and then twice the value $2m$. In Figure 61 we see three rectangles incasing each other. Their area apparently is

$$M\phi(M), (M+m)\phi(M+m), (M+2m)\phi(M+2m) ,$$

respectively. Their differences, figures of a kind which the ancients called gnomon, are decisive for the previously given quantities. The big gnomon

$$(M+2m)\phi(M+2m)-M\phi(M)$$

apparently approaches being twice as large as its part

$$(M+m)\phi(M+m)-M\phi(M),$$

243 as m decreases. This gives us

$$\frac{(M+2m)\phi(M+2m)-M\phi(M)}{2m}=\frac{(M+m)\phi(M+m)-M\phi(M)}{m},$$

and this equation is the basis of the independence which we have asserted.

The function

$$f(M)=\frac{(M+m)\phi(M+m)-M\phi(M)}{m}$$

shall be called the function of agglomeration. Our previous formula is now transformed into

$$AsR=f(M),$$

and this is the basic formula of agglomeration. It shows that the radius within which the agglomerating force of a production of the quantum M is effective, is directly proportional to the value of the function of agglomeration, while it is inversely proportional to the locational weight and the transport rate.

§ 3. *Diagram of the function of agglomeration.*—In order to get a clear survey, we shall imagine now that the function of agglomeration, as the function of economy before, is presented in a diagram (Fig. 62). In this diagram the perpendiculars upon the axis raised at the extreme points of the several M have the length $f(M)$. Above a small segment having the length m which has been laid out from the extreme point of M, there lies a strip of plane. This plane is bounded on both sides by the ordinates $f(M)$ and $f(M+m)$ and on top by the curve of our diagram. We will be able to calculate this strip as a rectangle having the base m and the altitude $f(M)$ the more accurately the smaller m is. This strip had the area

244
$$mf(M)=(M+m)\phi(M+m)-M\phi(M),$$

and thus represents the increment of daily economies which results when agglomeration progresses from the values M to the value $M+m$.

If we now look at the entire plane above the abscissa M which is bounded by the curve of the diagram and the ordinates, we can see that it is possible to conceive it as being divided into a whole series of strips. The value of this plane is, therefore, nothing but the sum of all the increments of economies from the beginning of the process of agglomeration up to the altitude M; in other words, the total economies of agglomeration at M. It equals

$$M\phi(M).$$

Finally we may even get an idea of $\phi(M)$ itself. Let us imagine (Fig. 62) the two axes and the ordinate of M being impermeable walls and

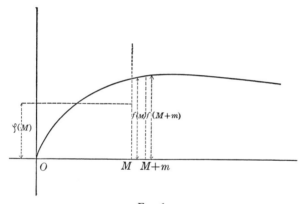

FIG. 62

the plane just mentioned as consisting of inflexible metal bounded in front and in back by parallel plates. If the metal would be liquefied now, it will readjust itself so as to have a horizontal surface. Since the area of the resulting rectangular figure is $M\phi(M)$, and its base is M, the altitude gives us $\phi(M)$.[9]

[9] Higher mathematics will express the relations which we have discussed and which exist between the function of economy and that of agglomeration by saying: The function of agglomeration is the differential quotient of the function of economy multiplied by M:

$$f(M) = \frac{d(M\phi)}{dM}.$$

§ 4. *Agglomeration of small units of production which have been uniformly distributed.*—Let us imagine small units of production which are distributed uniformly throughout a certain area. If a large unit of production develops within this area it will absorb the existing smaller units within a certain radius. If we wish to calculate the radius with the help of our formula of agglomeration, we must keep in mind that M itself changes and increases under the influence of the process of agglomeration. We designate as ρ the amount of daily production which is produced per unit of area under the original uniform distribution. This we shall call density of production. If then (Fig. 63) a large unit of production at G has absorbed all production just up to the circumference of the circle with the radius R, it must have reached the quantity

FIG. 63

245

$$\pi R^2 \rho .$$

Therefore this value for M must be introduced into the formula of agglomeration, or R must be calculated from

$$\pi R^2 \rho = M :$$

$$R = \frac{\sqrt{M}}{\pi \rho} ,$$

and then introduced. We thus get

$$ARs = f(\pi R^2 \rho) ,$$

or respectively

$$As \sqrt{\frac{M}{\pi \rho}} = f(M) .$$

From this equation we shall have to calculate M. This is of course possible only if the function of agglomeration $f(M)$ is known. But if we have found the value of M, the quantum of agglomeration, then it is easy to give the approximate number of large units of production which have come into existence in the area dealt with. For if Ω indicates the amount of daily production in the entire area, the number will apparently be

$$\frac{\Omega}{M} .$$

§ 5. *Ascertaining the quantum of agglomeration through the diagram of the function of agglomeration.*—According to what has been said the problem is now to determine M in such a way that

$$\frac{As}{\sqrt{\pi\rho}} \cdot \sqrt{M} = f(M) \ .$$

We shall imagine that we had laid out a second curve in the figure which contains the graphic presentation of $f(M)$ by co-ordinating to each abscissa M the ordinate

$$N = \frac{As}{\sqrt{\pi\rho}} \sqrt{M}$$

(Fig. 64). The points which we get compose a well-known curve, called parabola. *The required abscissa is that abscissa for which the*

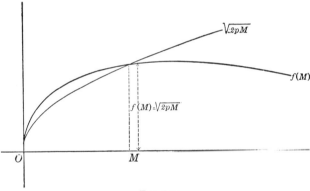

$$\sqrt{2pM}$$

$$f(M)$$

$$f(M) = \sqrt{2pM}$$

$$O \qquad M$$

FIG. 64[10]

curve of $f(M)$ and the parabola have equal ordinates; in other words, where both curves meet.

There exist several possibilities. The curve of $f(M)$ may right from the beginning extend beneath the parabola and remain beneath it. In **246** that case the equation is never fulfilled and always

$$N \rangle f(M) \ ,$$

[10] For brevity's sake the designation $2p = \dfrac{A^2 s^2}{\pi\rho}$ is used for the so-called parameter ($2p$) of the parabola.

which means obviously that the increments of transport costs are never reached by the economies of agglomeration for any quantum of agglomeration. In this case agglomeration is impossible.

Second, the curve of $f(M)$ may in the beginning run above the parabola and then cross it at some place remaining beneath it after that. In this case agglomeration will occur up to that quantum which is indicated by the abscissa of the point of intersection of the two curves.

The third case in which $f(M)$ runs from the beginning and always above the parabola does not, it seems, correspond to any actual cases.

INDEX

med on or before
below.